D1546339

Following the Sun

Tales (and Fails) From a Year Around the World With Our Kids

Margaret Bensfield Sullivan

Little Friday Press
www.LittleFridayPress.com

ISBN (paperback): 979-8-218-28050-5
ISBN (e-book): 979-8-218-28051-2

Cover art by Margaret Bensfield Sullivan

Dedication

Writing this book was a way of prolonging one of the best years of my life. It was also a form of grieving: The more I wrote, the more deeply I understood how places remain but time does not.

Teddy, Willa, and James: This is for us.

PROLOGUE

This is a book about the year my husband and I quit our jobs, gave up our New York City apartment, pulled our two kids (four and six) out of school, and left the country to travel as a family to twenty-nine countries across six continents. Our adventure spanned 2019, the last year anyone would be able to do such a thing before COVID.

"A real live case of *carpe diem,*" is how a friend described our trip after we returned home. COVID had landed in the U.S. a month after we had, and our friend was one of many people who expressed amazement at our timing. Messages by email, text, and social media poured in as we returned, many with questions about our adjustment to pandemic life, but most revealing a broader curiosity about our trip itself. Whether rooted in bewilderment *(why would you do such a thing?)* or inspiration *(I want to do such a thing!)*, their questions probed every mile of our experience.

What were our favorite cities and best meals? How about the details of our daily life—managing laundry, for instance, or dealing with sickness? Several people went deep: How had we managed to stay present? What enduring yet intangible lessons had we returned with? How had we changed? A few were even roused to plan their own big adventures one day and looked for specific guidance on matters like homeschooling and mobile phone plans and how we'd dealt with mail and our bills. Almost everyone, it seemed, asked how the hell we had stayed sane with our kids around all the time.

The year away *had* turned our family into a well-oiled travel machine—seasoned, efficient, clear-eyed—but it hadn't happened right away. There had been so much bumbling in the beginning. (And in the middle.) So many mishaps, mistakes, and misguided assumptions! It wasn't until the final months of the year that we really figured things out and hit our stride. Once I sat down and replied to all those questions, I could see how far we'd come, and how all the lessons we had learned the hard way—about travel, about the world, about ourselves—just might be interesting for others too.

So, I decided to put them in a book. Sometimes I changed names, sometimes I merged experiences for the sake of efficiency. But otherwise, this was our lived experience. It's the book I wish I'd had, back when I needed straight talk from someone like me, who's neither a lifestyle expert nor, to be sure, an influencer with millions of followers. Someone who could answer my three biggest questions with complete authority and candor:

What will this be like?

Can we actually pull it off?

Are we making a huge mistake?

The simple answers are: life-changing, yes, and definitely not. But that's not really enough, is it?

This book shouldn't be considered one of those "anyone-can-do-this" inspirational guides. Clearly not everyone *can* do what we did. At that point in our lives, we could afford to take a year off from earning a living and still manage the flights, meals, accommodations, and activities. Also, my husband and I were both in a transitional moment professionally and therefore didn't need to negotiate time off with bosses.

There were other fortuitous factors, less obvious to us at first, that we grew to recognize and appreciate as the year went on. Like how we were all free to just … leave. The kids didn't require support for learning differences, for instance, nor did they need regular in-person medical treatments or sessions with specialists. None of us had worrisome health conditions. Our parents, while getting older, were still strong and did not rely on us for care.

As the year wore on, we recognized that for a family like ours—straight, able-bodied, white, native-English speakers clutching American passports (and dollars)—things were relatively easy. We could glide around the planet, not just hassle free, but warmly welcomed. This, I witnessed, is not a given for every traveler.

If you're pondering your own radical departure, so to speak, I invite you to treat this book as something of a reference, and in doing so, find helpful answers. In the likelier case you're an armchair adventurer with no immediate plans to put your life in storage and board a plane, that works too. Enjoy our travels vicariously, no passport needed.

Part One

CHAPTER ONE:

Anatomy of a Life Swerve

My husband, Teddy, and I did not fit the image of a couple who would take a year off to travel the world with their small children. We all know those people. Travel is their "thing." Their intrepid babies have passports; they post grinning selfies from Southeast Asian noodle stands wearing bandanas and toddlers in back carriers. That wasn't us.

It's not that we didn't like to travel. We had visited many places together— from Cuba to Turkey, Argentina to Thailand—but not with kids. What would be the point? They wouldn't remember the sights much less appreciate the adventure, and we'd have to endure all the inevitable whining and schlepping. Travel was something we liked to do together, as a couple. We'd wait till the kids were older (maybe).

Besides, life was good. We lived in New York City with two healthy and thriving kids: Five-year-old Willa, inquisitive and earnest, and James, two years younger and more of a dumpling, always with a ball in his hand. We employed Didi, a doting nanny from Jamaica who had raised two children and several grandbabies of her own. When she was off, Teddy and I evenly split parenting and household duties. We had a tight group of friends, a cherished apartment in Lower Manhattan, a car for weekend outings, and, to complete the picture, a dog named Molly.

Our promising careers consumed most of our waking hours. I was into my twelfth year at the marketing and communications agency I'd joined when the place was just a startup. After more than a decade of late nights and vacation days not taken, I'd helped grow it into a thriving company that was eventually acquired by a major holding company.

Meanwhile, Teddy had turned his love of baseball and experience as a professional pitcher into a business, founding a software company for the amateur sports market at the dawn of the iPhone era. After his own slog, he'd grown the product into one of American youth sports' most beloved products. A major retailer acquired it, naming him an executive.

Our marriage was the bedrock to all of this. We had grown up one mile and two years apart in Washington, DC. As teenagers we'd volunteered for the same nonprofit and bonded over a mutual appreciation for Jim Carrey's oeuvre, but romance hadn't come until much later, when we reconnected in New York as grownups. Now, combined with our shared roots, it translated into a marriage that worked very well.

We weren't restless or unfulfilled. We were on a "track" that was conventional, sure, but it felt gratifying, not constraining. We were doing what we were supposed to be doing.

Sometimes I imagine what it would be like if an old version of myself, somewhere in the past, suddenly learned specific details about her future. Like, how would the sixth grade me respond if someone told her, midway through that 1991 field trip to New York City, fanny pack full of souvenirs, that she'd raise her family right there in the South Street Seaport? Or how would teenage Margaret react if she learned that in fifteen years she'd marry that handsome upperclassman who pitched for the varsity baseball team?

There's something about this thought experiment that I love. Maybe it's how little we see coming. Or the reminder that seemingly permanent plans rarely are. But I think what I find most fascinating is how humans aren't nearly imaginative enough to predict what the future holds. Which leads me to a work trip I took in 2017.

I traveled a lot for my job in those days, usually to places like Minneapolis but occasionally overseas to cities like Rio, Edinburgh, and Paris. In fall 2017, I flew to Arusha, Tanzania, a temperate city of about half a million people near Mount Kilimanjaro, to oversee media relations for a conference hosted by my client. It was a long way to go for five days, but I didn't mind. I got to experience a new place, not to mention enjoy twenty hours on a plane by myself uninterrupted.

The event got off to a familiar start. I had worked with this client for years and their conference format was routine by now: stage lineup of brilliant pioneers and thinker-types. Speeches and "fireside chats" on big ideas and breaking news. Audience of connected, deep-pocketed attendees. This particular event promised to spotlight exciting developments and inventions brewing around the world while also "challenging the prevailing wisdom about Africa." As usual, I sat perched in the back of the venue with reporters, listening to the talks while fielding press requests on my laptop.

But as the days went on, I started to pay more attention. There was something different about this program. None of the power players on stage, for instance, were referencing Wall Street or Silicon Valley, the two "power" tentpoles back home. And it seemed odd that the new Trump administration never came up once, despite its domination of every U.S. headline. Come to think of it, very little of the news being broken onstage related to my life or to the "major" topics I followed at all.

Instead, the room was abuzz with chatter about billion-dollar startups I'd never heard of from places like Nigeria and Kenya and scientific research from labs in the world's largest cities, which it turned out weren't American. When an urban planner discussed social issues in Lagos, everyone in the room nodded along except for me. I didn't know the first thing about Lagos.

As I sat in the back of that theater, a creeping embarrassment about my worldview started to take hold. Not so much that it was wrong, really, but that it was painfully limited. Provincial, almost. Was that possible? I had lived and worked in France! I had traveled! Didn't the fact that I was at this very moment on a work trip in *Arusha, Tanzania,* automatically set me apart as an astute citizen of the world?

According to the thought bubble forming over my head, the answer was no. Hazy at first, the message came into focus until it was unmistakable: *I don't even know what I don't know.*

More humbling was the fact that this event had indeed challenged my personal prevailing "wisdom" about Africa. Despite three prior visits to the continent, there was a chasm between "Africa," a place shaped in my mind by the news I read and the movies I watched, and the actual continent, made up of autonomous cultures and complex politics and, like everywhere else on the planet apparently, brilliant people solving hard problems.

As all this was dawning on me, innocuous details about my surroundings took on greater significance: A billboard on the highway touted an infrastructure alliance between Tanzania and Japan *(Tanzania and Japan are hanging out without us?).* A TV ad in my hotel room featured a happy Middle Eastern family enjoying a new vacation property in Azerbaijan *(people are buying vacation properties in Azerbaijan?).*

All this zooming out, all this new context made my little life back home seem, well, little. Not inconsequential, just kind of puny. All these years I'd had my head down, doing what I thought I was supposed to be doing, and even succeeding, only to look up one day in Tanzania and realize that there was a whole world out here—and that I'd been operating in it with only a fraction of information.

Disoriented, I packed my bags at the close of the conference and boarded a flight from Arusha to Dar Es Salaam, the first of three legs back to New York. My laptop, so important just a few days ago, now sat powered off somewhere at the bottom of my bag as I stared out the window, wishing Teddy had been with me for all this. I thought of writer Fran Lebowitz, who once observed, "When you're young, you think the world is how you find it." All of a sudden, I needed my kids—but also their parents—to find it much wider.

Just then I heard the sound of children speaking English with American accents. Coming down the aisle was a familiar-looking family: A mom, dad, and two kids a little older than ours. Under different circumstances I might not have paid them any attention, but that day I stared. Who were these Americans traveling in Tanzania with their small kids in the middle of a school year? What was their story? They took seats in the row behind me, and I spent the next hour eavesdropping as they flipped through workbooks solving math problems together before deplaning in Zanzibar.

I watched them walk away across the tarmac, all tans and backpacks and traveling hats, and the possibilities took hold. Should my family … take a sabbatical? Move abroad? Go on some extended trip? Is that what these people were up to? I started googling family world travel. I didn't know what I was looking for—I didn't know what I didn't know. But the more I searched, the more I saw terms like "family gap year," "round the world travel," and "roadschooling."

Over the many hours of flights, I read about families, mostly European, who traveled from country to country together, homeschooling and adventuring as they went. *People do this?* I thought. It seemed the kind of fringe behavior those grinning couples with toddlers at the noodle stand in Southeast Asia could pull off, but not me. Until, of course, that moment, when it seemed nothing could be more important.

By the time I reached the Doha, Qatar, airport, I was already rehearsing dialogue for a conversation with Teddy.

What about our jobs? We have to work! Or did we? Now that I thought about it, both of our current jobs did have possible stopping points coming up. We didn't need to leave tomorrow. If we planned our departure far enough in advance, we could wrap things up and use a trip like this as an intermission between professional acts.

What about money! We could never afford this! Actually, we might have enough to pull this off. I started ticking off the budget line items: Manhattan rent, our nanny's salary, private school tuition. If we eliminated all of those costs and used the money we had to travel instead, we could probably swing it, even without income. It might even cost less than a year in Manhattan.

And the kids? They're in school! I suppose we *could* homeschool them—a daunting thought but maybe not so daunting? Those kids on the flight seemed pretty serene with their math workbooks. I could imagine Willa and James doing the same.

But we have an apartment with lots of furniture and stuff! It's a rental. We could end our lease. Put our stuff in storage.

But-but our parents! They'd be devastated and distraught with worry! They are still healthy and don't need our care. It's only a year. They can visit.

Won't this look awful on our resumes? Sure, a suspicious "gap year" has to be explained, but the world is changing. Aren't employers more encouraging, even appreciative, of swerves like this?

The realization that we were so mobile stunned me. I spent the subsequent twelve-hour flight to JFK scribbling notes, ideas, a list of pros and cons, a timeline, even a starter itinerary. The more I thought about it, the more possible it began to seem and the more excited I got.

By the time I landed in New York, I'd distilled the idea down to a headline in my notebook: "A full year of global travel, with the kids, without jobs, on the move, seeing and learning as much as we can about the rest of the world. Not someday, but now."

Beneath that I jotted, "This would be the scariest thing we've ever done."

In my mind, it was happening.

At last I walked through the door to my apartment to cheers from Willa and James, dressed in pajamas, their hair still wet from a bath and jumping up and down with excitement at my return. I knelt into their little arms and embraced them tightly, then stood to kiss Teddy, who welcomed me back with a big smile as he took my bag. I looked around at our familiar apartment. Everything was exactly as I had left it. But I was different.

When we finally got the kids to sleep a few hours later, Teddy and I sat on our couch and I started talking. And didn't stop. I described the people I had heard and met. I talked about the impressions their talks had made on me, and how the questions they provoked stopped me in my tracks. "What other assumptions have I made?" I asked, not looking for an answer. "What other narratives have I blindly accepted?"

I told him that I wanted him to have the same "a-ha" I'd had. I wanted him to realize that he, too, had everything wrong—or at least, not nearly all the information he thought he did. Didn't we need to give our kids a chance to see the world with a wide lens from the start, so they wouldn't have to unlearn and relearn things later, the way we clearly needed to?

Teddy listened patiently, bristling only slightly at the suggestion that he had "everything wrong." Then I dropped the bomb: "And so, in conclusion— *don't say no!*—I think we should take a year off to travel abroad."

Oh, that blank face staring back at me. The memory of it makes me chuckle. What, exactly, had I been expecting him to say? "Sure! When do we leave?" When at last he spoke, there was no yes or no. Just a few polite nods and some clarifying questions. "You know I have a job, right?" he asked, only half-teasing.

The next morning, Teddy said nothing about our conversation as we got the kids ready for school. Perhaps he was hoping I'd forget about it, and if he stayed quiet, this whole harebrained idea would go away. He was out of luck. I had vowed to mention the plan aloud once daily until we'd very deliberately weighed all options and concluded, "Yes, we are doing this," or "No, it's not going to happen." I could play the long game. I just wasn't going to let the idea fade away because we got busy.

Tucking the kids into bed, I'd ask everyone, including Teddy, to name a place in the world they'd love to visit. In the car, I'd remind him how a couple he respected had uprooted their four kids and moved permanently to San Juan, Puerto Rico, for a change of scenery. If a nature documentary featured faraway panoramas, I'd point out that we could go see them in person if we had a year to travel.

For a long time, though, the conversation didn't take root. It became clear that for all my mental calculations, I had failed to acknowledge that while I was ready to leave my job, Teddy was not ready to leave his. He loved the company he'd founded and the team he'd spent years building. "People are counting on me," he would say. Sure, everything I described sounded intriguing, but he just couldn't see a year-sized hole in his career trajectory.

But then, a few months into my campaign, something changed.

"Why a whole year?" he asked one night over dinner. "Why not, like, six months?" A full year, I explained, trying to keep the excitement out of my voice, meant we would be all in. I had no rational basis for this conviction, just a feeling. He changed the subject.

A few days later, another sign of interest: "What would we do with Molly?" referring to our dog. We could find a relative who'd take her in, I suggested, or maybe our dog-walker Rodney would board her at his place in the burbs. (*Promising*, I thought.)

A few weeks later, unprompted: "How would it work? Would we have a home base somewhere?"

"I don't know," I punted. "We'd have to figure that out."

The next week: "Would the kids have to repeat a grade?"

Later on: "I *have* always wanted to ski in Japan."

These questions didn't appear out of nowhere. A year after his company had been acquired, it was thriving within its new parent company, and Teddy felt less personal responsibility for its growth. For the first time in years he could pause and take stock. One evening he came home from the office, grabbed a beer from the fridge, and said, "I mentioned your idea to Jeff."

Jeff was his most trusted coach, mentor, confidante, whose opinions on business and life mattered. Over years of weekly chats, Jeff had evolved from paid consultant to close friend as he helped Teddy hash out the management and business challenges of being a startup founder and CEO. Lately, their talks had steered further into "life chat" territory, covering things like balance and personal relationships.

"Oh?" I asked, trying to sound half-interested. I busied myself with a stack of mail but realized this was a new level. I could only think, *"Come on, Jeff."*

"I asked him if he thought it was nuts," Teddy said.

I held my breath. If Jeff had rolled his eyes or shared any of Teddy's misgivings, that might have been it. As Teddy began to talk, though, I exhaled. Not only had Jeff not thought it was nuts, Teddy told me that he proclaimed it a must-do. *What's holding you back?* he asked. *How could this be harder than starting a company? Why would it be any riskier?* He seemed to be pushing Teddy to close his current chapter at work and use a year of travel as a kind of essential transition.

Here was someone Teddy had always viewed as not just reasonable, but visionary, one of those people who could see the whole field of play and knew what mattered versus what was distraction. Now he was emphatically backing a proposal some might see as far-fetched. "It would be challenging, sure," Jeff had said. "But it wouldn't be *irresponsible*."

Then Teddy said Jeff had asked him a simple question: "What could possibly be more valuable than spending a year away with your family?"

Right.

Time with our family.

I had been so consumed with the idea of breaking out of our bubble and giving our kids (and ourselves) the chance to learn more about the world, that, honestly, I hadn't really thought about the time with our children and with each other.

In hindsight I can see how this oversight probably reveals something about our family at the time. We spent plenty of time together, didn't we? We loved each other, of course, and were totally committed, but Jeff's question, and more so, the fact that we hadn't thought to ask it ourselves, forced us to acknowledge that maybe our days and weeks had become a bit too transactional: commute, work, bedtime, playground, socializing, rinse, repeat. We were so entrenched in our individual and collective routines that we were just kind of passing and waving to each other as we went about our days. The kind of behavior James's preschool teachers called "parallel play."

This framing lent a new clarity to the conversation, which had finally gained momentum now that Teddy seemed open to leaving his job. We started to talk more earnestly about how a trip like this might mean we'd all get to know each other, not just better but more deeply. As parents, we would have the highly concentrated and accelerated chance to teach and model for Willa and James all the things we believed were most important.

More than anything, it would allow us to make the most of this fleeting chapter of our young family's story. Suddenly a big trip felt like a way to future-proof against regret.

What could be more valuable? The question diminished our financial worries, career concerns, and school angst. Teddy suggested we pause any long-term planning, just in case—things like job searches and vacation bookings. The more Teddy inched toward leaving his job, the more he began to talk about a year of travel using "if" and "when" interchangeably. Links to backpack brands and hotels in Asia started appearing from him in my inbox.

Yet every time I'd ask, "So does that mean we're doing this?" he hesitated.

"I think so?"

We were making progress, but I hung back, afraid of jinxing anything. I played devil's advocate in our now constant debates, even though I knew deep-down that we both wanted to take this leap.

And then, one night in the spring of 2018 after more than nine months of dissecting and analyzing the possibility often late into the night, we had at last reached a decision point. We were sitting on the couch where the conversation first began, chatting about destinations to visit and the possibilities of who might come visit us. I asked the question again.

"So does that mean we're doing this?"

A deep inhale. "Guess so!"

CHAPTER TWO:

How Do You Plan for a Year Around the World?

Note: If you are fond of logistics, this chapter is for you! If you are vaguely curious about how we managed to get ourselves organized, ditto. If these matters make your eyes glaze over, see you for the travels in Part II.

Arriving at "yes" was the biggest hurdle. The rest was a lot of logistics. We had six months to get ready for our departure on January 7, 2019, a date we picked somewhat arbitrarily to give us a little breathing room after the holidays.

I used a project management software we both knew well from work to take a first stab at organizing the many details and tasks and lingering questions. When I thought it was in a good place, I showed it to Teddy, who took one look, cracked his knuckles, and reorganized the entire thing. I wasn't offended, I was thrilled: He was *in* and bringing his type-A logistical mastery to this trip.

The first item on our list was to tell family, starting with our parents. I had mentioned all this to my parents back when the idea first dawned on me. They loved travel, especially the spontaneous kind, and if it hadn't been for four pesky kids and my dad's long legal career, they too might have done something like this. I knew they'd be thrilled, even jealous, and when I made the call to tell them that we were on, they were delighted.

Where my parents still held a seventies-era view on things like seatbelts (which is to say, they didn't always wear them), and had never once in my life asked me to "call when you get there," Teddy's were acutely more aware of life's dangers, quick to point out the potential for injury or disaster in even the most benign scenarios. We were nervous to tell them, afraid our plans would only worry them. Plus, we were taking their beloved grandchildren away for a year. Teddy's mom, Lila, visited New York so often to babysit that she'd created her own mom and nanny friends in town. His dad rallied the whole family—four couples and eight grandkids—each summer for a family beach vacation, despite not loving to travel (a fact which, of course, only further underscored our worry that they might not love this plan).

I was sure they'd suspect this terrible idea was all mine (which, of course, it was) and resent me for it. But when we dropped the news, there was no outrage, no calls for Teddy to divorce me. Just a couple of bemused smiles and an acknowledgement that we sure were doing things differently than they had. They had concerns, of course. What about school? Careers? Safety? But

Teddy had reassuring answers. Lila, who Willa and James called Lobsy, even pulled out a calendar to mark weeks she could come visit. Their disapproval wouldn't have stopped us from going, but even as grownups with kids of our own, we were glad to have our parents' blessing.

Back in New York, we started to inform our friends. Those who'd known us for a long time were incredulous at first—*Wait, what?*—then supportive, which buoyed us even more. So many wanted to share recommendations of places to go and people to meet up with along the way. Some of them even made immediate plans to join us on the road.

We asked the kids' school if Willa and James would need to repeat their grades when (if?) we returned. The head of enrollment assured us in a phone meeting that they wouldn't need to repeat if we homeschooled them. She added that all the teachers and administrators admired our plan, and later, the school's founders echoed that support, telling us that they "wished more families would do this."

That summer, we quit our jobs. Teddy went first, resigning in person at corporate headquarters, then gathering his staff back in New York. By that point the team of about seventy employees were more like dear friends than colleagues. His company had been his creation, and even as he knew leaving was the right decision, it was still difficult. As for me, I gave four months' notice, more than enough time to transition clients and tie up loose ends. Leaving felt as good as I'd always fantasized.

The announcement we were most excited about was telling Willa and James, a scenario I had played out in my mind for almost a year. They were the last to know, and I couldn't wait any longer. The moment arrived in early September, when Willa had just started first grade and James preschool. It was a Saturday, the late summer air still warm. We walked to a pub down the street and sat at a high-top table where we ordered mozzarella sticks and chicken fingers. A Yankees game played overhead.

We suspected our observant Willa, now six, had already sensed something afoot, but knew that James, who'd just turned four, didn't have a clue. I looked at Teddy, who nodded, then I turned to the kids.

"Hey guys!"

They both looked up from their plates.

"We have a question for you. How would you like to go on a trip allllll around the world for a whoooole year with Mommy and Daddy?"

Willa's eyes opened wide. She started giggling loudly, then wrapped her twiggy arms around me in a tight embrace. She didn't say anything, just kept laughing and hugging. *I'll take that as a yes.* James cocked his head to the side and shrugged as he poked at his mozzarella sticks—thrilled, we thought, in his own way.

Here were two kids accustomed to thirty hours a week with a nanny—a loving nanny, but still, a nanny—and we'd just told them they were about to spend a whole year at our sides, basking in our undivided attention.

Telling them made it real. Afterward, we walked home up the street in the shadow of the Stock Exchange, Willa's hand in mine, James riding on Teddy's hip, already chattering about the adventures ahead.

What could be more valuable?

In his outstanding memoir *Barbarian Days: A Surfing Life,* William Finnegan recalled his own goal as a young globe-trotting surfer, writing that he was chasing, "[n]ot the exotic, but a broad-beamed understanding of what is what." That was exactly what we were after.

After my "aha" moment in Tanzania, I was determined to see the world as it actually was—malls and ads for Azerbaijani vacation properties included—and avoid wherever possible the "authentic" version of places concocted by the media or the travel industry.

With that loose objective in mind, our plan was to make our way around the world observing what people were doing in non-touristy, foreign places on, say, a Tuesday night in November. We wanted to chat with barbers, watch subway riders on their morning commute, check out the local playgrounds—that kind of thing. Statues and temples and, yes, even a museum, fine, but also suburbs and farms and Sunday night dinners at someone's home. We took to calling our vision "real life, elsewhere."

This mantra grounded us as we prepped. We did not need thrills and adventure, nor prepackaged tours designed for well-to-do Americans. We wouldn't deny ourselves a few splurges, we decided, because in our real life we *did* enjoy the occasional nice vacation and upscale restaurant. On the flip side, we wouldn't become backpackers for the sake of some pseudo-authentic "roughing-it" experience. The idea of camping and hosteling *sounded* cool, but we would never do that in real life, so why start now? We'd stay in places at about the same comfort level as our own home, with a few exceptions in both directions on the spectrum.

Of course, our decision to not work could hardly be characterized as "real life." And if there was one snag in Teddy's complete commitment to this plan, it was his unease with the notion of idleness, not to mention no income. As far back as he could remember, he'd always been engaged in some money-making venture, even if it was giving pitching lessons as a teenager. Many of our conversations would default to his concern that we were being reckless. Or that we'd be bored in the absence of purpose. They'd usually wrap with a plea for compromise: Maybe just a *little* consulting on the side?

"I know myself," he would say. "I need to be challenged."

Repeatedly, I made my case: We had a rare twenty-first century opportunity to unplug and be present. Let's not poison it with email inbox distractions and nagging deadlines (thankfully Jeff backed me up here). Finally, by October, he agreed. No work in 2019.

To create a budget, we added "back of the envelope" numbers to a spreadsheet, including what we felt might be an average cost of accommodations per night, projected cost per flight, meals and tours, giving us a rough total budget figure for the year. Also, while we wouldn't have income, we were eliminating 100% of our current costs, including childcare, rent, tuition, and bills, so our travels would not be an added expense the way a vacation would.

There were two major cost centers for our trip: Accommodations and air travel. Cheaper stays and fewer flights than the seventy-nine we took would have lowered the price tag. Destinations impacted cost, too. A week in a Santiago, Chile, apartment cost a fraction of what we paid for four nights at a safari lodge in South Africa. Colombia and Vietnam were not expensive, but Australia, New Zealand, and Sweden were. Consider the wash 'n' fold laundromat in Stockholm that charged $75 for two loads, compared to one in Cambodia that charged $5.50 for the same pile of clothes.

The key to it all was making peace at the outset about spending so much money. We could afford the big-picture estimate and made the conscious decision not to obsess about the price of every line item. *This adventure is not fiscally responsible,* we thought, *but it's the best investment we'll ever make in ourselves and our family.*

James summed it up best once we started traveling, scrawling an all-caps pro-con list of "Being a Grownup":

Pro: "GET TO DO WHATEVR THEY WANT."

Con: "HAV TO PAY."

But note that large sums of money aren't necessarily required to make extended travel accessible. Especially if the goal is time with family, not far-flung locales. Some families take a year off to explore the U.S. via camper van, for example, and others put off big purchases like houses in order to save for world travel. We heard of couples who worked remotely, sold or rented out their homes for extra income, stuck to low-cost places like Southeast Asia—or all of the above.

We bought an oversized map of the world and hung it in the kids' bedroom. The more we stared at it, the more places we wanted to visit. I'd envisioned traveling exclusively to hard-to-reach destinations that required extended time, like Asia and Australia and New Zealand. I'd lived in France for three years after college and traveled throughout Europe, so the well-trod and relatively accessible Amsterdams weren't part of my vision.

But the realization that this once-in-a-lifetime trip was happening had stoked a desire in all of us to see as much as possible. Especially Teddy, it seemed. He told me that since he'd "spent his life on a pitcher's mound," he had hardly seen Europe at all. So, we added it. South America, too, after he revealed that he'd like to use his high school Spanish. Oh, and he'd always dreamed of going on safari in Africa. Teddy was the disciplined and measured one, so watching this transformation from Mr. Let's-Not-Get-Carried-Away to Señor Giddy Traveler wasn't just fun to witness, it was also turning our year into a full-blown trip *around the world*.

Our strategy was to "follow the sun," wending our way along a seasonal path of warm springs and summers, which had the added advantage of simplifying our packing. In some cases, we were very specific about where we wanted to go. In Brazil, for instance, we knew we wanted to get to Rio, the Amazon rainforest, and Bahia on the northern coast, a place my sister-in-law had told me was unmissable. But in Southeast Asia? Whole countries seemed up for grabs. Laos? Malaysia? Vietnam? Thailand? The world was ours for the picking.

People often ask how we factored safety into our decisions, especially when they saw that we had several cities on our growing wish list that many Americans might consider "iffy," like, say, Bogota and Rio. I was more conscious than ever of how the media's monolithic portrayals of places were often "scarier" than they actually were—see: *Africa is poor and war-torn!*— and really didn't want to fall into that trap again. As for Teddy, his practical side prevailed: He didn't let the negative cliches that dominated the conversations about certain cities put him off when the facts, according to his careful research, told a different story.

Besides, we weren't going to be out late at night, drunk, stumbling home wearing flashy jewelry. We'd be a family of four, wearing stained t-shirts and sneakers, getting ready for bed by 8 p.m. Sure, even then something *might* happen. But bad things happened everywhere. In just a few years, our own neighborhood in Lower Manhattan had been devastated by Hurricane Sandy and a deadly West Side Highway van terrorist attack. Not to mention September 11th.

Teddy called up a friend and former Navy Seal who ran a security company that specialized in monitoring risk abroad and advising (and even sometimes evacuating) clients who lived, worked, and traveled outside the U.S. We paid them a small fee to keep tabs on our itinerary and flag any brewing coups or monsoons we should know about. A free alternative would have been to register our itinerary with the U.S. State Department so that in the event of an international incident, American authorities would know to look for us.

At a certain point, all this daydreaming needed to become actual plans. We called up a family someone introduced us to, one that had taken a similar trip a few years before. We wanted to know: How had they tackled the planning? They told us how they had loved blowing with the breeze, booking one country at a time. Their routine, they said, was to sit down after dinner and research possible next countries, then book flights and house rentals or hotels on the fly. More of a "where to next?" year. For them, winging it was the recipe for a perfect adventure.

We knew our family was different and would be better off planning as many of our stops in advance as possible, ideally about three months out at all times. We suspected that this would free us to relax, enjoy the trip, and not spend all our precious time sweating the next destination. We could still "schedule" free days and weeks of leisure, leaving them open to explore a city or place on our own.

All that prebooking sounded great, but the reality didn't take long to sink in: Making all those plans ourselves required a ton of work. With about four months left before our departure, Teddy and I would sit down at our laptops after dinner, the kids asleep, and try to divide and conquer the firehose of nagging, small-scale but crucial decisions that began to pile up.

Where to? Which neighborhood? Which hotel? Which room? Standard double or connecting? Should we book a place closer to the subway? Is breakfast included? Maybe we should rent a car? Could we use points? Have we looked into the train? What tours should we sign up for? Private or group?

Inevitably, each question would devolve into a hellish algorithm of "if this, then ... what?"

If we go here, then can we not go there? If this flight is booked, then can we take the next one and still make our connection? If we miss the connection will we then miss our ferry? If the hotel has no vacancy for our exact dates, then do we need to change our rental car booking?

I'd start out strong and focused, certain that this time I could check a few to-dos off the list. But two hours later I'd be nowhere, having spent the whole time scrolling, say, an endless list of farmhouse rentals in France. Teddy was hitting just as many walls, often cursing the error messages he'd gotten while trying to book connecting flights using frequent flier miles or credit card points.

"Real" travelers loved to do this work, right? But nobody warned us about the endless digressions, the setbacks, the innumerable options, and the nightly bouts of decision paralysis and self-doubt. If the point of booking everything in advance was to help us relax, it was backfiring; the nitty gritty stressed us out.

"Maybe we should just send Bobby an email," glassy-eyed Teddy said one evening. There was no shame in calling up the travel agent who'd helped us with a few special trips over the years like our honeymoon. Why wouldn't we turn to a pro now that we had a much bigger project?

Sure enough, one chat with Bobby simplified everything. He pointed us to people in his network who could help, and we started researching new agents on our own. Why had we waited so long to seek professional help? Yes, it cost more. Most agents worked on commissions earned from bookings, and some we paid additional fees, but these were expenses we agreed to file under "peace of mind."

The agent we used in Africa, for instance, needed just a few days before she came back to us with a down-to-the-day nine-week itinerary that thoughtfully incorporated everything we'd told her we wanted, all within budget. Four countries, a road trip, fresh thinking, places I'd never heard of, lodges with owners she knew personally, a house rental in a neighborhood handpicked by her team—all of it, just like that. I clung to the phone, listening to her describe each stop, thinking, *My god, this woman just saved us so much time and agony.* We barely changed a thing about her proposal.

From there we went all in, fully embracing the help of not one but many, many agents over the course of the year who kept things from falling apart, including one group we eventually tapped to manage the entire second half of our year across Asia and Australia.

Agents booked our flights, which may seem straightforward, but a trip of this scale went far beyond simple route planning and prices. It included strategizing connections, securing seats together as a family on crowded flights, dealing with cancellations and missed planes, and applying miles. Not to mention the bush plane charters we hired in Africa. Planning seventy-nine flights alone would have taken up all of our time, not to mention exhaust our enthusiasm for this project. Ditto for the accommodations. Our agent heroes found appropriate, vetted places to stay and then took on the brain-busting exercise of solving hotel room configurations and bed setups, including connecting rooms, extra cots, foldout couches, and more.

Plus, they handled all visas and complicated paperwork and even sometimes expedited our airport arrival in places like Indonesia or Egypt where the immigration and visa lines were notoriously long. They helped us get free upgrades, like breakfast in hotels. We relied on them to tell us which places were safe to visit, and which weren't, and they handled securing travel insurance, which, among other things, covered us in case we needed to change or cancel any of those many flights.

Perhaps most valuable of all, when someone else was doing the research and coming back with fully-baked plans, we were more likely to agree to them. When *we* did the research, the details paralyzed us. We'd drag our feet or abandon the ideas entirely, unable to pull the trigger in the face of so many dollar signs and stupid details. Having someone else do the legwork just made making decisions and committing to them immeasurably easier.

As if we needed a reminder why we were grateful we had engaged these agents, we got this text from a New York family we'd been introduced to who had just set out on a similar trip, opting to do most of the planning and booking themselves:

> *The thing I'm struggling with at the moment is being able to be fully present in the moment as a family/the kids and just BE together in the downtime/as we experience all these amazing new places. Like, small but meaningful example: We have all these little games that we've brought with us to play together and we haven't even taken them out of the package! Right now, we have this "shadow" hanging over us of needing to plan a bunch of stuff (mainly route and lodging) in SE Asia starting at the end of Nov to mid Jan. We're pretty full on btw now and then [with touring/travel], which means virtually no chill family bonding time. Make sense? I mean, that's so much of what we hoped to gain this year: Being apart from our "busy lives" ... more bonding time. I'm jonesing for more of the chill, game-playing, giggling in the moment variety.*

In the end, they, too, wound up engaging professionals for guidance.

As the days until our departure dwindled, we kicked our prep into high gear. There were the big details, like getting the kids passports and ordering fresh ones for ourselves, all with extra pages. Many of the countries we were traveling to required visitors to have X number of blank pages in their passports, and we knew they'd fill quickly. We booked weekly swim lessons for the kids and Spanish tutoring for ourselves. I found a guy who offered in-home CPR and first-aid classes; he came over one evening for a full-family refresher of the Heimlich and other life-saving tips.

Our school offered some advice on homeschooling. James's preschool teachers emphasized that academics weren't a concern at this age ("Just keep reading to him"), but peer socialization was vital: *Make sure you create as many opportunities for him to play with other kids as you can—we can't stress this enough.* Willa's first grade teachers gave us a helpful list of learning milestones the school expected her to reach by the time she returned as a second-grader. We registered both kids with the New York City Department of Education as "homeschooled."

Willa and James needed to get acclimated to walking long distances, so we ventured out on more stroller-free weekend treks around the city than usual, with plenty of subway rides and visits to museums and street festivals. We asked them to carry their own backpacks each time we left the apartment, packed with a water bottle, snack, and hand sanitizer, to get used to doing so.

Then came the physicals and dental checkups to get clean bills of health. We booked a lengthy appointment at the chain operation Passport Health for our vaccines. We brought our detailed itinerary with exact destinations and dates,another benefit of planning ahead, and received all the shots those countries required (as well as any the State Department and/or CDC recommended). We got malaria pills there, too.

We swapped our iPhones for Google Pixels, so we could use a Google phone plan that automatically covered data and texting abroad in 150-plus countries. The Pixel phone camera was superior to the one we'd been used to, too.

When it came time to address the big question, "How do you pack for a year away?" Teddy and I agreed that our overall approach should be to bring as little as possible. A trip around the world seemed hard enough, we thought. Why add the burden of huge duffels filled with unnecessary crap? We vowed to go very, very light. One carry-on suitcase and one backpack that could fit under an airplane seat per person. In them would be a week's worth of clothing, mostly solid-colored tees and soft pants that we could easily zip into packing cubes. (See appendix for packing details.)

We had to decide if and how we would chronicle our travels online. Teddy and I had both quit Instagram years before because it had started to suck up too much of our time and attention, so the idea of bringing it back into our lives, especially during a year when we were supposed to disconnect, made us uneasy. We needed a way to share the experience with friends and family, but didn't want the distraction and really didn't want to fall into the trap of posting airbrushed Instagram versions of a year abroad, all sunsets and melt-down-free children. But it was important to stay in touch, and this seemed to be the best option.

"I better see barfing," one friend told me.

We created a dedicated private Instagram account and vowed to keep it real, barfing and all. We also set up a password-protected blog on Wordpress. Where Instagram would help us maintain connections with people, the blog would be where we kept a detailed, daily log of What Happened. A record for us, our kids, and *their* kids to read in ten, twenty, fifty years.

Teddy canceled most of our recurring monthly bills (that was fun) and forwarded our mail to a trusted friend who promised to keep an eye out for anything important. I drafted a light-hearted FAQ that we could send in response to the emails now arriving regularly in our inboxes as more and more friends and colleagues caught wind of our trip. Here's some of what we shared:

Wait, *what* are you guys doing?! We're taking a "family gap year." For all of 2019, we will be traveling around the world.

With the kids? Yes, with the kids!

How old are they again? Willa's six and James is four.

Have you lost your minds? There are moments when it does feel like that, honestly, but we're confident and excited about this move.

Will you come back to New York? That's the plan. But this year might bring new paths and ideas for the future, and we're committed to being open to everything.

What will you do when you're back? Great question! We have 365 days to ponder that one and will let you know as soon as we figure it out.

What about your apartment? We're ending the lease.

What about all your stuff? There will be a giant purge, and the rest will go in storage.

What are you most excited about? Spending a ton of time with our kids. Disconnecting. Not having work worries lingering somewhere in our brains. The sights, yes, but also just how people live on an average Tuesday. Watching live sports in places like New Zealand and Brazil. Practicing our Spanish and French.

What are you most nervous about? See above: Spending a ton of time with our kids. Is that bad? The homeschooling on top of that seems daunting. And how is a year's worth of daily disposable contact lenses going to fit in our carry-ons? Oh, and how're we going to be motivated to exercise regularly? Also, Margaret is afraid of fish, so ocean activities will be interesting. Teddy also just realized he'll miss March Madness right when Duke has a shot at the Final Four.

One day, though, we no longer had a snappy answer to one of the most frequently asked questions of all: *What about Molly?*

Molly was our black lab-pitbull mix with a dear, graying face. Teddy and I had adopted her after getting married, treating her like our first baby. We hated to leave her behind, but we decided to put her in the care of a family member, paying for all her food and medical visits in exchange for a loving temporary home. But Molly developed incontinence that fall. It would be too much to ask a family member to play caregiver for a year. With only weeks left in NYC, we needed another option.

Surely there's some kind of "Manhattan dog retirement home," I thought while googling furiously. And there it was: A website for a farm in upstate New York that specialized in boarding "Manhattan dogs who can no longer withstand the hectic rigors of apartment living." The idea of sending our Molly off to a place filled with strangers for a year made me ill.

"Are we abandoning our girl?" I'd ask Teddy.

"Right when she needs us most?" he'd add.

But we both knew it was the most humane option. Even if we weren't leaving to travel, an apartment on the eighteenth floor wasn't going to work any longer for a dog who needed to go outside every hour.

We explained to Willa and James that Molly got to move somewhere where she'd be spoiled and happy. They loved hearing that she'd have a doggy door and be pampered with canned dog food, her absolute favorite, at every meal. But we knew this was probably goodbye for good.

On her last morning with us, we gave her hugs and treats, but I could barely look her in her big trusting eyes. Teddy drove her four hours north to the farm, and when he finally walked back through our door that night, the kids asleep, he said, "She knew I wasn't coming back," and we spent the rest of the evening sobbing.

The remaining New York goodbyes could only be easier. Neither Willa nor James appeared to have any trepidation about leaving their buddies and relished the attention this trip had earned them. Grownups gushed over their big adventure and friends from school sent them off with classroom parties. At a going away party with our friends, a few were genuinely sad. "You guys are going to look up in a year and say, 'You're back already?'" Teddy told them. With new babies and busy jobs, they were all familiar with how time had a way of flying. When the night ended, our old friend Jon leaned over to me. "I don't think Teddy has any idea what's about to happen to him," he said. To be honest, I felt the same about myself.

As renters, saying goodbye to our two-bedroom apartment simply meant ending our lease. I worried I'd be emotional handing over the keys to the place where we brought both babies home from the hospital, where they had taken their first steps and said their first words. But my overwhelming emotion was giddiness. My most precious belongings were my husband and kids, and they were coming with me. After the movers boxed our stuff off to storage, we turned out the lights and rode the elevator down with a rush of excitement. We were off to DC for the holidays with our families. Then, it was happening.

The night before our departure, Teddy and I lay awake in twin beds at my in-laws'. The chaos of cousins and presents and big meals over Christmas and New Year's had sped by. Everything for the trip was now neatly organized and zipped away in our four suitcases, which sat waiting by the door. They looked impossibly small.

We stared at the ceiling.

"Not gonna lie," Teddy said. "I'm nervous."

"Yeah, but I bet we'll look back on this night a year from now and feel so jealous," I replied.

On Monday morning, January 7, at 5:30 in the morning, the four of us gave Lobsy a hug goodbye and climbed into my father-in-law's car to head to Reagan Airport. None of us talked much. My father-in-law is strictly business when it came to airport logistics, so there were no drawn-out hugs or tears when we pulled up to the departures terminal to board the first of many, many flights. We said goodbye, he reminded us to be safe and nodded from behind his window as he pulled away.

The yellow-beamed terminals of Reagan Airport dwarfed the kids, proud and excited, as they ran ahead pulling their new rollers behind them. *Were we really taking these tiny humans out there into the world?* One year and four months after this wild idea gripped my imagination, we were off.

Part Two

ITINERARY

SOUTH AMERICA

Seven weeks: Jamaica (Kingston) → Colombia (Bogota, Cartagena) → Peru (Lima, Lake Titicaca, Machu Picchu, Cusco) → Chile (Santiago, Valparaíso) → Brazil (Rio de Janeiro, Manaus, Amazon Rainforest, Salvador, Praia do Forte, São Paulo)

AFRICA

Nine weeks: South Africa (Cape Town, road trip along the Garden Route) → Zimbabwe (Lake Kariba, Hwange National Park) → Zambia (Victoria Falls, Katambora) → South Africa (Timbavati National Park, Durban, Johannesburg) → Mozambique (Vilanculos)

MIDDLE EAST

Two weeks: Jordan (Amman, Dead Sea, Petra, Wadi Rum) → Egypt (Cairo, Aswan, Luxor) → United Arab Emirates (Dubai)

EUROPE

Seven weeks: Spain (Madrid, Mijas) → France (Paris, Bordeaux, Disneyland Paris, Corsica, Vence) → Germany (Berlin) → Netherlands (Amsterdam) → Denmark (Copenhagen) → Norway (Fjordland) → Sweden (Stockholm)

ASIA

Three months: Mongolia (Ulaanbaatar, Gobi Desert) → China (Hong Kong, Beijing, Xi'an, Chengdu, Lijiang, Shanghai) → Vietnam (Hanoi, Ninh Binh, Halong Bay, Hoi An, Hue, Saigon) → Cambodia (Siem Reap) → Singapore → Indonesia (Amed, Ubud, Manggis, Sideman, Flores)

AUSTRALIA + NEW ZEALAND

Two months: Australia (Sydney, Far North Queensland, Tasmania) → New Zealand (Bay of Islands, Auckland, Wellington, Kaikoura, Queenstown, Nelson)

ASIA (again)

Two weeks: Japan (Kyoto, Hakone, Tokyo)

NORTH AMERICA

One week: United States (Kauai, Hawaii)

JAMAICA
Kingston

"We're really doin' it, aren't we buddy?" I said, quoting *Dumb and Dumber* to Teddy from across the aisle of a taxi bus we'd boarded at Kingston, Jamaica's Norman Manley International Airport. I didn't have a chipped front tooth, but my new fanny pack and crisp tee suggested Jim Carrey's same goofiness.

We'd invited ourselves to Kingston to visit our now former nanny Didi, whom we knew would be on the island for the Christmas holidays. What better way to kick off our year than with someone we loved? We passed a billboard on the highway imploring people not to litter—"Nah Dutty Up Jamaica!"—as Willa pressed her face against the window, amazed at cars that drove on the left side of the road. James stared ahead at the seat in front of him, inscrutable behind sunglasses. He wore a fresh buzzcut and a spotless Baltimore Orioles baseball hat we'd bought for the trip, an homage to our DC roots that I allowed despite a "no logos on travel clothes" rule.

We checked into a hotel that catered to Jamaican business travelers and stopped by the pool so the kids could take a dip. We were the only ones there besides a lifeguard, who noted the kids' interest in some unfamiliar tree pods and cracked one open to show them the almond inside. A chatty Cayman Airlines pilot in aviators and swim trunks showed up for a break between flights.

"Wow, you're traveling for a whole year?" he asked in a Caymanian lilt from the shallow end. "How long have you been at it?"

"About six hours," we replied.

On the morning of our first full day, Teddy stood at the curb clutching our two new travel booster seats, which he had inflated for the ride into town. When Didi and her friend Delroy rounded the corner in a low-rider station wagon with just enough room in back for the four of us to squeeze into two slack seatbelts, I saw him quietly let the air out and fold them away into his backpack.

"Didiiiii!" Willa and James screamed. The kids' joy at reuniting with their beloved nanny was ratcheted up by all the sugar they'd eaten at breakfast. It had been their first-ever hotel buffet, and the concept of unlimited cereal and beverages had so excited James that he tripped and spilled a full cup of cherry juice all over the tiled floor. (Perhaps if he'd known how many buffets awaited him that year he might have played it cooler). We buckled in as best we could and headed out for the day to explore.

Some people had been skeptical about us taking our kids to Kingston, a city many Americans associate with drugs and crime. I admit I had shared some concern. But the people we had encountered so far were warm and welcoming: The lifeguard with his botany lesson; a dreadlocked jogger who cheered "Ya Messi!" as James kicked the ball in a park; a smiling woman who called Willa "Cinderella" as they washed hands side by side in the restroom. All the business travelers at breakfast who had made James feel better about the cherry juice.

The only whiff of danger we would experience at all came that morning at Bob Marley's house, now a museum. Not the sign in the parking lot warning people to "Please Be Careful of Falling Mangoes," but rather a moment toward the end of the tour, when our guide described a 1976 assassination attempt that almost took Marley's life. "As you can see," she pointed out, reciting her memorized script, "these are bullet holes from the day armed men raided the residence and tried to kill Bob." I held my breath and eyed Willa and James. I didn't think they knew what murder was, and they were hanging on this woman's every word.

When it was time to move on, our group shuffled to the next room, but Willa and James wouldn't budge. "Someone tried to *kill* Bob?" Willa hissed.

James peered over his shoulder and asked, "Is the gun people still here?" Just as the low-rider station wagon demonstrated how the world wouldn't be catering to our fretful American notions about safety, this little history lesson indicated there would be no trigger warnings, either.

Delroy and Didi chauffeured us all over town, showing us places far from the tourist enclaves. We strolled Hope Botanical gardens and played pickup soccer in Emancipation Park. We ate ice cream cones at one favorite local spot and roadside jerk chicken from another. We capped our time with a meal at Didi's place on the outskirts of town, pulling up just as storm clouds rolled in, her electric pink house even more pronounced against the gathering black clouds. We took cover inside around her table with other family members, a framed portrait of Bob Marley hanging Jesus-style on the wall over us as we tucked into the traditional home-cooked feast: Jamaica's national dish—ackee fruit and saltfish—and sides of fresh avocado, mangoes, breadfruit, fried plantains, lemonade, and Red Stripe.

The rain on the metal roof offered a soothing accompaniment to the sounds of our laughter as Didi, Delroy, and the kids recounted the many stops we'd made. Willa explained how someone tried to kill Bob Marley with a gun. James mentioned that our buffet had a lot of cereals to try. Didi and her family described life in Kingston, everything from what various grandchildren were studying at university to the types of trees growing in their yard. Yes, I thought, this was the best part of the visit. Travel that was personal and low-key in the most gratifying ways.

When Delroy took us to the airport on our last morning, we took a final moment of comfort in Didi's grandmotherly embrace. It seemed appropriate that we would find our initial footing for this adventure with her. *This is going to work,* I thought, grateful to her and to Delroy for giving us a strong start. We peeled ourselves away, shed a few tears, and boarded a flight to Colombia.

SOUTH AMERICA

Seven weeks: Colombia (Bogota, Cartagena) → Peru (Lima, Lake Titicaca, Machu Picchu, Cusco) → Chile (Santiago, Valparaíso) → Brazil (Rio de Janeiro, Manaus, Amazon Rainforest, Salvador, Praia do Forte, São Paulo)

Colombia

Bogota

We had scrutinized the listing photos for our two-bedroom Airbnb apartment in Bogota so many times it felt surreal to now be standing in it, unpacked and settled. Our leafy neighborhood was dotted with coffee shops and fitness studios and stylish young people who looked like they worked at ad agencies. It looked nothing like the Pablo Escobar miniseries we'd recently watched, but it did feel far from home. Bogota was the official start to our year.

Our first morning, a shiny van with a sign reading "Sullivan" in the window pulled up to our building. Behind the wheel was a private driver and, in the passenger seat, an eager tour guide named Andres. This was no low-rider station wagon. We piled into the leather seats, boosters inflated, and set out for a day of sightseeing—unaware that this would be the last time Willa and James would ever again leave on such an outing without a fight. Indeed, the day would highlight all the reasons why, when traveling with small children, organized tours should be regarded with extreme wariness, if not avoided altogether.

We were hardly away from the curb before Andres began describing in great, great detail the origins of the city, beginning five hundred years ago. Willa and James were immediately bored. About ten minutes in, one of them asked me loudly when "this" was gonna be over. We still had nearly three more hours to go. Just as Andres would finish explaining, say, the significance of the *Museo Quinta de Bolívar* in front of us, one of the kids would point at the very same building as we drove away and ask, "What's that?" as if Andres hadn't just delivered a spiel. As if Andres wasn't there at all.

When we arrived at Monserrate, a towering peak more than 10,000 feet above Bogota that we ascended via steep funicular, Willa and James's complaints escalated: Tired, hungry, bored, hungry, tired, bored, when is this going to be over? At first I was relieved that Andres didn't seem to notice. I didn't want to come off as boorish Americans indifferent to culture or history. Indeed, he hardly took a breath (impressive at that altitude) as he described settlement patterns, the Catholic influence, various topographical details ("I want a snaaaaack," the kids moaned). There was something about a nearby quarry, details regarding the church's architect, and a tangent about local flora. None of this was in any way adjusted for his preschool audience.

It was literally and figuratively downhill from there. We traversed miles of Bogota's colonial-era neighborhoods on foot, James and his Orioles hat jouncing across the cobblestones as we pushed the stroller. We made stops at Simón Bolívar's former residence, some statues, a garden, and innumerable plaques. It was going terribly but we kept nodding and smiling at Andres as he lectured, politely ignoring the whines, even as Willa draped her wet noodle body against my legs, her eyes rolling back in her head, moaning loudly to "pick me uuuuuupp," and James cried for lunch, which was, admittedly, long overdue.

At last, Willa collapsed in a rage, sobbing that there was, "TOO MUCH GROWNUP TALK!" and we threw in the towel. "This has been lovely," I told Andres. "But we need to go."

On paper, this outing had made sense. An efficient way to learn the history, get the lay of the land and, since we were new to exploring faraway places with kids, play it safe. Only now could we see how preposterously ill-advised a three-hour historical tour was for a four-year-old like James, who may or may not have thought the day after Tuesday was "threesday." He could not have cared less about power struggles within Bolivar's army. He wanted a balloon!

None of the other tourists we'd seen had had a private minder. Why? Because Bogota was a modern, easy-to-navigate city. Yes, dangerous drug cartels had once made the place unsafe, but that was decades ago. Today it was a cosmopolitan metropolis with dog parks and trendy restaurants and Uber. The hundreds of people we saw on Monserrate had gotten up there all by themselves!

When we returned to our Airbnb having finally gotten some lunch, it was time for a little self-flagellation. "Why did we do that to ourselves?" I asked.

"I have no idea," Teddy replied, shaking his head. "We do *not* need to see every landmark in these places." Barely three days in and we'd already strayed from the way we said we were going to do things. We canceled our remaining Bogota tours.

Instead, the next morning, after breakfast in our PJs, we attempted our first homeschool session. This, I think, was supposed to make us feel better about the sightseeing snafu—the kickoff to a magical exercise we could all look forward to every day! We had no reason to think that teaching our own kids how to read and do math would be anything but fantastic. *Imagine the fun we'll have doing word problems as a family!*

Within minutes it was clear that not only did our children dislike touring, they despised homeschooling. There were too many distractions, too fierce a level of competition between them, and too much punching. Within minutes we pivoted to a one-on-one approach that would last all year. I taught Willa first grade in one room, and Teddy taught James preschool in another. But even that didn't address the bigger, irreducible issue: Our kids didn't want to be taught anything by their parents. The harder we tried, the more they rebelled. We saw for the first time how we might actually be in for a world of hurt.

We quit early and headed to a playground for our big afternoon outing. A "no dogs" sign hung on the park's gate, but goofy mutts romped around inside with the local kids, some of them pets, some of them strays. When a shaggy brown dog named Cora tried to scamper up a slide, only to slip and slide like Scooby Doo, all the kids laughed, including ours—an ice-breaker that led to them spinning and being spun by new buddies on a carousel, no common language necessary.

Playing was, to state the obvious, more fun than touring. For everyone. This was how we had envisioned our year. Hanging out, people-watching— *dog*-watching! We vowed to stick to our "real life elsewhere" goal and did so over our remaining days in town. I joined a neighborhood spin class, and we wandered through a mall where the prices were low and the electricity went out three times, stranding nonplussed shoppers in the dark halfway up escalators. We found more playgrounds and made stops for interesting-looking snacks. Willa, who loved citrus, discovered that restaurants always offered a shot glass of fresh-squeezed lemon juice for patrons to add to water (or, in her case, drink straight). I liked how Bogota didn't seem to have any global commercial retail and food chains, only Colombian brands.

We learned why when we went to the home of Ari, a business school buddy of Teddy's who lived in Bogota with his wife, Camila, and their three kids. We were Shabbat dinner guests along with a few neighbors at their apartment on a Friday night, and while the kids played together, the grownups answered all our questions.

Everyone around the table had grown up in Colombia during Escobar's reign of terror and told us they each knew at least one person directly harmed by his drug wars. It had been nearly two decades since the violent drug cartels he created were dismantled, they told us, but global businesses remained gun shy. The people around the table were baffled by the world's increased interest in, even glorification of, Escobar's story. Colombia may be safe for visitors, they said, but it was still way too soon to treat the bloody history as binge-worthy TV.

They told us about their quotidian lives. If you owned a car, it had to be registered to drive only on even dates or odd dates, but not both—a municipal measure to control traffic. But Camila explained that those who could afford it skirted the rule by buying two cars and alternating their even-date vehicle with their odd-date one. It was a revealing quirk of the city that wouldn't be included on a tour like Andres's. Nor would a drive out to the countryside for a cup of sangria at Camila's mother's house, or the chance to experience the carnival-like restaurant Carne Andres de Res, where the kids got face paint and jumped on trampolines. We wouldn't have rented bikes and joined thousands of cyclists for *La Ciclovia*, a citywide bike ride on Sundays for which Bogota closed miles of its boulevards.

People talk a lot about the difference between "tourists" and "travelers," the former being those who sightsee along a comfortable circuit, the latter more likely to wander off the beaten path, making friends and eating local food. We wanted to be, and would eventually become, proficient at both. But finding the right balance between the two styles wasn't easy. On the one hand, we wanted to see *what was what*. A shopping mall! Dog parks! The unvarnished, unsexy, real-life gas stations, public pools, fitness classes, convenience stores, and city buses that made up people's real lives. The equivalent of going to a little league game in Memphis or a farmers' market in Milwaukee instead of to the Statue of Liberty.

Still, though, weren't we *supposed* to see the Statues of Liberty of the world? Were we really going to travel all that way and not check these boxes? And, also, weren't private guides and drivers in unknown countries a wise precaution? With this dichotomy unresolved after five days in Bogota, we flew 650 miles north to the coastal city of Cartagena.

Cartagena

Cartagena's hot Caribbean sun offered a welcome contrast to Bogota's brisk mountain air and gray skies. As soon as we landed, we stripped off our sweaters to reveal arms the color of pancake batter. At our small hotel in the heart of Cartagena's historic walled city, a receptionist used tongs to offer us each a chilled hand towel. James hesitated, looking at the woman and then around the lobby for clues. "You wash your body here?" he whispered to me as he accepted the towel. "With your clothes on?" He and Willa had only ever stayed in a hotel once in their life before this year, and breakfast buffets, tiny shampoo bottles, room keycards, minibars—and, yes, the occasional chilled hand towel—fascinated them.

Cartagena is a former Spanish colony dating back to the fifteenth century that served as a key port city and gateway to the rest of Colombia. Over the centuries it had seen everything from pirate attacks to slave ships from Africa. "If these cobblestones could talk," I said to Teddy.

"I'm not sure I'd want to hear it," he replied. There were plazas with fountains and baroque palaces, colonial rowhouses painted gold, turquoise, and violet, wooden balconies and bright flowers spilling over their edges. Street vendors sold $1 plates of heaping sliced mangoes and papayas that would have run $20 in a Manhattan grocery store.

Mere days after renouncing organized tours forever, a shiny van with a "Sullivan" sign in the window pulled up to our hotel. Willa and James looked at it, then us. "This is going to be different from Bogota, we promise," I assured them. After all, this outing had been billed as a kid-friendly activity: A private "chocolate-making" class! We bounced along the cobblestones in the leather embrace of an air-conditioned Sprinter van, watching everyone outside make their way around town just fine on foot.

The "class" turned out to be little more than a gimmick at a tourist-trap "chocolate museum" more interested in steering us toward the gift shop than actually instructing us. James's favorite part wasn't the lecture on the life cycle of a cacao crop or the twenty-step cooking demonstration. It was karate kicking strips of plastic that hung in a doorway to keep the AC inside. When he got bored with that, as one does, he walked in desultory laps around the room, shoulders slumped, whining to no one in particular. Eventually, he tripped on Willa's stool, which sent cacao beans—and both kids—to the floor. They burst into loud sobs.

My eyes met Teddy's across the room. It was our ninth wedding anniversary, a milestone James referred to as our "university" when he wasn't busy ruining it. I was frustrated with myself and mildly distracted by Teddy, who, like me, was wearing a saggy brown chef's hat stitched with the museum's logo as he dutifully stirred a pot of melted chocolate. Once again, despite all signs that we needed to bail, we were hanging in there.

"What is wrong with us," I asked Teddy later at lunch. It was already 1:30 pm and everyone was "hangry." James rested his chin on the table and his four-year-old jowls drooped into a pathetic expression already so commonplace that it had earned a name: Restaurant Face. Not only had we subjected ourselves to more touring nonsense, we had once again forgotten to feed our children on time.

"I'll cancel the fortress tour this afternoon," Teddy said, pulling out his phone to type an email to our agent.

"Definitely," I agreed.

We spent the rest of the lunch talking with two American guys at the next table, a couple in town for their friend's bachelorette. I found myself hanging on every detail of their weekend plans: Dinners, dancing, carousing. "I'm jealous," Teddy said after they got up.

When we got back to the hotel, Teddy had an email from our travel agent in Colombia. He really, really did not want us to cancel the fortress tour. Teddy politely explained that their itinerary just hadn't been a good fit for our kids, and we'd be fine on our own. "We will make the tour kid-friendly!" he insisted. We decided to give it one last shot.

When a shiny van with "Sullivan" in the window returned at 3 p.m. to pick us up, we took a deep breath and opened the sliding door. "Arrr!" bellowed a man in a pirate costume seated inside, pointing a plastic sword at Willa's and James's faces. "Welcome to the treasurrrrre hunt!"

This man in a do-rag and striped shirt was no kid performer, we learned on the drive. He was Fernando, a historian with a graduate degree in Colombian history who had dressed up this way at the request of his boss, who was apparently desperate to make the Sullivans happy. During his tour, Willa and James scurried through the fort's labyrinth of underground tunnels, low-ceilinged and dark, not listening to Fernando, but looking for "treasures" he had hidden before we arrived, like an "Elsa" tiara from *Frozen* and light-up plastic swords. Every time they found something (a tube of bubbles! A light-up bouncy ball!), Fernando interrupted his talk to feign glee and offer another *"Arrrr!"*

Teddy and I cringed at the spectacle, embarrassed for Fernando and appalled at the pile of plastic crap our children were accumulating. Yet, we did learn the Spanish built the *Castillo San Felipe de Barajas* in 1536 to protect the strategic city of Cartagena from other European powers—and, of course, pirates. Its walls were constructed with limestone, brick, corral, shells and, of all things, cattle blood. Most fascinating for me was this handy (and perhaps apocryphal) colonial Spanish life hack: The purpose of eye-patches wasn't, as I'd always assumed, to cover injured eyeballs. Rather, the Spanish used them so they could always have one eye accustomed to the dark in case sword fights tumbled from daylight into the dark fortress.

After two hours of this, we told Fernando we could skip the remaining two stops on his itinerary (was that relief I saw in his eyes?). It was already 5 p.m. and we needed to start thinking about dinner before Restaurant Face set in. I wish I could say that was when we learned a lesson about booking such tours and activities, but we weren't even close.

⌢

By now we were beginning to understand the deep chasm between being working parents, which we'd been pretty good at, and being full-time caregivers, which did not come naturally to us at all. I'm not sure we realized just how little of our time in New York had been spent alone together as a family. In our minds, we had devoted plenty of time to Willa and James. But when we switched to full-time caregiving, it was obvious we didn't know their rhythms, their subtle cues, their quirks. And now, after just two weeks on the road, Teddy and I were struggling to adjust to life with them around all the time. Our stamina was pathetic and our attitude even worse.

Until then, we'd relied on a team of grandparents, sitters, a nanny, and school to provide loving stability in a household where both parents worked long hours. Now that the reins were firmly and exclusively in our grip, we realized how unprepared we were. We'd never really taken our kids anywhere before, and I wasn't used to travel companions who whined to be picked up or who needed so many snacks.

When our Colombian friends from Bogota told us about La Vitrola, an iconic restaurant in Cartagena, they demanded we make a reservation. "You have to experience this place," they said, describing bow-tied waiters and patrons who danced on tables into the wee hours of the night. Going there was a rite of passage for any newcomer. Excited, we booked a table for lunch. But when we showed up, a lone server seemed surprised to see anyone walk through the door. The place was empty, save for us and our backpacks. The only sound as we waited for our meal to arrive was Willa's and James's crayons scratching in a coloring book. A drop cloth covered the bandstand, which Teddy and I both stared at, imagining the bacchanal we wouldn't be joining later that night. *This would be so much more fun if the kids weren't here,* I thought. The look on Teddy's face told me he was thinking the same thing.

Cartagena was a sexy place. I love my kids, but I also wanted to dine on moonlit terraces with my husband, cocktails in hand, salsa music drifting through the palms. I wanted to read García Márquez in peace at an outdoor cafe and spend hours shooting street scenes with my new camera. These tables around us? I wanted to dance on one! Instead, we had spent the morning inventing games like, "find a house for every color of the rainbow!" to curb the kids' whining and answering so many unanswerable questions like, "Why's this plate so big when the scrambled eggs are so small?" Every time we walked around, I imagined a giant invisible clock ticking down the minutes until a meltdown.

For all my good intentions and "real life, elsewhere" mantra-ing, I was still equating international travel with "kid-free vacation." In spite of myself, I felt a snag of resentment at how my darlings, with their short legs, early bedtimes, and many, many needs, were holding me back.

"We're the ones dragging Willa and James around, not the other way around," I said, mostly to myself, as we lay awake in bed one night. Was it even 9 p.m.? Horse-drawn carriages clopped by outside our window, no doubt whisking revelers off to La Vitrola. By now we'd both admitted our frustration with the constraints of full-time parenting. Of leaving so much of a place like Cartagena undiscovered. The irony was obvious: A trip designed to prevent us from missing out on time with our family was giving us FOMO.

We needed to banish the I-want-to-dance-on-a-table-but-can't bitterness and recast the year in our minds back to its true purpose: Not a couple's vacation, but a family adventure. We needed to shed any longing for kid-free dates and meet our kids where they were—and get to know them while we were at it.

"We signed up for this," Teddy said.

"We signed up for this," I repeated.

That conversation was a kind of pact. Tailoring our days to suit the kids' needs did not mean we were missing out. Nor did it mean we were indulging them to become one of those families where kids seemed to call the shots while parents meekly obliged. We needed to fully inhabit the idea of a different kind of travel.

You'd rather watch the street performer a little longer before hitting the museum? I'm good with that.

Your feet hurt? Thanks for telling me, let's sit down for a rest.

From that point forward, any time we found ourselves in places like Cartagena, which would be so much fun without little kids, we'd just smile and say: "Let's come back here one day."

Peru

Lima

The blog post I wrote after flying from Cartagena to Lima, Peru, was titled, "Travel day from Colombia to Peru – Approx 6 Meltdowns." While flights themselves had proven easy so far—Willa and James happily equated them with uninterrupted screen time—airports themselves were hard. Our kids had only flown a handful of times before this year, and the airport gauntlet, from security lines to baggage claim, mystified them. They were slow. They whined. They repeated: *What are we waiting for? How come we have to stand here? Why do we have to walk so far/fast?* The only entertainment they could come up with besides punching each other were those retractable-belt line dividers. "Guys, for the hundredth time," I'd beg, "please don't play with th—" *SNAP!!*

When we finally landed in Lima, Peru's capital city on the Pacific coast, the straw hat I'd bought on the street in Cartagena sat in a rumpled wad on my head, an apt representation of everything we had endured. But just as I despaired, the kids perked up: Teddy's mom, Lila, "Lobsy" to the kids, was landing in one hour!

Not only had my mother-in-law surprised us by embracing the idea of our year-long trip, she had already proven herself one of its greatest cheerleaders and most engaged participants, having booked not one but several flights to be part of our itinerary. We realized this trip gave her a way to safely parachute into bucket list travel destinations she'd always dreamed of. Places like, say, Peru's Machu Picchu. She'd already started telling her friends she had a "year of living dangerously" ahead. (My father-in-law, indifferent to travel, was glad to support her from afar.)

We heard a crowd cheering and looked up to see a woman walking out of the "Arrivals" gate to a boyfriend waiting on one knee. He'd popped the question in front of dozens of balloon-toting friends and family, and she had said yes. Behind her came Lobsy, rolling her tiny suitcase and cheered by a welcome crowd of her own: Willa and James, who broke free from our grips to sprint into hers. "Hello, hello!" she beamed.

At our hotel in Lima's trendy Miraflores neighborhood, which looked like Santa Monica perched on a steep, dramatic cliff over the Pacific, I updated Instagram. My nightly routine by this point was to publish a single photo from the day with a postcard-ish caption, ideally something that told a story about us and about the place we were visiting. I would also share Stories, offering daily recaps with observations and the occasional funny moment. That evening, I had an Instagram message from a friend of my parents' saying something like, "I see you're in Lima. My nephew and his wife live there! Here's his number. You should call him!"

Teddy and I were nice, affable people, who could be neighborly and social, but we weren't the types to go out of our way to meet a stranger. Calling up a friend of a friend's nephew in a foreign country? That just wasn't … us.

But this time, I didn't come up with a reason to reply with some politer version of what I was actually thinking, which was, "Nah." I picked up the phone and invited this nephew, an American named Greg, and his Peruvian wife, Bea, to dinner.

They made a reservation at a favorite neighborhood restaurant and, while Lobsy babysat our kids, we sat for hours over drinks and dinner, listening to them talk about their lives and about modern-day Peru. They were charming and fun, eager to answer all our questions about their jobs and apartment, their social lives and weekend plans. Once again, we learned far more about everyday life in a place from one dinner out with locals than we could have from a three-hour tour.

From then on, Teddy and I vowed to set aside our introverted instincts and embrace a new status as bumbling-but-eager tourists, ready to call up random nephews and be their new best friends. We didn't know it yet, but this conscious shift would make for a much easier way of moving through the world.

Lake Titicaca

Lobsy would see Machu Picchu, but first we flew north from Lima to the rural, remote shores of Lake Titicaca, the world's highest altitude lake. To be honest, I wouldn't have thought to include this stop, having seen lakes before, but I stopped questioning it when we pulled up.

Located between Peru and Bolivia at 12,500 feet above sea level, Titicaca's deep blue waters mirrored an even deeper blue sky overhead. The boulders outside our lodge were marked with curves and divots from millions of years of lapping waves, and the moss that swirled around in its shallow tide pools radiated an electric green. The light in that thin air made it look like Willa and James were joined by two crisp silhouetted playmates, the foursome bounding across the rocks and searching for flat stones to skip.

A guide from our lodge named Alberth seemed relieved when we asked him if he could take us to wander some nearby farms. The day before we'd visited the indigenous Uros people, and while we had enjoyed seeing the "floating island" habitats constructed of dried grass, we sensed that Willa and James now needed a looser day spent giggling at piglets and smelling interesting flowers close by.

Alberth and James held hands as we walked through farmland, passing older women herding flocks of sheep and tending their quinoa farms wearing bright colored skirts and tall brimmed hats. I admitted I was surprised that people in the world still wore traditional clothes like these. "Their daughters don't wear these clothes," he said.

All of this would have been perfect were it not for the altitude sickness. Nothing in our precious little bag of medicine and bandaids was going to save me or Teddy when we got clobbered one night out of nowhere. Imagine the worst hangover you've ever had combined with the flu, sprinkled with morning sickness, then add a dash of food poisoning. The same thin air that had made for such spectacular light had me and Teddy huffing on an oxygen tank. At least we pulled out of it; other guests at the lodge never even came out of their rooms, they were so ill. Somehow, the kids were spared, as was Lobsy, who'd packed altitude sickness pills.

Machu Picchu

An overnight train took us through the high Andean plateau across farmland and over mountainous peaks to deliver us from Lake Titicaca down into the lush Sacred Valley, home of Machu Picchu. Storm clouds added drama to the landscape as we chugged along, cozy in our cabins. Our travel agent may have inflicted the Cartagena chocolate museum on us, but we forgave him as we curved through the Andes at dusk on that extraordinary ride.

On our first night at a lodge nestled in the Sacred Valley, the five of us walked home from dinner in the kind of dark uncontaminated by ambient light. "Guys, look up," I said to Willa and James. Willa craned her neck skyward and let out a cartoonish gasp, then began shrieking in delight. I guess if you're going to show someone stars for the first time, this would be the place to do it. She hadn't spent much time outside after dark, and when she had, Manhattan nights revealed nothing but the glow of skyscrapers. Here in the valley, the sky looked like someone had taken a canister of incandescent salt, dumped it onto a black countertop, and spread it around with a few swipes.

The next morning, we watched as a shiny van pulled up to our hotel, "Sullivan" sign and all. James eyed it with suspicion as he held a tissue to his bloody nose and lip. Five minutes before, he had gone skidding face-first across some flagstones while running around. We assumed that this injury plus his bad night of sleep meant we were in for it.

Quickly, though, our guide Boris revealed himself to be a superstar; a dad of small boys, he was immediately engrossed in Willa's and James's stories. We boarded a train for a two-hour ride through the Andean foothills that featured breakfast and, for some inexplicable reason, a live cover band crooning American Seventies rock at 9 a.m. (*"Cracey lee-tel theeng called love..."*). Boris played cards with the kids and listened intently when they talked about their stuffed animals back home, using lulls in their conversation to point out tidbits of information for the grownups. We ascended the last leg to Machu Picchu on an hour-long bus ride, rumbling up a one-lane road with no guardrails, looking straight down over the edge at a forest buried in clouds. Willa and James dozed with their mouths open.

Anyone who's ever visited a major tourist destination knows the disappointment of discovering that the stock photos from the guidebook look nothing like the ugly reality of a site covered with crowds and t-shirt stands. But that didn't happen at Machu Picchu. If anything, this fifteenth century Incan citadel, perched nearly 8,000 feet above sea level on a sweeping mountain top above the clouds, was even more spectacular in person. Green, immaculate, otherworldly. It was so much larger than I imagined; we felt as if we were among the only people there.

We had strict regulations to thank. In addition to "metering" traffic to prevent crowds, authorities at Machu Picchu enforced rules like no selfie sticks, vendors, food, smoking/vaping, large backpacks, booze, littering, climbing on ruins, speakers, loud noises, or, my favorite, drones (nothing helps you savor the magic of a place quite like having someone's camera drone hover loudly over your head).

Also prohibited? Singing, whistling, tripods, running, sharp objects, metal-tipped canes, hard-soled shoes, lying down, undressing, "generating tumult," and "any kind of activity that distorts the sacred character of Machu Picchu." Attendants kept us moving, prodding us along the pristine pathways if we lingered too long. It would take us many more months, but eventually we'd fully grasp how unusual that level of TLC was for a World Heritage Site.

Neither Willa nor James whined because Boris kept his explanations brief and his feet moving. In fact, James held Boris's hand for most of the tour, just like he had Alberth's, walking ahead of the pack. Occasionally we'd see Lobsy, typically a woman in perpetual motion, stopped in her tracks, soaking up the experience. By the end, once we'd finally exited the protected area, Willa slumped against a boulder and began shedding a few tired tears after so much walking. A passing tourist stopped to crouch down and hand her a candy bar. "Chocolate always makes *me* feel better when I'm sad," she said with a British accent and a smile before walking away. And it did.

Chile

Santiago

We said goodbye to Lobsy at the Lima airport, already looking forward to seeing her again in South Africa, and traveled to Santiago, Chile, where we had booked a small but clean apartment on the eighth floor of a concrete high-rise apartment building in the city's bohemian *Lastarria* neighborhood.

It had a washing machine and a pool on the roof—but no AC. February in the Southern Hemisphere was the height of summer and we had arrived at the start of a historic heatwave to a stifling apartment. Willa lay on top of her sheets in her undies at night, a small fan pointed at her bed. "Mama?" she gasped. "If Airbnb starts with 'air,' how come they don't have air conditioning?" Details like AC got lost when Teddy and I, full of misplaced confidence, arranged the booking.

I doubt many American travel agents would have proposed spending a week in Santiago, which is typically a one-night stop for tourists en route to more scenic Chilean destinations like Patagonia or the Atacama Desert (where we did not go). And sure, the city was not considered especially beautiful, and it certainly wasn't known as a culinary draw unless you really like mayonnaise, but that absence of major tourist infrastructure is exactly what made it the kind of destination I envisioned when planning this trip: A faraway land where we could be anonymous wanderers, observing the goings-on of everyday people.

We made whole afternoons out of visiting UniMarc, just another *supermercado* to locals but an exciting stop for us with its unrefrigerated eggs, piped-in Chilean pop music, and unfamiliar cereal brands. I went to a spin studio in an office park and exercised alongside corporate types on their lunch break. We watched pickup basketball games and groups of teenagers attempting hip-hop dance routines in the reflection of a glass office building. We stumbled across a Beatles cover band ("Los Beetles") crooning from the roof of an office building one Wednesday afternoon and hummed along with the lunch crowd, marginally less self-conscious than we'd been back when a tour guide at Bob Marley's house had led us in "One Love."

By now we'd given this kind of travel a name: "Interloping." It wasn't quite the right word, but it stuck. Not glamorous or sexy or Instagrammable, interloping was the art of parachuting, Zelig-like, into someone else's quotidian existence. The opposite of riding in a private van with a tour guide to see famous landmarks, and nothing like doing "authentic local experiences" cooked up by the tourism industry. No travel influencer was going to post about the frozen yogurt we ate at that Santiago mall; no travel mag would carry a spread about the subways we took; no guidebook would ever devote pages to Los Beetles.

People weren't putting on a show for tourists in these places, but living their lives that day in their corner of the world. And we got to feel their rhythms, what mattered, and experienced a taste of what it would be like to be from there. We were imposters as much as interlopers, but we learned more about a country traveling this way than we could ever have imagined.

And we wanted more. "Anyone have friends in Santiago, Chile, we should meet up with?" I posted to Instagram, making good on our recent vow to seek out new people. I was surprised to get a hit: The next day we were guests at the home of a friend of a friend's ex-boyfriend in a high-rise apartment building. He and his wife ran a wedding planning business and hosted us with such generosity we were forced to wonder if we would be this nice were the tables turned. We stayed late into the night, drinking wine and eating grilled sausages on their balcony while our kids played together and, later, watched the Spanish-language *Moana* in a heap on the couch.

Before we left New York, one of our worries was that Willa and James might struggle to adjust to a year without structure. They'd only ever existed on a tight eating and sleeping schedule, a *Groundhog Day* lifestyle that had made for calm and content kids but hardly flexible ones. Would they be okay when we blew up their comfort zone? Added new foods and bedrooms?

The answer appeared to be yes, partly because without really meaning to, we'd started to find a daily rhythm, a routine that stuck no matter where we were. It always began with Teddy waking at 7 a.m. to exercise. He usually jogged, swam, or did bodyweight workouts—the discipline of a 25-year habit and former pro athlete. I'd relied on group fitness classes for exercise back in New York and, in their absence, found myself working out far less. Occasionally, though, I'd find an indoor cycling class in new cities and sign up. I was shy about these at first, but by the time I signed up for Titanium Cycling Box in Santiago, I was participating with gusto.

Then we'd have breakfast and settle in for homeschooling, which our teachers had told us, astutely, we should get out of the way first thing and not spend more than 30 minutes each on reading, writing, and math. "Don't try to do more than that," they'd insisted, worried we'd burn the kids out. *(Don't worry about that.)* We homeschooled every day that we weren't flying somewhere.

Homeschooling was still a struggle in those early days, but we stuck with it despite the histrionics. Willa in particular hated everything about it, especially her teacher. Work that she had loved back in school—reading aloud! Math games! Story writing!—she suddenly loathed. Each day was a test of wills. Our mild-mannered little angel snapped pencils in half and collapsed in sobs, shredding her worksheets in Oscar-worthy performances. One morning in Lima she hurled pillows across the hotel room while shouting, "You are NOT A TEACHER!" as if I needed the reminder.

James wasn't quite as dramatic. Teddy could usually trick him into playing some math games and sitting down with his Marvel-themed I Can Read books. But he could be exasperating in his own way, flipping pencils in the air for fun instead of counting, or melting into a heap on the floor when asked to write one damn sentence in his journal.

Our objective was simple: Willa and James needed to comfortably hit the ground running with their peers when we returned. Our school had packed us off with a checklist of milestones to hit—stuff like, "be able to tell time" or "add and subtract within 100"—and we made up our lessons as we went, using games, random workbooks picked up in bookstores along the way, and occasional online explainer videos from Khan Academy.

We'd set off around 11 a.m. to find lunch and explore, usually with some vague destination like a neighborhood or playground to anchor the afternoon. Sometimes we had a laundry mission. After about ten days, each of our medium-sized drawstring laundry bags were nearly filled and we had to figure out a plan. Apartment and house stays were easiest, as we usually had a washer. If there were no dryer, we used a portable clothesline we'd packed. When staying at hotels, we ventured to nearby wash 'n' folds and learned to seek out places that charged by the kilo, not by the item. While such services were pretty easy to find in South America, there were still times when we had no choice but to pay the astronomical hotel laundry service fees. We became skilled at washing our undies in the sink.

Because we were living in hotels or, if we had a kitchen of our own, weren't in town long enough to stock much beyond cereal and milk, lunch and dinner were almost always in a restaurant. Not only were restaurants convenient, they allowed us to eat local food. If we stayed in, we'd be preparing pasta or chicken staples.

Early on, Teddy and I would either overeat or order way too much food— or both. We spent a lot of time scanning menus for dishes that the kids, especially picky James, would eat. And of course, there was always Restaurant Face when the wait was too long before a meal appeared.

Keeping small kids under control at a restaurant multiple times a day was hard work no matter how many distractions we packed. And we probably made things harder on ourselves by having a low tolerance for loud and disruptive behavior. We were on them constantly: *Don't play with that, sit down, lower your voice, say please, say thank you, shhh!* One day at lunch, James picked at his food with his fingers. When I told him to use his fork, he shot me a look and asked, "Why do you always have so many *announcements?"*

By 7:30 p.m. we had them bathed and in bed listening to a chapter or two of whatever book we were reading. They were usually asleep by 8:30. Teddy and I used the remaining hours of the day to write our blog, post pictures, and check out the plan for the next day. The setting for all of this varied almost daily, yet there was a familiar order that the kids had started to count on no matter where we were.

I'd thought chaotic, unfamiliar cities might be alarming for Willa and James, but they hardly fazed them at all. Stars in a Peruvian night sky made them scream, but no amount of honking or yelling seemed to rattle them. Our young New Yorkers weren't intimidated on crowded subways, either. They'd elbow through straphangers to get seats and then fall asleep, mouths open, as if they'd done that commute for years.

Before we'd left, I'd had visions of getting separated from the kids in crowded, foreign streets, a nightmarish hypothetical that drove us to pack emergency whistles and lanyards printed with contact information for their necks. Pretty quickly, though, we developed a few critical habits: staying together, holding hands and always being aware of each other's whereabouts. Willa and James never wandered off, and Teddy and I learned to trust them to stay close, jettisoning the lanyards somewhere between Machu Picchu and Santiago. We'd lightened up.

Or had we? A small Santiago playground made me wonder. The place wasn't much—a gated patch of dust featuring a few swings and a slide with peeling paint. We should have felt right at home, but, for starters, the place had seesaws, which New York City had phased out for safety reasons long before we had kids. The seesaw fulcrums at this playground barely came off the ground, but that night in my journal I described how "they made me so nervous." I imagined serious injuries.

But the seesaws weren't the biggest challenge there. A little girl who looked like she was about four years old walked through the gates holding hands with her grandpa. We learned her name was Sophia, and her grandpa answered to *Papito.* Sophia had a contagious laugh and somehow convinced both Willa and James, despite no shared language, to push her on the swings. Everyone was having fun, shrieking and giggling, all very sweet and normal.

Papito watched for a bit, then did something unexpected. He walked out the gate and disappeared into an apartment building down the block. Maybe small children get dropped off to play alone where you live, but where we were from, parents and nannies were always present. Always. Sentinels along the sandbox, they monitored all the children, especially their own.

This was probably Papito and Sophia's routine. She seemed content, but being so American, we found ourselves unable to go anywhere until he returned. What if something happened to her? What if she got hurt? Willa and James were confused as well. "Where's Sophia's grownup?" they wanted to know. We hung around for another hour, getting hungry, wanting to go, debating whether we were being ridiculous. Finally, *Papito* waved Sophia home for lunch, and she scampered off with one last giggle. Had jettisoning the whistles and lanyards really meant we were relaxing? Was it possible that we parents didn't need to be quite so afraid?

Valparaiso

We escaped the heat of Santiago after a week and headed for the coast to Valparaiso, a port city once critical to global trade, now an artist's haven known for street art and stray dogs. We checked into another apartment with no air-conditioning, but this time it didn't matter. The temperature was twenty degrees cooler and an ocean breeze coursed through our windows.

We didn't have a plan in "Valpo," which meant aimless walks characterized by a barrage of questions from Willa and James: Where were we going? How long would it take? What would we do when we got there? How long would we stay? *Can we have a snaaack?*

The first morning, we attempted to get our bearings amid miles of Valpo's steep, maze-like streets, which were lined with crumbling colonial-era buildings coated in bright murals and graffiti. We had a loose destination—downhill toward the water's edge, which had shops and restaurants—but first we needed to figure out the best path. The kids asked their usual questions and a stray dog ambled over, probably wondering some of the same things. Teddy and I tuned them out as we opened Google Maps on our phones.

This had been our deeply flawed MO: Both of us consulting individual maps then following whoever got the navigation sorted first. When Teddy got the route, I'd follow trustingly, holding one of the kids' hands, enjoying the scenery. When I took the helm, however, Teddy would follow closely behind me, nose still in his own map, wondering aloud if this was really the best way to go. It irritated me. Not because I felt controlled, but because I felt judged. I knew that his "trust but verify" approach came from years of enduring my meandering, perhaps sometimes unreliable, navigational style.

Teddy is the detail-oriented one who actually reads the step-by-step instructions when doing things like assembling furniture or following a recipe. I am a slightly more Type-B personality. Why read the instructions when you can wing it? I load the dishwasher the same way I load the washing machine—just throw it all in and push the button! His methodical ways are a perfect yin to my *it'll-be-fiiiiiine* yang, and thanks to a deep mutual respect, our *Odd Couple* tendencies had, over the course of our marriage, drawn us closer to common ground. But it's not always seamless.

That morning, I got the directions on my phone before Teddy did and started downhill. Teddy, the kids, and the stray dog followed behind. We hadn't walked half a block before I heard it: "Are you sure we don't go left here?" I stopped and took a deep breath. Turning to face him, I zipped my phone into my fanny pack with a flare of my nostrils.

"Why don't you do the map thing from now on," I said, the slightest edge to my voice. He looked up from his map. There was a pause when I thought he might be on the brink of apologizing, or even taking the bait to ignite a fight. But instead he was just checking to see if I was serious. Noting that I was, he took the lead down the street, dog at his heels.

Yes, this was mildly annoying. But ultimately, I was grateful we could solve a source of friction: Two people handling navigation was, apparently, one too many. I had no interest in being the cliche couple bickering over a map in a foreign city. Teddy relished studying where we were and getting oriented. Fine! He could have it!

This was part of our learning curve. Keeping the marital peace meant embracing "jobs" like this one ("Chief Navigator" or "Map Guy" as we came to call Teddy). We were developing a system in which we each had distinct roles and responsibilities. Much like the homeschooling division of labor, Teddy was in charge of James's suitcase and I for Willa's, which meant packing, unpacking, and being responsible for any lost items or clothing in need of replacement.

Teddy had become Minister of Finance, which included withdrawing local currency and tipping, but more important, he was Keeper of the Itinerary, a role he'd assumed in New York because he'd quit his job first and had had more time. And, given my track record for misplacing things, he carried our important documents.

As the amateur photographer and (now former) communications professional, I oversaw all things "content." While we alternated blog-writing duties each night, I was responsible for recording our trip, the photo-taking and archiving, all social media posts, and any kind of historical documentation. Whenever I wanted Teddy to take a few pictures, I delegated with specific instructions. Teddy took pride in referring to himself as the "Content Intern."

Some of these jobs were natural holdovers from our New York life, when I'd made the annual family photo album and Teddy made sure we had things like wills; I wrote the school admissions essays while he filed our taxes. For six years we had designated days to be on bedtime duty. When we took the train to visit grandparents in DC, we traded shifts, with one parent managing both kids while the other got to put on headphones and relax for thirty glorious minutes at a time.

This allocation of responsibility saved us a lot of pain. It didn't just prevent travel logistics from falling through the cracks, it helped us avoid resentment, or the "How-come-*I*-end-up-doing-all-the-work?" bickering. Since we both had our equal share of unglamorous assignments, we were always grateful to the other person for dealing with this or that task.

Most of the time, that is. Teddy usually still asked if I'd done a thorough last-look of any hotel room before checkout, which drove me nuts, especially when, as was often the case, I *did* find something I'd overlooked, like a sock. Or a laptop.

Brazil

Rio

When we pulled up to our hotel in Rio, our taxi driver opened the back door and reached in with a smile to pull James out with some kind words in Portuguese. He then tossed our son high in the air to squeals of delight. It was so affectionate, so familiar. And so odd. Before we could talk about it, the man behind the hotel reception desk took one look at James and disappeared into the back, returning with a gift: A soccer ball. He invited James to play pickup with him in the lobby.

We were happy to be back in a hotel after two weeks in Airbnbs. Air conditioning! A breakfast buffet! Clean towels! It was a contrast to the thrill we'd felt about switching back to Airbnbs after two weeks of hotels in Peru, when we were excited about eating cereal in our pajamas! Having our own kitchen! Living like locals!

Teddy and I had both spent time in Brazil, but I'd forgotten how it was so enormous, so culturally rich, so apart from the rest of South America that it may as well be its own continent. Top 50 music charts in Jamaica, Colombia, Peru, and Chile had all featured the same mix of American pop, Puerto Rican reggaeton, and Euro dance hits from home, but Brazil's list only featured tracks performed by Brazilian artists we'd never heard of, each with *hundreds of millions* of plays. Brazil did not import culture. It was doing just fine on its own, thank you very much.

We made a quick gondola trip up the verdant skyscraper of a hill called Sugarloaf Mountain on our first morning to check out the view, ecstatic to be free of shiny "Sullivan" vans and tour guides, then walked to Copacabana

Beach. If any other beach had the same amount of plastic in its waves, shoulder-to-shoulder crowds, unrelenting 95-degree heat, and hawkers, it's hard to imagine we would have bothered renting chairs and an umbrella. But we loved it and stayed for hours, James in swim goggles and a colorful UV-protection rash-guard tee tight over his potbelly, playing in the waves alongside thonged beauties and groups of young men juggling *futeballs* in a circle.

The days that followed weren't much different. We wandered in markets. Watched footvolley and weightlifting on beach gyms. We joined a food tour we found online, eating tapioca and acai bowls and fish croquettes until we were stuffed. We bought the kids flip flops so they could fit in, only to be reminded as they shuffled along why we had always resisted doing so. Everywhere we went, men we had never seen before ruffled James's hair and gave him fist bumps as they passed on the street.

The Amazon

We knew we wanted to see the Amazon rainforest, but the travel agent we'd used in Colombia and Peru kept proposing air-conditioned boats with white-glove service, which just seemed silly. Teddy found a different agent whose style was more low-key. Her itinerary began in Manaus, an industrial port city on the Amazon River, and we flew there from Rio, checking in for a few nights to a hostel-ish spot called Casa Teatro, located near an unlikely pink Belle Epoque opera house known as the "Amazon Theater."

Casa Teatro featured wall-to-wall shag carpet, which smelled like mildew from the humidity, and somehow all-night party noise kept us awake even though our room had no windows (unless you counted a porthole to the hallway outside our door). A fluorescent light flickered over our beds. We were happy when a local taxi arranged by the travel agent arrived to drive us away, two hours deeper into the rainforest.

The Amazon footprint is the size of mainland U.S. and accounts for 20% of the world's oxygen. The sheer scale of it is too much to comprehend. We stared out the window as we rocketed down a wet and empty two-lane highway that cut through lush, remote jungle, flimsy ribbons of old seatbelt draped over the kids' chests. (Our precious inflatable booster seats had burst in the Peruvian high altitude and been discarded long ago.)

Eventually we reached a small fishing town, where our home for the next few days was tied to a pier: the Jacare Tinga, a two-story wooden river boat like something out of *Swiss Family Robinson*. We got out of the taxi and met the crew, only one of whom, a guide named Josue, spoke English. The one other paying passenger was Laura, a retiree from Sao Paulo. A fellow city slicker with a little English.

The boat's bottom deck held a kitchen and an open-air common area with a large table for meals. Upstairs, we ducked into our little family cabin and saw two bunk beds and a small bathroom with toilet and "shower," which was really just a handheld sprayer of river water.

The kids thought it was cozy, a little bears' house on water, but Teddy and I unpacked in silence. The Amazon rainforest had sounded cool. Toucans! Trees! A chance to see it before it disappears! But we're not particularly outdoorsy and here we were, about to ride a rough-hewn boat into the unknown, leaving behind any trace of Wi-Fi and cell signal for the first time that year. Make that since 1995.

The kids wanted to explore the lower and upper decks, and we tailed them, already on edge. Were these low railings safe? Were our excited children going to tumble over into the Rio Negro? We made sure we knew where the life jackets were and debated whether we should just put them on to be extra safe. Teddy kept smacking his head on the low ceiling beams.

When the sun set, the kids went from excited to clingy. We couldn't blame them. Night falls quickly near the equator, and the view over our low boat railing disappeared into blackness. There wasn't even a moon. We had a few fluorescent bulbs on board, but only really sensed that we were moving because of the breeze and the hum of our engine. If I'd hoped for some "jungle sounds"—how about a few bird calls or the rush of a waterfall?—I was out of luck. It felt like the trees on either side of our boat were closing in on us as we crawled along. We were only one hour into an overnight ride that would take us much, much deeper into narrowing waters.

Suddenly, a splash! I looked over. About ten feet away, a small black fish the size of a matchbox car lay flopping on the deck of our boat. One of the guys walked over and tossed it back, saying something to Laura in Portuguese. She explained in broken English that, apparently, fish were attracted to boat lights the same way moths were to a flame, and it was common for them to fling themselves onboard like that.

Now would be a good time to share that I am terrified of fish. I'm unsure where the phobia comes from. Perhaps the memory of my big brother chasing me around our house with my pet goldfish in a net when we were little? But the idea that a fish, and an Amazonian one at that, might fly out of thin air into my human space without warning did little to comfort me that night. We retired by 8 p.m. after a light dinner at the communal table, the crew to their hammocks outside our door and we to our little cabin, where we folded our bodies into the tiny bunk beds. *Let's just get this over with,* I thought to myself.

The following morning we ate breakfast with the cheerful crew at 7:30 a.m. We passed around strong coffee, homemade corn cake still warm from the oven, a tray of sliced tropical fruit, traditional cheese bread known as *pao de queijo,* and juice. The spread and the lush forest around our boat had us feeling better already. We did not, could not, check our phones.

James turned to Laura and explained that adding different fruits to plain yogurt was like adding single digit numbers to ten. You could turn it into something, like mango yogurt or, say, seventeen! She found this hysterical. Casual chit-chat with grownups wasn't something we'd seen from James before. Not to mention these math fundamentals. Teddy and I looked at each other and laughed with a mutual look of "Huh?" It's like we'd missed something about our son, only now seeing it for the first time.

Josue pulled out a jumbo map and explained that we'd be setting out in aluminum dinghies, our destination "here." He pointed to some spot. Map Guy stepped forward to review the situation. We descended into two boats, our family and Laura in one, a few additional crew and coolers in a second. Feeling smaller and more vulnerable than ever, off we went, up a narrow stream flanked on both sides by trees 150 feet tall.

The water was clear but tea-colored, the trees draped with serpentine vines. Every half mile or so we'd encounter a fallen limb or white water, and the guys would have us hop out and hike along the banks while they chopped through the mess with machetes. Sometimes they had to pull the boats fully out of the water and carry them behind us through the bush. Mostly, though, we'd just lower to the floor and limbo under the trunks.

Watching Josue and his crew's superhuman instincts and encyclopedic knowledge of the rainforest put us at ease. These guys weren't trained to pamper or baby us. There were no Elsa tiaras hidden in these woods. They were just there to show us their home and, while they were at it, keep us alive. Clearly, they were up to the task. They didn't even wear shoes.

By lunch we arrived at a place I'd heard Josue refer to as a "swimming hole." The shallow water was sandy and appeared canary yellow, then, as it got deeper, turned orange then red then black as it stretched toward a roaring waterfall. A cool-looking ombre effect, but ... *swimming hole?* Josue chuckled at the look on my face, assuring us that because of the rushing water there was little to no life beneath the surface—no snakes, no alligators, no fish. He stripped to a Speedo and ran in. Before we could react, Willa and James sprinted past us after him and belly flopped into the water, laughing as they came to the surface.

I cringed, but their splashing and playing was pure joy, and I had to smile. They were in heaven, unafraid. If they could do it, I guess we could too.

Teddy started to wade in, and I followed, the sand under my feet soft. When the water reached our waists, we each took a deep breath and sank backward until the water flowed over our heads. It was warm and lovely.

When we finished swimming, Josue grilled a whole fish for lunch on a barbecue constructed out of fallen branches, and while we waited to eat, prepared caipirinhas made with limes he sliced with a machete and muddled with a whittled stick. "Jungle juice," he said, handing out the cups. Laura grabbed the bottle of cachaça and topped everyone off.

Meanwhile, James, usually modest, strutted around shirtless in his trunks, wearing a necklace of leaves Willa wove for him. He found a staff and used it to jab holes in the mud. Was this the same child I had referred to as a "stuffed shirt" in my journal only two days before? Every once in a while, Willa would stand up, run to the water, and leap back in just for the hell of it. When it was time to eat, we sat down with plates of white fish coated in a layer of coarse and salty cassava flour.

Back on the boat that night, tucked away in our little cabin on a river in the middle of nowhere, we slept—hard.

The next day, emboldened, we pulled on long sleeves, closed-toed shoes, sun hats, and DEET and set out for a trek led by Jose (not to be confused with Josue), a strong and youthful crew member our captain had stopped to pick up the morning before. The kids had watched in astonishment as he'd bounded barefoot out of a solitary one-room dwelling on stilts, the only sign of human life we'd seen for miles, carrying nothing but a small backpack over his shoulder. Now he was whacking vines and branches with a machete to clear our path.

"This guy's such a badass," Teddy said as we walked behind him. The first rule of hiking in the Amazon is never touch a tree trunk because spikes and barbs among the flora were vicious. Hands at our sides, we lumbered along, trying to keep up. We were so focused on our feet that we almost didn't see Jose stop and hold up his hand for us to pause. He pointed to a spot overhead in the towering canopy: a family of spider monkeys.

Spider monkeys! A real *National Geographic* moment! We stared at them, craning our necks skyward. The monkeys stared back, cautious and unsure what to make of us. Jose spoke to us in hushed Portuguese, while Josue translated, his words confirming a dim memory I had about these creatures: They're extremely territorial.

One of the monkeys took a branch in his hands. He held it for a moment, then threw it at us. "They want us to leave," Josue noted. Sure enough, more monkeys in the group were now cracking off limbs and hurling them our way as if to say, *Hey! You in the fanny pack! Scram!* They were too high in the canopy for their "attack" to be effective, so we just continued, unscathed and chuckling. (The monkeys trailed us to make sure we never came back. *And stay away!*)

We had booked less than a full week in the Amazon, but the longer we stayed with Josue and the guys, the more we relaxed. We hiked, swam, and bird-watched. We jumped off the boat into the Rio Negro for more swimming when we got hot, Teddy even cannonballing from the top of the boat. I spotted a toucan, a giant freshwater stingray, and some rare pink river dolphins. We got to know our guides, laughing at their stories over delicious home-cooked meals together.

I knew I had relaxed more than I realized when I agreed to go piranha fishing. We descended again into that aluminum dinghy, Jose in back steering us in his strong and silent way through a watery mangrove forest, while Josue explained in English how piranhas live near submerged clumps of trees in deep, still waters like these. It was the rainy season, he said, so the river was especially high, creating optimal fishing conditions. When we found a quiet spot, Jose cut off the engine and Josue baited rods made of bamboo and string with cubes of raw steak and passed one to everyone in the boat, including me.

There I was, the ultimate good sport, setting aside my fear of fish for the sake of adventure. We dropped our lines and listened as Josue laid out detailed instructions that could not have been clearer: *Piranhas are smart. They know how to nibble the bait off a hook and slip away undetected. If you feel anything at all, jerk your line upward with only the slightest flick of the wrist and you'll be able to snag one.*

We waited in silence, our lines in the water, repeating the instructions to ourselves.

After just a few minutes, Laura's line went taut. "I think I feel something," she whispered with urgency. I whipped around to see her line stretching away from our boat and felt the back of my neck tingle. How is it that only then, when it was way, way too late, did it dawn on me that "going piranha fishing" meant catching actual live piranhas and sharing a tiny boat space with them? Laura adjusted her grip and stuck out her tongue in concentration. My mouth went dry. *This is it,* I thought. *Here comes the flick.*

Only Laura didn't flick her wrist. In fact, Laura didn't do any of the steps on Josue's list. For whatever reason, Laura instead summoned the kind of strength one might need to reel in a 300-pound marlin and hauled back so hard that the piranha she'd hooked shot straight to the sky. We jerked our faces up in horror, freezing at the sight of it sailing over our heads. It seemed to hover, the sun glinting off its silver body. *Maybe it will just stay up there,* I thought. But Laura's piranha smacked a tree branch and came hurtling back down, directly at our boat.

Now, my composure has always ranked among my greatest assets. "Unflappable," "steady," "cool as a cucumber"—this is how friends and colleagues have described me, especially under pressure. A busy doctor once interrupted herself mid-exam to say, "You know, you have *the most* calming presence."

But when that piranha landed in my lap, someone was screaming bloody murder, and it was definitely me. As soon as it touched my thighs, I crashed backward to the floor of the boat, clawing Willa with me so that we both smacked our heads loudly on the metal. Face up in the boat, we imagined the flesh-eating piranha gnashing its teeth somewhere beneath our backs and our cries went from panicked to blood-curdling.

Over our screams, Jose and Josue barked orders to each other in Portuguese and lunged to pull us upright, sending the dinghy lurching side to side. Eagle-eyed Teddy spotted the fish and pinned it with his backpack long enough for Jose to scoop it into a cooler.

As quickly as it began, it was over. The seven of us breathed hard. The boat rocked and our guides looked at each other with wide eyes. Willa sobbed into Teddy's shoulder, while James's face froze in a thousand-yard stare. I panted, "I'm sorry!" to no one in particular as Laura repeated an equally winded, "No, *I'm* sorry!"

How could I have been such an idiot? What if I'd fallen overboard? What if *Willa* had? *What if I'd capsized the whole damn boat into piranha-infested waters hundreds of miles from the nearest hospital?* While I pondered the terrifying possibilities, a flock of parrots overhead squawked in a panicked frenzy, hopping along a branch flapping their wings. The piranha had startled them as much as it had us. Watching them, the absurdity of the situation sank in.

I'm not sure who started laughing first, but once we started, we couldn't stop. Teddy, Laura, and I had tears streaming down our faces, while the guides bent at the waist, gasping for air. Willa and James, surprised at this twist, quickly joined in too. The parrots went even more bonkers, which only made us laugh harder. Jose, red in the face and wiping his eyes, pointed at them and choked out a pretend bird call at my expense: "Gringo! Gringo!" before convulsing again.

Just when we'd try to catch our breath, someone would do an impersonation of my flailing and we'd start up again. When Jose reached into a cooler to pass out a few much-needed beers, I jumped out of my seat at the sound of his hand digging into the ice, another display of goofiness that sent us back into tears. It was the hardest any of us could ever remember laughing.

Eventually we regained our composure and even caught three more piranhas, though the guides were quick to take the rods whenever we felt a nibble. I joined everyone in eating our catch for dinner back on the boat, then later, as we crawled into our bunks after dessert, the four of us were still cracking up. So was the crew. We could hear their hysterical laughter drifting up from the kitchen, where Josue and Jose were apparently offering a play-by-play in Portuguese for the cook and captain. Their howling carried for miles in the darkness.

Up until the Amazon, our nice tidy trip had been going well. Across ten different stays in Jamaica, Colombia, Peru, and Chile, we'd learned to designate roles and manage kids in restaurants. We had the laundry routine down. We knew how to befriend strangers! We were better about navigating our children's mood and needs, their likes and dislikes. We were all getting to know each other better.

But when I look back at our family as we were in the days before the Amazon, I see the same people that lived in New York. Yes, we were "road-schooling" and yes, we were together all the time. But there was a quality to our dynamic that differed very little from the ways we had interacted back in New York. Teddy and I were the married couple. The kids were the kids. The world out there was still the world out there. None of it was particularly enmeshed.

The Amazon shook all that up. For the first time, we saw Willa and James differently. No longer were we divided into Those Who Know Stuff (grownups) and Those Who Don't (kids). Out there, we'd all been equal in the eyes of the Amazon, and Willa and James had surprised us with their bravery. Who were these cool people laughing alongside us, at ease in the world, game for whatever? The ones who chatted up new friends and leapt into mystery waters? Who recovered easily from piranha attacks?

And while getting more comfortable with risk wasn't on our to-do list, that happened, too. It was hard to imagine that just a few weeks before, I'd fretted about the seesaws in Santiago. Compared to the Amazon, when the four of us were jumping off a boat into black river water and trekking without cell service among god knows how many hairy spiders, concern about a playground seemed ludicrous.

After five days, we didn't want to leave. We'd grown attached to the boat and our new "family" out there. It had been our first major leap of faith, and we felt a deep sense of gratitude to Josue and the others for everything they'd shown us, including that we were tougher than we thought and capable of more than we'd given ourselves credit for.

Bahia/Salvador

Right when we started to wonder if our kids would ever get better at airports, they started to. Not surprisingly, the change in behavior came after our Amazon week, when everyone seemed to mature by a decade.

On day forty-six, with fifteen flights already under their belts, as we flew from Manaus to Salvador with a stop in Fortaleza, we noted in our blog that, "Our kids are getting the hang of the travel thing. Waiting in airports didn't faze them today. This serenity would have been unheard of even a few weeks ago. We sat at the airline counter for forty-five minutes in Manaus and they didn't whine, complain, or punch each other once. They knew the drill at security. They sensed when to ask questions and when to let the grownups figure things out in peace."

We had two nights in Salvador, a major city that confirmed a fact about the year that we hadn't anticipated when planning it: *Taking four- and six-year-olds around the globe will expose them to complex issues and concepts earlier than anticipated. Be ready to answer tough questions.*

On our first day, Map Guy began leading us down a side street when a local street vendor in his sixties whistled at us to halt. He'd sized up our map-searching, fanny-pack-wearing gringo-ness and signaled with a wagging finger and some Portuguese that we shouldn't walk that way. This six-second interaction and the subsequent glance between Teddy and me prompted a flood of questions from Willa and James about what possible danger might have lurked down that street.

Despite raising kids in New York, we hadn't felt it necessary at their age to talk about crime. Now, though, it was just another topic in a growing list of "Tough Questions" that Willa and James asked as we traveled. The potential for Tough Questions lurked everywhere, even when we intentionally tried to keep things light and age appropriate. Like Bob Marley's house, which had seemed innocent enough—we sang "One Love" and got to see his recording studio!—but had ended with us fumbling to explain the words "assassination attempt."

When we'd set out to explore South America's many churches, we thought we'd be admiring archways and gargoyles, not explaining what those life-like Jesus mannequins, anguished and bloody, were all about. "What happened to that man?" they'd ask. We hadn't done much in the way of Sunday school, and the story of his life was new to them. Our attempts at responses only drew more questions. "So people can come back alive after they die?"

In Colombia, Chile, and Peru, there were questions about Europeans and indigenous people, like Willa's repeated question at Machu Picchu: "How come they say [American explorer] Hiram Bingham 'discovered' Machu Picchu when my book says a local boy showed him where it was?" Simple question, complicated answer. Or amidst Salvador's colorful colonial streets, which played host to impromptu Afro-Caribbean drum performances. When we explained to Willa and James the history of its *Pelourinho* main plaza, which had once been a notorious slave-trading square, they wanted to know: *What was slavery again?* After she heard our answer, Willa forgot all about the music and looked out the window of an old church, lost in thought.

"What came first?" she finally asked. "Jesus or slavery?"

Pollution and conservation and respecting different cultures were subjects I was prepared for, but seeing the world apparently meant talking about murder, torture, slavery, street crime, and white supremacy, too. Obvious in hindsight, but these topics somehow caught us off guard every time. We didn't know what else to say, so our responses were usually blunt. *Here's what happened. Here's what this means. Here's what people did.*

When we arrived in Praia do Forte, a beach one hour north of Salvador by car, we were ready to rest. I know that sounds ridiculous, but we'd spent seven weeks in constant motion in South America and now understood the silly phrase "I need a vacation from my vacation." Back when we'd baked a few periods of R&R into our year-long itinerary, we'd assumed they wouldn't actually be necessary. It turned out they were. Plus, it was Teddy's birthday.

The place we booked for five nights was a Florida-ish resort with 250 rooms and a fleet of golf carts to shuttle sunburned São Paulistano families on school break from pool to buffet and back again. There was a spa and nightly activities like bingo and live music. It might have been an adventurer's hell, but it was an interloper's heaven. I felt like we'd snuck into a real-life Brazilian vacation, not some American travel agent's creation of a Perfect Brazilian Stay. There were no outsiders there because, as Teddy noted, "They'd have to fly over a lot of water sports resorts to reach this one." No one spoke much English and our presence confounded people.

That particular week in February was a big one for vacationing Brazilians, kind of like the last week of August in the U.S. Many families were there to escape the chaos of Carnaval in their cities and enjoy a getaway before back-to-school season kicked off the following week (in March). This meant we saw a lot of unhappy, sniping, exhausted-looking parents who all shared the same dazed stare. *Why did we think it was a good idea to bring our toddler here?* Every table in the buffet hall had at least one propped-up iPad blaring Portuguese-language cartoons to tranquilize preschoolers. Parents bickered or sat without talking to each other, zoned out on too-little sleep. When packs of monkeys descended from the rafters at breakfast to steal fruit and bread, it barely registered.

As we walked to dinner on our first night, someone called out to us in accented English. It was a German man with his wife and six-year-old daughter, clearly as surprised to see another non-Sao Paulo family as we were. They introduced themselves as Bjorn and Eva from Berlin, a radio personality and a TV actress, and explained they were in the country visiting extended family. We ate dinner together most nights after that, a table of outsiders at the buffet, toasting birthday rounds of caipirinhas and celebrating the fact that we didn't have babies or toddlers.

Willa and James learned to surf with help from a couple of teenage instructors with braces. The lack of shared language did not seem to matter. By the end, Willa had learned enough pantomiming to book her own lesson with the water sports desk, a bit of independence we hadn't seen much of before. "I like surfing because I'm good at it," Willa informed us at lunch one day between bites of a lime slice. She'd figured out how to order a small plate of them at meals and would eat them one by one.

One afternoon, Teddy and I brought our laptops out to the pool, which we had not done much of that year so far. We had housekeeping to do before we left South America—answering travel agent questions about upcoming stops in Africa, updating the blog, replying to emails—and thought it made sense to let the kids swim while we knocked out some to-dos. "When are you coming *iiiiiiiiin,*" James whined. "Yeah, what are you *doooooing?*" Willa asked.

This fool's errand confirmed how one assumption we'd made about the year had been laughably off. Not homeschooling, which we'd thought would be easy but was actually a nightmare, nor homesickness, which we'd assumed would kick in at some point but hadn't at all. Rather, we saw how foolish we had been to assume that this year of travel without jobs would translate to lots of free time. We had no free time.

Obviously, the palpable absence of work from our lives felt incredible. We'd worked at such a burnout pace for so long that the quiet had a record-scratch abruptness to it. It reminded me of that glorious feeling you get when you step out into a hot summer day after sitting for hours in arctic air-conditioning; your shoulders relax, your body unclenches. It was only once you started thawing that you understood how uncomfortable you'd been. Sundays weren't "scary." Teddy and I would start breakfast on Monday mornings by shaking our heads in disbelief that we had nowhere to be, saying "Monday morning" aloud just to remind ourselves to appreciate the peace.

We had not, however, anticipated how this trip would be a full-time job. With our children around all day and night, requiring meals, schooling, and support in unfamiliar environments, it seemed as if we couldn't write or read one sentence without one of them hollering at us from the pool or the couch to show us a trick, tattle on the other, or ask when we were going to join their game. How was it impossible for them to *just play on their own for thirty freaking minutes?*

Even when we were sitting around doing quiet independent activities like coloring, there were the questions. (So many questions!) "Will I have my same hair when I'm a grownup?" "If you stacked everything in the world on top of each other, how tall would it be?" "Is it true that food is better in November?" "What is powder?" When they finally went to sleep, we had our own reading up to do, planning, blog writing, and photos to edit.

Which meant that despite everything I'd imagined, there would be no uninterrupted "flow" time for things like writing, drawing, and photography. No use for the precious little watercolor set and sketchbook I'd packed, nor the fancy DSLR camera. And Teddy? His concern that he might be bored in the "absence of a challenge" now seemed laughable.

We had abandoned notions of a "couples getaway" back in Cartagena (see: "We signed up for this"). But by now we had added another mantra, this one about free time: *That's another trip.* As in, "Oh you want to spend a few hours shooting street photography? Sketching? Enjoying long stretches of deep thought while staring at a view? *That's another trip.*" One where we didn't have a four-year-old tugging on our pant legs, asking where his pencil sharpener was.

São Paulo

I expected that the concierge at our hotel in Sao Paulo, the final stop on our South America itinerary, would be able to help me box and ship home all the souvenirs we'd collected so far. There were some wooden bowls, a bottle of perfume from Colombia, two Peruvian ponchos, and even the cleaned jaws of that infamous piranha. Sending it all back was our last bit of housekeeping before leaving the continent the next morning.

At first we were ambivalent about souvenirs. How could we collect them if we were trying to travel light? Did we even need them? Wouldn't shipping them be expensive? But then we spoke with a guy who'd taken a similar trip with his young family years before. Their only regret, he said, was that they'd considered souvenirs too costly and burdensome and didn't buy any. Now, ten years on, they had "nothing tangible to show for our experience."

That's all the convincing we needed. We collected items we couldn't find in the U.S. and treasures that reminded us of a specific moment, staying away from cheap and cheesy junk, even though our kids begged for it at every gift shop. (We managed to fend them off by channeling their focus into specific collections like stacks of plastic hotel key cards and coins, which they still have.)

Eventually we started carrying a spare tote bag just for souvenirs. Just as a full laundry bag meant it was time to find a laundromat, a full souvenir tote meant it was time to find a DHL. Sao Paulo was our first experience trying this out, and we had things to learn. Bottles of alcohol (perfume) couldn't always be shipped internationally. Countries have rules about what can't leave its borders—like Amazon artifacts. Our concierge frowned as she inspected a traditional wooden blowgun that Josue had whittled for Willa and James. He had stayed up late wearing a headlamp to finish it, then trained the kids to spit darts at a makeshift target. The concierge warned me that customs might not like the looks of it.

I kept the perfume with me and packed the rest, trying my luck. Sure enough, DHL dropped the box on my parents' porch a few weeks later. Today the blowgun hangs on our wall in NYC near the piranha jaws, which we framed. As for the perfume, I wound up carrying it with me the rest of the year, wearing it almost every day. I can barely open the bottle today without being immediately transported back to that time in my life.

We were preparing for Africa, where we'd settle into a new chapter of our adventure—or "Season 2" as one Instagram follower called it—for the next nine weeks. It was hard to imagine we were leaving one foreign continent for another and not heading home. Back in those early days of the trip, our brains still hadn't adjusted to the concept of a *full year* of travels. When we'd pack up on the last day in a spot, we'd experience the gut-punch you get at the end of an awesome trip. *I guess it's back to reality!* Then, in the same second, we'd remember: We were packing to go on another trip.

Before we left New York, people always asked if we thought moving so frequently would be exhausting. We'd wondered the same thing. By the end of South America we'd already stayed in twenty-two different places, including an airport Holiday Inn, an overnight train, the Amazon riverboat, a ranch, an un-AC'd Airbnb apartment, and that Orlando-style mega resort. And, of course, shag-carpeted Casa Teatro in Manaus.

Meanwhile, Willa and James easily adapted to all the moving around. Any unease they felt when falling asleep in new beds was dispelled by the fact that we were all so close together, Teddy and I in the same room or just on the other side of a wall. Willa and James often shared a bed, which helped too. In fact, changing "homes" every few days seemed to excite them more than anything else.

We also weren't doing many painfully early wake-up calls, which eliminated a lot of dread and exhaustion from each transition. Unconcerned about missing chunks of the day to travel, we opted for late morning or midday flights. And while "living out of a suitcase" implied frustration about being away from a homebase, the fact that a small suitcase *was* our homebase made life feel more manageable, not less. The few items we packed each had their proper place, the exercise of zipping up like tidying a very small apartment. Plus, constant newness energized us. Each time we moved on, we did so with the excitement of people about to go on vacation. We understood exactly what travel writer Bill Bryson meant when he wrote, "I could spend my life arriving each evening in a new city."

Before we left for South Africa, we still had two people to see. The first was Laura, our Amazon river boat buddy. She lived in Sao Paulo, not far from our hotel, and came to pick us up, all of us giddy about our reunion with the only other person who could relate to our Amazon experience. We adored her, even if she *had* slung a piranha into my lap.

Laura drove us to her favorite restaurant, explaining that Brazil had the largest number of people with full or partial Italian ancestry outside Italy and that Sao Paulo was known for its absurdly good Italian food. Braz Pizzaria did not disappoint. We ordered a few pies from their wood-burning oven and washed them down with caipirinhas, toasting Jose and Josue. Then she presented Willa and James with a little stuffed animal jaguar named Juma and asked if they would carry her around the world and snap photos on

WhatsApp. This, she told them, would be her way of tagging along on our adventure vicariously since she wasn't on Instagram. We found a special spot for Juma in James's suitcase.

The second person we saw was Brendan, Teddy's father, the one who disliked travel so much we weren't sure we'd see him at all that year. Coincidentally, a trip he had to take to Sao Paulo for work overlapped with ours for twenty minutes. We had just enough time before our flight to South Africa to catch up at his hotel and unwrap a card game called Rat-a-Tat-Cat from Lobsy. It was disorienting, but somehow fitting: Just as we were about to go to Africa, we were with the last person to see us off in Washington. And sure enough, he gave us that same loving nod and reminder to be safe.

AFRICA

Nine weeks: South Africa (Cape Town, Road trip along the Garden Route) → Zimbabwe (Lake Kariba, Hwange National Park) → Zambia (Victoria Falls, Katambora) → South Africa (Timbavati National Park, Durban, Johannesburg) → Mozambique (Vilanculos)

South Africa

Cape Town

In his memoir *Love, Africa*, former *New York Times* East Africa correspondent Jeffrey Gettleman asked, "Is it even possible for an outsider to look at Africa, to see it as it really is, without eyes jaundiced by all that we have read and heard about it?" After my experience in Tanzania, I wanted to approach our itinerary across South Africa, Zambia, Zimbabwe, and Mozambique as objectively as possible.

"I want to see the real South Africa," I told a South African friend when we were still in New York. "I want to see the *authentic* place."

"Be careful with that word 'authentic,'" she cautioned. "It's ... tricky." I had meant I wanted to interlope in its cities—see the gyms and schools and markets and movie theaters and observe all the people in and around them. I suspected this was her way of telling me not to go searching for, say, people in tribal robes.

At almost ten hours, the redeye from Sao Paulo to Johannesburg marked our first long-haul flight and a grueling sleepless marathon. After a connection to Cape Town, we arrived squinting in the late summer morning light. (The concept of March being late summer still made my brain hurt.) Teddy tentatively navigated our rental car along the left side of the highway all the way to the quiet Oranjezicht neighborhood, our home for the next two and a half weeks and our single longest stay of the year.

Spending so much time in Cape Town was the inspired idea of Tamsyn, our travel agent in Africa. A South African who lived in the U.S., Tamsyn was the agent who'd rescued us from the depths of our logistics hell back when we were attempting to plan everything ourselves. She delivered a nine-week itinerary with a bow on top, complete with house rentals, road trips, small independent lodges where she personally knew the owners, and bush plane charters. Exhausted by our many failures, we'd taken one look and said: "Book it."

When we pulled up, we saw a historic three-bedroom bungalow perched on a very steep, tree-lined street in the foothills of Table Mountain, Cape Town's iconic landmark. The neighborhood was walking distance to shops and cafes farther down the hill and, according to the agent who greeted us with keys, catered to an arty set.

Someone named Justine, according to a piece of junk mail we found in the slot, owned the place and was effortlessly cool. Wide-plank pine floors original to the 1920s house ran throughout; a renovated kitchen opened into a little yard with a tree and plunge pool. Justine had delightfully faded needlepoint upholstery, well-worn mid-century Danish leather chairs, a farm table with bright, mismatched chairs, and a 1980s diesel Mercedes station wagon in the garage—with a surfboard strapped to the roof. For New Yorkers used to a box in the sky, this felt like a real home.

The first thing we noticed about Cape Town was the wind. A complicated combination of pressure systems, proximity to the mountains, and swirling ocean currents made it one of the windiest cities on earth, and we'd arrived at the end of its most intense season. Our old house rattled so unrelentingly that it would trigger the burglar alarm, so we stopped setting it before bed. Not that Willa and James noticed—their window panes shook all night yet they never woke up once.

Willa noted in her journal that week that a "con" of house rentals was "no bofay," but as we settled into our new house we welcomed the break from hotel breakfasts. We'd sit around in our pajamas making plans for each day's post-homeschooling outing. Something about having two whole empty weeks, our own car, our own house felt indulgent. Being "settled" wasn't just a superficial reference to unpacking for a relatively extended period. We could slow down and pretend to be locals.

We started with Cafe Paradiso on Kloof Street, which sat at the bottom of our hill and offered indoor and outdoor seating for neighborhood diners. Our first afternoon, we wandered up. "Do the kids want to come back with me and make some pizza?" our server asked. She explained that for $4 a child, Paradiso invited kid patrons into the kitchen to make personal pizzas, decorate cookies, and hang out with the other kids and waitstaff while parents relaxed alone. The place's many two-top tables were filled with parents enjoying $6 gin and tonics and uninterrupted conversation while their kids baked in the back. Willa and James disappeared with our server.

We established a grocery routine, making regular stops at our local Woolworth's, which everyone called Woolies. During one of my first trips, just when I reached the front of the long, after-work weekday line, I realized I'd forgotten to get charcoal for the grill. When I mentioned it off-hand to the cashier—totally prepared to give up the whole barbecue thing because of the hassle—she replied, "Oh I'll grab it for you!" and ran off. Two minutes later she was back with a huge bag of charcoal. I couldn't imagine such a thing happening in New York.

Teddy's increasingly confident left-side-of-the-road driving skills added to the sense that we were part of the local mix. We rode around town in our Rav-4, exploring new neighborhoods, testing different playgrounds and lunch spots, the scene out our window like B-roll from the documentary *Searching for Sugarman*—stunning cliffside roads woven in and out of huge aquamarine swells crashing into boulders below. One day we drove to a beach where Willa and James played for hours in the sand. When a gust of Cape Town's famous wind sent a vendor's baseball cap careening down the beach, they sprinted after it, performing two heroic diving tackles to pin the hat down and proudly return it to the man.

All that exploring and driving around the city introduced us to Cape Town's unique parking situation. Everywhere we went, a local guy in a pseudo-official fluorescent green vest would wave us over to a parking spot. First we groaned, viewing these "helpers" as some kind of squeegee nuisance, but when we had no idea where to park, what was legal, where to go or how to find the shop we were looking for, these green-vested guys would help. We began to look for them and had our tips handy whenever we knew we'd have to park.

We walked so much everyday that an actual fitness routine seemed redundant, but in Cape Town I signed up for regular "heated boxing" classes. The boxing class was just as much for the people watching as the sweat. Cape Town boasted a thriving modeling industry, and my fellow boxers were all six-foot-tall stunners in their twenties, more interested, it seemed, in juicing their social media likes with sweaty workout selfies. Multiple times per class, a leggy participant would stop hitting the heavy bag and ask the instructor to capture video of her delivering uppercuts while pouting seductively. No one seemed to notice the American mom in the corner, grunting away.

In the afternoons, Teddy would drive us to De Waal Park, a local grassy stretch with a few swings. Willa and James grew to love throwing balls for assorted sheepdogs, dobermans, collies, and labs who congregated after work hours. A sign reading "Dogs must be on a leash" dangled upside down from a nail. One day they befriended a little girl their age named Mia. The three of them took turns lobbing tennis balls for the dogs, laughing the whole time. When it was time to leave, Willa walked up to Mia's parents. "We'll be back," she said. "I live nearby!"

The first few months of our trip were a much larger percentage of Willa's and James's young lives than ours, and the changes in them became more pronounced around this time. Maybe it was just the fact that in Cape Town we weren't as much on the move, and I could be more attuned to subtle shifts.

The pain of homeschooling, for instance, had begun to dissipate, if only a little. We were nearing day one hundred and had realized somewhere along the way that rewards worked. We initially hated the idea of a transactional relationship with learning. *Why would I offer kickbacks for work they're supposed to be doing?* Yet, after we dangled a new iPad game for every six school days completed without a snarky attitude or tears, Willa responded so well that we changed our tune.

Or perhaps Willa, and to some extent, James, simply surrendered. They'd fought valiantly, but we broke them in the end. Our unwavering consistency—ninety minutes of schooling each morning on non-travel days no matter what—showed them school would happen, whether they threw a tantrum or not.

In Cape Town, Willa and I would arrange ourselves on one of Justine's couches in her sun-drenched living room, faded surf photo books lining the shelves, and practice reading aloud or decorate flashcards she used for sight words. At the kitchen table, James and Teddy played a version of Blackjack called "Twenty-One or Bust" and read his beginner Spiderman and Hulk comics. Not always perfect, but most mornings had a nice, productive hum to them.

The most unexpected dividend from this breakthrough wasn't that homeschooling had become easier, it was realizing that despite all the drama, it had propelled both kids past their grade level. James could now read those comics himself and Willa was easily adding and subtracting large sums in her head. It turned out that one-on-one customized teaching, even when it was going *very, very badly,* worked.

After months of eating in restaurants, I had to make fewer "announcements" about putting napkins in laps and keeping elbows off tables. A middle-aged British woman even walked over to compliment Willa and James on their manners at one restaurant. Teddy and I improved our restaurant habits, too. We always had a plan for where and what we were eating before someone uttered those two dreaded words, "I'm hungry." Where once we'd scanned menus for familiar items they would eat, even allowing the kids to select what they wanted, we took over all food decision-making to get them trying new cuisines and eating a healthier variety. We stopped wasting food, too, having learned that two dishes—three at the maximum—was plenty of food for four of us.

Willa and James brought their new restaurant know-how to a local bed and breakfast in the Imizamo Yethu township near Hout Bay, a place run by community matriarch Mama Miriam. We had questions about all facets of Cape Town and South Africa and felt that a walk and shared meal with local guide and resident Mhinti could offer a window into township life. Townships were ghettos for Black South Africans during apartheid. Today many still exist, some as established suburbs with deep roots, others as impoverished towns with a revolving door of locals and immigrants. Imizamo Yethu had new government-built houses at its town center as well as paved roads, but sprawling around its outskirts were hundreds, maybe thousands, of metal shacks without plumbing or electricity, corrugated roofs pinned down against vicious wind by rocks, tires, and other heavy objects.

We joined four Germans and a Swedish couple with a ten-month-old baby named Ines as Mhinti walked us from a local pub to a school to her church. We met volunteer members of a safety patrol who kept crime and school truancy down, and then Miriam, a community leader who ran a popular boarding house and restaurant. Our group stepped into her living room hungry, ready to eat whatever Miriam was stirring on the stovetop. Willa and James stood in line with their plates outstretched as Miriam piled them up with home-cooked chicken, spinach greens, and a traditional tomato and bean side called *chakalaka*. I couldn't help but think how much the meal tasted like Southern American comfort food, especially when paired with liter bottles of Coca-Cola Miriam had set out on each table. Willa and James said "please" and "thank you" and politely tucked in with everyone else, eventually clearing their plates.

Before arriving in South Africa, I reached out to Luke, an American college buddy of mine who lived in Cape Town. "Marge," he wrote back. "Great to hear from you, you old bat." He had a house and a career and had married Meg, a woman from Johannesburg. The two of them showed us around their city, including sunset barbecues on the beach and picnics at the famed botanical gardens, teaching us local slang and driving etiquette as we went. They explained how locals coped with the wind by downloading special apps that showed which specific parts of the city's topography would be affected on any given day.

Then Luke and Meg invited us out for a grownup dinner. "Willa and James are welcome to join," Meg said. "But I do have the name of a sitter if you want a night out without them?"

Some people might consider it irresponsible to even consider leaving kids with a stranger in a faraway country. Others might ask, "What the hell took you so long?" But everyone wanted to know how we managed without childcare.

The unbroken togetherness hadn't come naturally to us, but, like anything, we got used to it with time and practice. Any worries we'd once had that a lack of childcare might mean no couple quality time had long disappeared, too. Teddy and I were spending more time together than we ever had in our relationship, chit chatting on playground benches, shooting the breeze while the kids played. It's how I imagine retired couples might be, just enjoying each other's company in an unhurried fashion. (And as for our more, um, intimate life, that was fine, too. Uninterrupted. This was made easier since we usually stayed in places where we had our own room—with a door that locked.)

Which brings me back to a night out with friends. Wasn't it time? We took Meg up on her babysitter introduction and as soon as twenty-something Melissa showed up at our door all smiles and coloring books, Willa and James mobbed her before she'd even taken off her jacket. James had hated new sitters before this trip, but now he and his sister were talking over each other, breathlessly recounting every obscure detail of their lives. It dawned on us that maybe Willa and James had needed a break from *us*. They didn't even notice when we walked out.

⌣⟋

Having our kids around to watch everything we did and hear everything we said was part of what convinced us to take this trip. It was a golden opportunity to model our values, behaviors, and beliefs, like being considerate, listening, showing respect, saying please and thank you, knowing how to behave in public spaces, showing gratitude, asking questions, being curious, being on time, telling a story, acknowledging differences, trying new things, respecting the environment, having a firm handshake, accepting new cultures and ways of life, being gracious—you get the idea.

What we hadn't considered in all this, however, was how some of our rougher edges would also be on display. Cursing became a problem, for instance. One morning as I dealt a fresh hand for Rat-a-Tat-Cat, the kids' new favorite card game, Willa looked at me and said, "I'm going to kick your ass off." She mistook my speechlessness for confusion and leaned forward, speaking carefully for her slow mother: "That means I'm going to *win* you."

Earlier that same week, James had dismissed a gift shop's selection as "crap," and another time, after getting scolded, called me "a dammit."

Shit.

Rather than treat salty language as taboo and scold them, we told them what each word meant, and explained how and why they might offend people when used. We figured after so many tough conversations about violence, religion, and injustice, they could handle it. They were most enlightened by the definition of "asshole." Despite knowing what "ass" meant, they couldn't quite piece together what an *asshole* might be. "A hole filled with asses?" James wondered. After we cleared that up, he asked, "Is there a bad word for every letter in the alphabet?" referring to our use of "s-word" and "d-word." I assured him that no, I had not left any out.

Other times our actions, not our words, were the problem. Teddy and I often found ourselves on our devices for logistical reasons—maps, translations, figuring out where to get lunch, texting guides and contacts, or booking tickets. Willa and James were seeing us use our screens way more now than they had back home when we worked. We'd read enough parenting articles to know this was bad.

With the exquisitely tuned radar that children have for what they see as any kind of hypocrisy or parental foible, the kids started needling us. Willa began referring to our phones as "Plastic Metal Things," a six-year-old's attempt at a withering put-down. She must have gotten such a good reaction the first time she did this that she used it to shame us relentlessly for weeks. "Watch me jump in the pool instead of looking at your Plastic Metal Thing!" Or, "Mom, what's your favorite activity? Looking at your Plastic Metal Thing?"

When Teddy challenged James to a spelling game in homeschool one morning at our Cape Town kitchen table, James offered the odds. "If I win, I get a Nutella sandwich," he said. "If you win, you get to look at your computer all day."

As irritating as this was, it inspired a new protocol: If we needed to use our phone or laptop, we'd either go to another room or clearly say exactly what we were doing. "I'm looking up the price of aquarium tickets," for instance. No more zoned-out scrolling in their presence without explanation.

In Cape Town, we decided Willa and James needed to learn how to ride bikes. We were a little defensive that they couldn't already. "They're New Yorkers!" we told ourselves. "Kids don't *do* bikes there!" But of course that's not true. And with ample opportunities for family bike rides ahead, we decided to teach them once and for all.

Constantia, a suburb of Cape Town, was renowned for its vineyards, but it also had a bike park. The place featured a couple of dirt-packed acres with man-made hills large and small for kids of all levels. After 3 p.m. the place would fill with kids in helmets charging over humps and flying off ramps, but in the morning it was mostly empty. We rented two glider bikes from a guy at the desk named Blaise, and Willa and James spent the next three hours waddling gingerly around in the dust.

There were tears, bumps, and bruises. "Those *babies* can ride and I can't!" sobbed Willa, pounding her handlebars in high-drama mode as toddlers too young for school whizzed by. Occasionally a troop of baboons would wander around the course until Blaise shooed them off. "Why not let them stay?" we asked. "They're so cute!" Blaise gave us a funny look but didn't answer.

That night before bed I shared this bicycling effort with our Instagram following, which had recently crept past 500 people and continued to grow daily. They responded with cheers and advice, as if seated in bleachers right there in Constantia. "Gooo Willa!" "Raise James's seat!"

Social media was playing a more significant part in our travels than we anticipated, with one group of followers in particular becoming enthusiastic "regulars" who seemed personally invested in our days. These weren't just family and close friends, but also people we met on the road or contacts from the past who'd come out of the woodwork. The one thing they had in common was an earnest curiosity.

This wasn't a crowd that wanted sunsets and panoramas. They hankered for details about laundry missions and homeschooling meltdowns, Restaurant Face and packing tips—like the time we started using hotel shower caps as shoe covers. They liked being shown things like how Cape Town business owners seemed to love "punny" brand names such as Bed Fellows (mattress store), Stalk of the Town (flower shop), Off the Hook (seafood restaurant), and Afro Dizzy Acts (talent management). They were so actively engaged that sometimes it felt as though they were with us—which was weirdly comforting. Our motivation to post photos morphed from "staying in touch" to "bringing people with us."

I tried to keep our Instagram's written content postcard-ish, opting for facts and personal anecdotes, like a series about two kids learning to ride bikes in a suburban South African park, over gushing platitudes. Sometimes *not* posting at all became the story. When we signed off to head into the Amazon for five days, a friend described the radio silence as a drama of its own. *What was happening down there?*

My friend's insistence that our Instagram show "barfing" stayed with me as a reminder to keep things honest, especially when it came to the realities of parenting. There were more than a few posts of tired kids, lagging behind us and whining. We also made sure to laugh at ourselves. I embraced our dorkiness, posting photos of myself asleep on a long flight, mouth slung wide open, or wearing my fanny pack while using municipal exercise machines (the latter, incidentally, became a fan favorite, leading me to duplicate the act in dozens of public parks around the world).

Since Teddy the Content Intern had the idea to only follow people and places we encountered on our trip, our feed became a living rolodex of the restaurants, museums, hairdressers, guides, friends of friends, Uber drivers, restaurants, and people like Blaise and places like this bike park that had filled our days. And yes, in that Cape Town bike park, both Willa and James learned to ride bikes.

Cape Town had just recently recovered from a historic drought, which, by some accounts, had nearly cratered its economy. Though Cape Town had survived, its citizens had dramatically altered their behavior and encouraged visitors to do the same. Signs everywhere reminded us to use hand sanitizer instead of soap and water, to take two-minute showers, to forgo car washing, and cover swimming pools to prevent evaporation. Someone we befriended told us about hosting houseguests from Johannesburg who flushed after each toilet use, an egregious violation that earned them the nickname "The Flushers."

The drought had hurt tourism. Visitors from Europe and the U.S. had canceled trips, and the hospitality industry was still suffering, its many servers and cooks out of work. Entire restaurants had gone under, and the effects were expected to last years beyond the actual drought recovery. We had learned the same lesson in Bogota: Negative news headlines discourage visitors and hurt economies.

For us, the lack of crowds gave our afternoons a leisurely feel. Some days our post-school excursions were touristy (aquarium), while others were pure interloping (bike park). One night we caught a rugby match between the Cape Town Stormers and the Jaguars from Argentina. We watched a "Rugby for Dummies" video on YouTube while Ubering to the famed Newlands Stadium, then cheered on the "scrums" and "hookers" from crude stands while wearing Stormers merch fresh from the shop, only barely understanding the spectacle before us.

To understand South Africa's complicated and troubled past, Teddy and I dug into memoirs and histories of the place, while Willa read books like, *"Who Was Nelson Mandela?"* an age-appropriate chapter book. In discussing it together, I saw how concepts like blatant racism and apartheid confused even a thoughtful six-year-old. Kids' brains try to make sense of the world and nothing about apartheid made sense.

Willa and I made the pilgrimage to Robben Island, the prison where Nelson Mandela and other anti-apartheid activists had been imprisoned. Eighteen of Mandela's twenty-seven years behind bars were spent at Robben Island. There were audible gasps when our elderly guide told us that he himself had been a political prisoner on the island for twelve years alongside Mandela. He described the harsh treatment and despair of his daily existence.

Nelson Mandela's cell was housed in the infamous Section B solitary confinement ward, which we reached by passing through a concrete barrier three feet thick. We peered into the narrow shaft, a space that was more tomb than cell, with only enough room inside to stand up and take a few steps. A thin mat on the floor. A small window high on the wall. Eighteen years. The crowded ferry ride back was nearly silent.

Five o'clock in Cape Town kicked off a daily ritual. Teddy and I would pull down a bottle of some craft gin we'd picked up and pour a gin and tonic. Some of the gins were pink, others purple. They came in beautiful bottles, sometimes signed by the distiller. Drink poured, we would start preparing dinner. The kids were in the tub, and when they were done, got in their pajamas to color and draw quietly at the big farm table Justine had placed just so in her kitchen.

We would open the French doors to our garden, where the sun would be setting, the temperature comfortable. Sun-El Musician, a South African recording artist Meg introduced us to thrummed on our soundsystem while I chopped vegetables. Teddy would walk out to the little tripod Weber grill and poke the charcoals we'd ignited, the smell of lighter fluid and smoke wafting back into the kitchen.

Those nights were magical. Etched on my brain. So beautiful, they make me cry just closing my eyes and recalling them. But why? To the casual observer, they looked a lot like our life back in New York. We'd often hung out together and cooked in the evenings at home. Sipping a cocktail while the kids colored was hardly a departure. But there was a profound difference: In the Cape Town version of our evening routine, every extraneous claim on our time had been stripped away. The outsider looking in wouldn't see how I *didn't* have a pit in my stomach about a meeting the next morning; how Teddy *wasn't* thinking about an upcoming work trip; how we *weren't* bracing ourselves for the week ahead.

We were just enjoying the comfortable motions of a family routine, the four of us alone with nowhere to be and nothing to do. I had never known that before. Neither had Teddy. It was the most profound feeling of peace we'd ever experienced in our adult lives. Does a family need to go halfway around the world to enjoy that simple feeling? No. Did *our* family need to go halfway around the world to discover it existed at all? Yes.

Western Cape Road Trip

Back in New York, we had explained to our Africa travel agent Tamsyn that we envisioned taking some kind of road trip while on the continent. Through Namibia, perhaps? She told us Namibia would be great, but not with a four-year-old. "Too many long stretches of … sand," she said. "He'll get bored." Her alternative was a more scenic two-week driving itinerary along 350 miles of roads that stretched east of Cape Town.

We packed up the car and took one last look at Justine's bungalow. Its sunny rooms and little courtyard had taught us more than how to "live like locals." It had given us the gift of peace and restored a sense of balance in our lives. I gave a little wave as Teddy pulled away from the curb.

As we merged onto the highway, I recalled the road etiquette rules Luke and Meg had explained before we left: If a car slowed to let us pass on a two-lane highway, they said, we needed to acknowledge the driver by flashing our hazards in "thank you" and could expect a double headlight flash "you're welcome" in response. It all seemed too elaborate and polite to be true, but sure enough, as soon as we got underway, the same scenario played out over and over without fail: Pass, hazards, headlights. It provided endless amusement for me, who added "hazard-thanker" (or "headlight-you're-welcomer") to my list of jobs.

Our itinerary included three stops, including a vineyard stay in a town called Franschhoek, "glamping" on a farm in Stanford Hills, and a hotel in Plettenberg Bay, a coastal weekend town that Meg had told us to call "Plett." Between each, Tamsyn had indicated places where we could let the kids run around, including a gas station that served homemade *roosterkoeks*, traditional South African bread baked on a charcoal grill.

The route took us into regions that had been overtaken and settled by Europeans since the 1600s, a mix that included French winemakers and Dutch farmers whose descendants had called this place home for generations. It was a history we were still trying to understand, despite my having already put a sizable dent in James Michener's saga of the Western Cape, *The Covenant*, and our close following of news about current land disputes.

Franschhoek is a small wine country town with architecture, and a demographic, that looks a lot like Santa Barbara. Our agent booked us a guest house for the next four nights on a twenty-five-acre working farm that included vineyards as well as plum orchards and an olive grove. The air was clear, the light on the distant mountains alternating between pink and golden, our house welcoming with a wide porch.

The spot offered a new setting for our familiar routine: Breakfast, schoolwork, lunch and afternoon activity, "sundowner" cocktail at 5 p.m., dinner, bed. Teddy and I would sit in the sunshine together on a bench and talk for hours as the kids peddled bikes in and out of rows of growing grapes, all of us proud of the progress they had made.

Angela and her three dogs owned the property, and we got to know them when they stopped by for visits. One afternoon after Angela left, Willa turned to us, her shoulders slumped. "Why did she have to go?" she asked. "I wish she'd stayed to talk." Our kids had both grown fond of conversation with new people, just as we had, and were clearly hungering for more human connections.

We hadn't flown for three weeks, and in the absence of luggage constraints, we had strayed from our minimalism. "I think we're at Peak Stuff," Teddy said as he loaded our trunk for the next stop. "This is proof humans will fill any allotted space with crap." Our rental car heaved with bags of groceries, reams of printer paper for drawing, a few puzzles, boxes of Legos, and two kid bikes we'd scored. Teddy could barely see out the rear window as we backed down Angela's driveway on our last day.

We headed farther east, where the rolling cropland was dotted with industrial irrigation machinery and the occasional silo. Most of the land in this region was owned by the descendants of Dutch colonizers who'd come to South Africa before the English. They spoke Afrikaans, a Creole mix of seventeenth century Dutch, Portuguese, and Malay, which was the first language of about seven million people of all races in South Africa and other African nations.

When we pictured traveling in South Africa, this rural white Afrikaner sub-culture hadn't factored much into the vision. But now we were curious. We checked into a cabin on a farm property with a rickety trampoline, a rusted tractor for kids to climb on, a tire swing, and a little family restaurant. Beyond that, farmland as far as you could see. A ruddy-cheeked woman greeted us, rattling off details about check-out time and parking. Her Afrikaans accent was thick, and an enormous pot-bellied pig snorted in the grass behind her. "That's Cracklin," the woman said. "She's kind of our mascot around here."

We roasted marshmallows that evening on our deck and listened to the sounds of other families gathering for dinner at their own cabins while their kids played in the fields, excited shouts in Afrikaans carrying over the property. Willa and James blinked their flashlights on and off in their direction hoping for a response. When none came, James shouted "POOP!" at them before ducking behind a wall. I made another note to get him some human contact.

At night the famous wind came, more deafening than ever, ransacking our tented cabin. Metal clanged, canvas walloped, and wind howled in great gusty, unpredictable bursts. At two in the morning, I lay awake, staring at the ceiling, convinced that if someone stood four feet from our bed and slammed a set of porcelain dishes on the floor, we would not hear it. Again, though, only the grownups woke up.

Reception told us that on Sunday, a popular local rock band called Watershed would be performing on the property for a casual afternoon with tractor rides and beer for sale. By 2 p.m. that day, cars started arriving, and we watched as about 200 families walked up the hill with their coolers and picnic blankets. We sat in the grass just off to the side, sipping plastic cups of keg beer and observing the scene while Willa and James surprised us by heading off on their own to do laps on the tractor ride. When the band kicked up, the crowd cheered and knew every lyric. A few tipsy moms danced barefoot with their kids.

When I posted a short recap that night to Instagram, one of our followers asked: "Where are the Black people?" It was more statement than question. There was no denying the complexity of social factors behind what we were witnessing, and it reminded me of my friend, the one who had cautioned against the "tricky" aspects of using the word "authentic" in South Africa. I wondered if this was what she meant.

Plettenberg Bay, known as "Plett" to locals, was our third and final stop of the road trip. We used our days in town to explore miles of pristine Indian Ocean coastline that stretched in either direction. As we drove, we were treated to craggy mountains and cliffs covered in a layer of the fynbos shrub endemic to the Western Cape. Nearly every day we spotted pods of dolphins leaping in the surf far below.

We were rewarded for visiting this part of the country when we visited the Robberg Nature Reserve, a World Heritage site on a peninsula surrounded by a thrashing, turquoise ocean. When we pulled into the gravel parking area after lunch one day, Willa and James had questions: "How long is this going to be?" "When is this going to be over?" "Do we have to?"

We ignored them and set out on what we believed would be a thirty-minute round-trip excursion, a little stroll to see a view of the ocean and then leave. We walked up a slight incline, the sun overhead. Occasionally hikers would pass us coming downhill, panting, their shirts soaked with sweat. *Hmm.*

Just when I assumed it was time to start circling back to the car, Map Guy realized he had made a mistake. "I think I missed a signpost or something," Teddy said. We squinted at his paper map. "I think we're actually on *this* path," he said, pointing to the three-mile route we had just hours ago deemed too challenging for Willa and James.

We considered retracing our steps, but we'd already come so far. I turned to the kids. "Okay. Here's the deal." They looked back at me, their cheeks pink, James's hair sticking to his neck. "This is actually going to be a long hike, not a short one."

"But!" I piped up, cutting off their groans. "If you do the whole thing? You can have your own can of *Coke* when we get back to the hotel."

This stopped them in their tracks. Coke was a forbidden pleasure only ever savored as a sip or, maybe once, as a heavy pour from Teddy's dad when we weren't looking. We weren't the kind of parents who banned junk food, but Willa's and James's bad track record of sugar-induced meltdowns had always made Coke off-limits. Until now. That chilled red can, with its swirls of white script and glittering droplets of condensation, could be theirs. Reenergized, we pressed on.

The trail quickly turned challenging. Narrow paths funneled upward through thick bush and opened up out across blustery clifftops made of rock dating back 120 million years, with steep drops down to colonies of seals below. We marveled at the vast Indian Ocean before continuing down a curve that eventually spit us out onto the top of a mountainous sand dune. Willa and James ran down its facade, the ocean seeming to retreat the more they jogged in its direction, the enormity of Robberg's coastline dwarfing them.

The last stretch took us single file along a slippery shoreline of boulders where occasionally we'd catch blasts of cooling sea spray as we plodded. Willa and James did not whine. When at last we made it back to the car, our water bottles empty, our noses red and all of us hungry, we had to admit: We had just witnessed one of the most beautiful places on the planet.

Back at the hotel, the kids cashed in on those Cokes and we got beers, telling the hotel manager, Matthew, all about our adventure as we sat with him and his young daughter by the pool. It was his day off and he was relaxing with the few other guests that week. When his daughter spied Willa and James chugging Cokes, she asked her dad if she could order ice cream. He chuckled and turned to us. "It's always ice cream for the little ones, isn't it!" he said.

"And beers for the big ones!" James shouted from somewhere behind us.

Our hike on the Robberg Reserve marked yet another turning point for our family. Had we known how difficult it would be, Teddy and I probably would have turned back as soon as we realized we were on the more challenging trail. But we hadn't, and now we knew a bit better what our kids were capable of. Why had we been selling them short?

We used our second hotel babysitter of the year in Plett. Miranda was a mother of three grown children and oversaw the housekeeping operation at our hotel. She had barely walked in the door before Willa and James told her all about Robberg, tried to teach her Rat-a-Tat-Cat, and showed her every item in their meager toy bag.

"We need to get them more babysitters," I told Teddy as we walked out the door unnoticed.

We headed to the spa for massages with "fynbos-infused oils" and soft music. A woman in her twenties tended to me. She had been raised on a farm in rural Botswana and talked about the many people she encountered in her job. The subject turned to the U.S. when I asked her if she had met many American visitors. Only a few, she said. Then, after a pause to dig her fists into my shoulder, she added: "I find it so strange that Black Americans try to pass as African."

"Pass?" I asked. "What do you mean?" She was white.

"They call themselves African-Americans!" she said.

"...and that's not okay?"

She stopped the massage for a moment.

"They're not African! They're *American*! *I'm* African!"

On our last full day in Plett, we packed sandwiches and walked down to the beach, which was mostly empty. A man in a white button-down shirt, black trousers, and black office shoes approached us as we ate. He smiled and introduced himself as Bilson, then crouched to chit chat. How did we like Plett? Where were we visiting from? And, oh, did we know that Jesus Christ had died for our sins?

We didn't blow him off the way we might have at home, perhaps starving in our own way for human connection. Why not make time for a Jehovah's Witness? The kids were preoccupied with a sand castle down by the water's edge or else they would have come over and talked his ear off. After listening to a cheery pitch, Teddy broke the news that we weren't going to convert. "I appreciate what you're doing, man," he said, extending his hand. "But it's not for us." Bilson shook it and stood to leave. Before he left, though, he wondered: "Could I say a prayer for your family?"

Who were we to turn down a blessing? "That would be nice," I told him. Teddy and I bowed our heads, a congregation of two. In soft tones, Bilson asked God to watch over us and keep us and our children safe as we traveled.

"Amen."

We had six hours to get from Plett to Cape Town to meet Lobsy at the airport, but there was a problem: Our soccer ball was missing. This was a very big deal. We'd had the ball since Bogota and kicked it all over South America, even recovering it once with help from some Good Samaritans after a street dog in Valparaiso ran off with it. We tore apart our hotel room and called Miranda, who told us her team hadn't seen it. This tortured Teddy, who hated to lose things. "It has to be here!" he said, looking under the bed for the fourth time. But we couldn't prolong our search; we had to go.

Five hours later, as we approached Cape Town's city limits, my phone rang. "We found the ball," said Matthew, the hotel manager, on speakerphone. "It was under the toilet."

"The toilet?" Teddy cried out, incredulous. I thanked Matthew and told him the ball now belonged to his daughter. Note to self: Always look under a toilet when leaving a hotel room.

That night, Lobsy breezed through the front door of our apartment-hotel door looking like a million bucks after having traveled twenty-four hours— DC to Dallas to Dakar to Johannesburg to Cape Town. "Hi guys!" she said with a smile as she hugged us hello, the kids beside themselves with joy at her arrival. This was her first time in Africa, and she arrived ready to join us for two weeks of safari in Zimbabwe.

I can think of plenty of people who might shudder at the thought of their mother-in-law joining an adventure like ours. But we'd seen back in Peru how she was a perfect addition, going with the flow, asking curious questions, apparently unaffected by jet lag, with energy that seemed to surpass her son's and daughter-in-law's—but not her grandchildren's. She was 5'9", yet insisted on sitting in the backseat scrunched between Willa and James so she could play car games with them like I Spy and "The animal guessing game."

She was impressed by how well we knew Cape Town, Teddy zipping around the city in our car, Sun-El Musician playing on repeat, the kids spewing facts as we stopped to see the beach penguins and the Cape of Good Hope. We wandered the lush botanical gardens and drank pink gin and tonics at 5 p.m. The night we took her to Cafe Paradiso, "our" neighborhood restaurant, she was amazed at the kids' independence as they dashed off to make their dinner in the kitchen.

"Excuse me," someone said as we settled into our table. I turned to see a woman my age leaning over to us. "Sorry to interrupt, but ... were you by any chance in Plett last weekend?"

"We were..." I said, trying to place her face.

"I think my daughter played with your children at Newstead Winery," she said, referring to a place we'd visited one afternoon. "I think they taught her a card game?"

Of course! Willa and James had corralled a girl there for Rat-a-Tat Cat. Little did we know the threesome had already reunited over pizzas back in the kitchen.

Lobsy turned to us, incredulous. "You *know* them?"

Zimbabwe

Lake Kariba

There had been plenty of motivations for coming to this part of the world, one of them Teddy's desire to go on a safari. Off we headed to two different Zimbabwe safari lodges for what one seasoned traveler friend called, "the budget-blowing part of the trip." This might have been an understatement, even in Zimbabwe—or "Zim" as locals called it—where visitors were only just beginning to return after decades of a dictatorship that had made the country a tourism pariah. These days, its lesser-known national parks offered excellent game-viewing and access to some of the best guides in the industry with a smaller price tag than counterparts in Tanzania's Serengeti or South Africa's Kruger National Park, which had benefited from years of glossy travel magazine spreads.

Safaris could be affordable. Families we met who lived in southern Africa told us about their regular weekends and school breaks in the bush camping and driving by themselves—the equivalent of American family camping trips in the Shenandoah Valley or Tahoe. It was the foreign tourists who were more likely to opt for the kind of fancy lodges where experts did all the driving (and pampering). How luxe could these places be? "There's only up," our friend Luke from Cape Town had said. We weren't entering that particular stratosphere, but even our upper mid-tier choices were still pricier than any-where else we'd been.

We flew to the musty Harare airport, Willa and James all tans and hats and backpacks, just like the American family I'd observed on that flight to Zanzi-bar. I looked at my kids watching cartoons on their iPads and wondered how those parents had accomplished homeschooling on a plane. In Harare, after a short layover in which we admired threadbare taxidermied lions displayed behind plexiglass, we boarded a second, smaller plane. A much smaller one.

Teddy, Lobsy, and I looked at each other as we walked toward our air-craft, all thinking the same thing: Teddy's dad would not approve. He had an outsized number of emphatic safety rules, but none topped "never board a single-engine plane." Not only did our plane in Harare have only one engine, it had only one pilot, one with a peach-fuzzed face. What was he, 22? 23? We buckled up in silence and, with one last look around at each other—*I won't tell if you don't*—took off down the runway, headed toward the Matusadona National Park on Zimbabwe's northern border.

I thought of the funny book series we were currently reading to the kids, in which a young character describes his parents as so safety-conscious that they install "fire alarms, flood alarms, burglar alarms, spider alarms, tiger alarms, vampire alarms, false-alarm alarms, and false-alarm alarm alarms." They were so nervous that they outfitted their son at all times in "emergency inflatable underpants." The realities of our next two weeks were coming into focus: We were taking my safety conscious mother-in-law on single-engine planes to remote lands far from any hospital so she could commingle with deadly predators while riding in open-topped jeeps in the wild. I suddenly felt the need for a lion alarm.

Our pilot made a perfect landing on a grassy strip, and we were greeted by Thando, a smiling, round-faced man in his fifties dressed in khaki. As we got settled at the lodge, one of his staff members passed around tea and clipboards bearing waivers and pens so we could sign on the dotted line accepting all responsibility for any injuries or attacks. "I wouldn't read that too closely," I said to Lobsy, a trained lawyer, as she squinted at the paper.

I had been on safari before with my family and knew that lodges all over southern and eastern Africa offered a variation of the same plan: Twice a day you climbed into an oversized Land Rover with stadium bench seating for "game drives," one at dawn and one at dusk, when it was cooler and animals were most likely to be out. The predawn wakeup calls would be tough for Willa and James, but by now we had devised a helpful trick—if we had to get the kids up earlier than 6 a.m., we played Woody Woodpecker cartoons on YouTube. Whenever the kids knew it'd be an early morning, they asked: Would it be early? Or *Woody Woodpecker* early?

Each game drive was about four hours of bumping along dirt paths enjoying the landscape while your eagle-eyed guide searched for footprints, broken branches, droppings—any clues that wildlife might be nearby to observe. If you were lucky, you could see lions, leopards, rhinos, and elephants, among others. Usually there would be a stop for coffee in the morning and one for "sundowner" cocktails in the evening, both timed to the golden hour for maximum enjoyment and photo ops. The jeeps have no windows or doors, the animals are not restricted in any way. As the guides explained it, predators are used to and familiar with the shape of the jeeps and regard them as big non-threatening animals (not mobile snack carts filled with tasty humans). There was no reason to worry.

At dawn the next morning, we set out for our first game drive. The sun rose over the horizon, a cheerful Thando at the wheel. We bounced along in the truck still half asleep, thought bubbles of "this is going to be great" drifting over our heads. Then we turned a corner and the jeep skidded to a halt. We sat up straight. Ten feet in front of us, standing on the dirt path as if he'd been waiting all morning for our arrival, was a solitary bull elephant.

With so much talk of lions, we hadn't thought much about elephants. We were unprepared for this fellow's sheer scale, the dimensions of his enormous tusks. Thando, oblivious to our alarm, did the one thing we did not want him to do: turned off the engine. While the elephant swayed in front of us, Thando settled into a whispered lecture about how this particular elephant appeared to be extremely distressed.

"See how his ears are flared wide?"

It sounded like he was recording a detached voiceover for some nature documentary, not describing the hostile elephant pawing dirt in front of us. I could see the headlines: "SAFARI BLOODBATH: Idiot American Couple Brings Kids, Grandma on Game Drive, All Five Slaughtered by Rampaging Elephant." There were a few nervous Sullivan laughs and white knuckles. *Hehe cool story, Thando, how and when are we going to get out of this?* When Thando was good and ready, he turned the jeep back on.

Just as he began to ease the vehicle forward, the elephant shot toward us, a full-on charge. Thando accelerated, swerving just far enough to the right to avoid its tusks, which came within a few feet of Lobsy's jaunty safari hat. He then gunned it up a hill and out of the way.

We were too stunned to speak. "Did that just happen?" Teddy finally asked, his baritone several octaves higher than I'd ever heard. Thando chuckled, dismissing him with a wave as he drove along.

"That elephant wasn't going to hurt us," he said.

"Why are you squeezing my hand so hard?" James asked me. I looked down at his fat little fingers twisted in my grip and let go.

"That was fun!" Willa exclaimed. They both seemed uninfected by our anxiety, enjoying the view and the wind in their hair.

Back at the lodge, we attempted to calm our nerves over breakfast. But a growing crowd of vervet monkeys gathered in the surrounding trees. They stared at us as we ate. We'd experienced badly behaving monkeys already that year: the "breakfast monkeys" at the Brazilian beach resort, the Amazon spider monkeys who threw branches at us, those trespassing baboons at our Cape Town bike park. At a sanctuary called Monkeyland in Plett, a vervet had snuck up behind me and tried to snatch my phone out of my hand.

But we'd never seen monkeys act with this degree of impunity. A few of them pounced down to pluck fruit and muffins off the buffet when they thought no one was looking. One snatched Lobsy's drink off the table and chugged it like a frat boy, while his buddy skipped off with her pool towel. We couldn't tell if the place was short-staffed or poorly managed, but there just weren't enough people around to shoo off the onslaught.

A man from the housekeeping staff caught up to us as we were leaving the breakfast table. He spoke softly in broken English, but seemed to be asking if we needed anything for our room. I looked at Teddy and shrugged. "Maybe some gin and tonic water for this evening?"

He gave me a strange look. "Gin and tonic?" he asked.

Just then, a troop of baboons showed up. We knew by now that male baboons, who had fangs like saber-tooth tigers, could be aggressive, particularly toward women and kids. We watched as one climbed down a trellis twenty feet away and made his way to the pool. He crouched at the shallow end, muscles ropey, and slurped a few gulps while eyeing us. We went elsewhere. But suddenly we heard frantic shouting. A male guest was locked in a standoff with that same baboon, shielding his wife and teenage kids. The guy was waving his arms to make himself look bigger, barking, "No! Go away!" over and over, thrusting out his chest. A staffer intervened and finally got the baboon to leave.

"This place is losing me," Teddy said under his breath. Lobsy and I nodded in agreement. Willa and James had seen everything but somehow weren't fazed. At that moment, the gentleman from housekeeping reappeared at my side. He was holding out a tray. On it was a freshly poured cocktail. "Gin and tonic?" he said. It was ten o'clock in the morning.

"I'm so sorry," I said after an awkward pause. "Could we have little bottles instead? To drink tonight in our room?" He walked away, nodding.

A few hours later, our jeep stopped to let a large herd of elephants with several babies plod across the road in front of us in silence. What should have been magical was now cause for anxious groans. One by one they passed. Some looked straight ahead, some turned to eye us, which made us suck in our breath. When at last they'd all crossed into the brush, Thando pulled away. We exhaled.

But that's when we heard it: An ear-splitting "Phhhrrrrooooooooooo!" directly over our shoulders. We spun around to see a full-grown female bearing down on us at a gallop.

"Goooooooooooo!" we screamed at Thando, the vein on Teddy's neck bulging. For the second time that day, our guide jammed the gas to flee an elephant in hot pursuit. Unlike the angry male from that morning, this one chased us hard down a long stretch of road until we finally outran her. We watched over our rear seat as she slowed to a walk on the horizon, still trumpeting through the dust.

The only other sound was Thando's belly laughing and the kids' giggling. "I thought elephants were gentle giants!" Lobsy said. Then, shaking her head, "I'll never think of Babar the same."

That night after dinner, we returned to our rooms only to discover that our toothbrushes, our shoes, and our full laundry bag were alive and writhing, coated in a black layer of ants. Teddy and I bickered. Had this seriously been our first day of safari? We had so many more game drives and lodges ahead of us, and we were totally freaked out. I tried to take deep breaths and opened the cabinet for a bottle of water. I stopped. Inside sat my gin and tonic from that morning, ice melted, lemon wedge sad, covered in plastic wrap. *Perfect.*

The following morning, things were conspicuously quiet at breakfast. When we asked where all the monkeys were, more than one staff member shrugged and offered an unconvincing explanation. "They just aren't hungry today!" and "Sometimes they're here, sometimes they're not!" But Thando gave it to us straight: "We sprayed."

Also missing that day was a game drive. Instead, our program was fishing from a pontoon boat on Lake Kariba while a never-ending parade of *Lion King* cast members made cameos on the nearby (but not too near) shore. There were herds of elephants on land, pods of hippos in the water, and a giant crocodile lurking near us, waiting for the four-legged antelope buffet options to move just a little bit closer to the edge.

James reeled in a tiger fish, a rare carnivorous species with long, razor sharp teeth that I wished I could unsee but which inspired Thando to jump up and down with conservationist glee before freeing it back in the lake. We returned after a golden sunset, at ease.

Hwange National Park

The planes to Hwange National Park in western Zimbabwe, Africa's fourth-largest protected area, were so tiny that our group of five had to split up into two aircraft in order to fit. I sat in the rear of one between suitcases, Willa and Lobsy in front. Again, no one spoke of the single engines nor the solitary pilots. When we landed, a guide named David was waiting for us at the airstrip.

Like Thando, David was in his fifties and had lived his whole life in this part of the world. He was a handsome man with grown children of his own, exuding quiet confidence as he over-explained everything, emphasizing safety protocols. Lobsy liked him right away.

The Hwange lodge where David worked was more rustic than the one we had just left, with only five tents and a main common area that included a small fire pit with outdoor seating, but no internet. A deck overlooked a man-made watering hole that David said was popular with elephants. He and his rifle would need to escort us to our tents after dark.

Just as we stepped down an elevated wooden walkway toward our tent, ready to drop our bags, James tripped and went tumbling over the side, cutting his scalp on the edge. He shrieked from the brush below, and Teddy leapt down to scoop him up, cradling his head. A patch of brown hair was already wet with blood.

This is it, I thought, in horror. *James has a concussion. He'll need stitches!* I did the calculations: We were at least one flight and several hours' drive from a hospital. David ran for a first aid kit while Teddy carried James to a chair so we could inspect the wound. Willa and Lobsy looked on with wide eyes.

"It's not actually that deep," Teddy said. David returned with the kit and handed us some antiseptic and gauze. Within minutes James was fine and our heartbeats back to normal.

"I'll see you when you see me!" a lodge host named Ronald called to us as we drove away on a game drive with David that afternoon. It was an expression we'd first heard from an official at the immigration desk in Harare and sounded like something Groucho Marx might say as he chomped a cigar.

We all felt secure with David. Cruising in his jeep, his protege Dophus sitting in the rear seat, we traversed miles of the park in exquisite afternoon sunlight that illuminated acacia trees to the horizon. After hours of this, which included several zebra, antelope, bird, and giraffe sightings, we pulled atop a small hill for a sundowner cocktail. Before us sprawled one of the most beautiful sunsets we'd seen so far, 360-degrees of pinks and blues and clouds and swirls.

David and Dophus told us about growing up in this part of Zimbabwe. At Willa's request, they rattled off a few tongue twisters in Shona, their native language (we'd learned this was a great ice breaker for kids visiting a new country). We were finally relaxed, safe in David's capable hands, captivated by the natural beauty around us.

Then a scream shattered the peace. James had climbed inside the jeep without anyone of us noticing and slammed his fat little hand in the door. For the second time that day, we scrambled to find out how bad the injury was. "I can't take it!" Lobsy sighed. There had been angry elephants, but injured grandchildren were worse, and the day's calamities were pushing her grandmotherly anxiety to the limits. Once again, though, we were lucky. As with his head wound, James's latest injury wasn't nearly as bad as we'd thought. Within minutes he had recovered with the help of some Sprite, and David returned to his story.

Over the next four days, we awoke each morning at 5:30 a.m. with a delivery of coffee to our tent and a message called through the canvas to be at breakfast in thirty minutes. After peeling Willa and James out of bed with a little help from Woody, we'd step out to find a breakfast buffet of toast and eggs arranged alongside a roaring fire pit, around which we would eat and chat before heading out for the morning.

Hwange National Park was the territory of Cecil, a lion whose untimely death at the hands of an American dentist-cum-hunter back in 2015 had led to an international incident and, for a moment at least, had made Cecil a household name. David explained that Cecil's two sons were now the dominant males in the area. Like Thando before him, he told us that lions on reserves were accustomed to safari vehicles and didn't see them as threats, nor their passengers as food. After the two elephant charges, we were skeptical, but he insisted. As long as you're calm and remain seated, he said, they ignore you.

"Can't you just drive away if they get too close?"

"Unfortunately, no," he said. "You have to stay put until they pass so as not to disturb them."

Not long after delivering this reminder, David spotted two female lions in the distance. Sensing the trepidation in our vehicle, he stopped far away. We took turns using his binoculars. But then one of the lions stood up and looked at us (or was that just me?). The other followed. Both began to walk in our direction.

"Um," I said. "Here they come."

"Stay still," David said in his steady way. "We must remain here." Those lions could have walked in any direction, but they chose the path directly towards us—eventually striding within feet of Lobsy's open door.

"I'm scared," she squeaked as they passed. The kids were statues. I was too afraid to look at the lions, certain I'd read somewhere that they responded badly to direct eye contact (or was that dogs?).

"You look like you're sucking on a lemon," Teddy whispered.

If the way to stay safe on safari is to remain silent and still in the presence of wild animals, *why did they allow four-year-olds to do this?* Had safari companies met this demographic? Most kids James's age lived in a permanent state of wiggling and blurting. Yes, thankfully ours was somehow rising to the occasion, but … *what if?*

When the two lionesses finally wandered off, we exhaled and spent the remainder of our drive delighting in a far less menacing creature: the dung beetle. These creatures, no larger than a ping pong ball, were everywhere elephants had left droppings. We would stop to watch dozens of them on the side of the road as they battled for choice hunks of the stuff, then pushed their putrid bounty down the road—guided by the sun's rays, apparently—until the dung smoothed into something akin to a donut hole, the perfect pod into which a waiting mate could deposit her eggs. My vision for safari hadn't included hovering over steaming mounds of elephant poop, enthralled, but the microcosm of millenia of evolution was endlessly entertaining.

As he sped us home in the dark that night, everyone ready for dinner, David suddenly slammed on the brakes. Sauntering just ahead of us in the same direction was a male lion in the headlights. Lobsy grabbed my knee just as I seized her shoulder—Scooby and Shaggy in a haunted house. He eventually turned off into the brush. When we got back to the lodge, excited staffers told us how Cecil's sons were, at that moment, dozing near our tent. They invited us to get a closer look. "Oof, no thank you," Lobsy said, settling into her seat in the main lodge, Sauvignon Blanc order placed. "I'll stay here with the kids."

Teddy, David, David's rifle, and I walked to our porch, where the beam of David's flashlight revealed two sets of yellow eyes staring back at us.

"Can they see us?" I whispered.

"Um, *yes*," David said, laughing out loud.

We spent one rainy morning at that Hwange lodge playing board games with David, Ronald, and a few of the other guides. We were the only guests that week and had their full attention. Ronald, a young guy with a class clown sense of humor and the patience of a saint, had already spent the morning lifting Willa and James overhead so they could probe the underside of our lodge's canvas ceiling with an umbrella, sending gushes of pooled rainwater cascading to the ground. When the three of them had emptied every sagging corner, Ronald took Willa and James to a table to teach them mancala, the ancient game played with stones or seeds progressing down a series of holes in a wooden board.

Eventually, Willa and James wanted to reciprocate. Willa went to her backpack and pulled out a card game Lobsy had brought from home called Spot It. The rules were simple: Players competed to spot and be the first to call out objects illustrated on a card. Like, "pencil" or "tree." It required sharp eyes and the ability to swiftly recall words. David, who'd observed the games from a distinguished distance all morning, surprised us by asking to join Spot It. He was a competitor, and the contest—David versus Willa and James—was irresistible. With a few of the other guides cheering, the matchup got underway.

Almost immediately, it became clear that objects we'd considered universally familiar were wildly out of context for David, born and raised in the nearby bush country. He recognized the top-hatted white figure with a carrot nose, for instance, but couldn't easily conjure its name in the intensity of the game. Snowmen did not feature prominently in Zimbabwe. Not that he was deterred. Cheered by the bellowing guides at his back, David was playing to win, and the game escalated loudly with each new card. He blurted out what he could, neck and neck with Willa and James.

The image of a dolphin appeared. He snapped his fingers in rapid bursts, as if it might help.

"*Fish!*" he cried.

"DOLPHIN!" countered Willa and James.

After that, there was a ladybug.

"*Ummmmm ... dung beetle!*" he shouted, jumping to his feet.

"LADYBUG!" James shouted, jumping to his feet as well.

A few more cards went by without incident—"car," "tree," "cat" in rapid succession. The score was getting close. Lobsy leaned in.

Then, a snowflake.

"*Gah!*" he yelled, laughing. "*ICE STAR?*"

The kids nearly collapsed. "SNOWFLAKE!" they yelled through their giggles.

An igloo was his doom. David took one look at the little white dome and shrieked in mock despair, "*What IS that?*" He knew that the game was lost.

We were all laughing so hard by this point, we had to wipe our eyes. David's fellow guides were busting his chops, howling at his pitiful performance. But the experience was illuminating: *My ladybug was someone else's dung beetle.*

That night during dinner, our last in Hwange, we were still chuckling about the game. But just as our laughter picked up, David put his hand in the air, suddenly quiet. He motioned for us to stop talking and listen. We were seated outside on the deck under the stars, and he pointed at the watering hole just feet from our table. A herd of elephants had arrived unnoticed and gathered like ghosts, barely visible in the dark. As we stood and moved toward them, we could hear the rhythmic sounds of their drinking grow more pronounced. When they dipped their trunks into the water it made a sound like covering a metal vacuum tube with your hand—suction and silence—and when they sprayed the water down into their mouths, it was as if bucketfuls of water were being emptied into giant, hollow rubber bags. We felt our fear of these creatures disappear until there was nothing left but awe, Babar's reputation restored.

"I'll see you when you see me!" we shouted the next morning as we pulled away from Hwange, feeling the same pangs of sadness we had experienced on our last morning with the Amazon river boat crew. We'd spent time without internet, with new friends David and Ronald whom we admired and respected, having bonded with them over rainy day laughs and heart-pounding injuries and lion sightings.

We said a hasty goodbye to Lobsy, too, this time on the tarmac of Zimbabwe's Victoria Falls airport, where she dashed to catch a flight to Johannesburg, the start of an epic thirty-hour journey home to DC. We were sad to see her go. She was part of this story—there with us at the peak of Machu Picchu, at our sides when we were charged by elephants in Zimbabwe, and in two months, back to see us in Spain.

South Africa (Again)

Timbavati

After a stop to see Victoria Falls, we drove into Zambia, where we stayed a few nights on the banks of the Zambezi River, famous for bird-watching and legendary sunsets. Willa and James filled their days with new friends, kicking a giant seed pod around a village for soccer with one group, and inventing a game called "elephant charge" at our lodge with another. Then it was time for our third safari, this time in South Africa. From there we would fly to Durban on South Africa's East Coast, a city I'd always been curious about, but before this trip assumed I would never actually visit. There would be several nights in Johannesburg after that, and then we would wrap our time in Africa with five nights in Vilanculos, Mozambique, a suggestion our travel agent made when we said we wanted to finish our Africa leg with a "vacation" at the beach.

Despite all this moving, despite the constant changing of homes and exposure to newness, Willa's and James's energy still had not flagged. We had been on the road for well over a hundred days, but they weren't run down or overwhelmed. If anything, the opposite. Traveling this way was just what they knew, our trip now representing an outsized chunk of their human experience. It was as if they had already forgotten what life was like before we left.

Now we were touching down on another grassy strip for our final safari adventure of the trip. We were in Timbavati, a reserve near Kruger National Park. This time, our lodge was someone's private vacation estate, rented out like a small hotel—with a staff of cooks and rangers—when the owner wasn't using it. We understood by now that some South Africans owned wildlife reserve weekend homes the same way Americans might have a lake cabin or ski chalet.

Our guide, Almero, or "Big Al," and his animal-tracking partner Sydney picked us up at the airstrip and quickly shot to the top of our list of favorite guides. Al was a tall Afrikaner who fist-pumped at the sight of lions and gladly shared his repertoire of Chuck Norris jokes. "When Alexander Graham Bell invented the telephone," he told us, "he already had two missed calls … from Chuck Norris." He loved the Stormers rugby team and the band Watershed. When we told him we'd seen both live, he couldn't believe it.

Sydney was his quiet counterpart. His instincts reminded us of Jose's back in the Amazon. He would signal with his hand for Al to stop the car (and stop talking) and hop down to examine the way a single tree branch was bent. "Elephants just passed through here," he might say. "They went this way." And off Al would drive in pursuit.

Sydney had trained in anti-poaching, which we learned made him a badass's badass, a kind of Chuck Norris of the bush. For months at a time, he would patrol the protected area, foraging for food, dodging lions, and finding his own water sources, all while stalking and arresting illegal rhino and elephant hunters. He was prepared to shoot them on the spot if necessary.

Poaching was a major problem, he explained. One kilo of rhino horn went for about $85,000 on the black market, usually in Vietnam and China, where it was used to "treat" everything from cancer to infertility. An entire adult rhino horn might fetch $1.5 million. Demand was putting a sizable dent in an already profound conservation problem.

We felt safe with Al and Sydney. Yet, even they acknowledged that no two days were ever the same on safari. That unpredictability, combined with the luck of being in the right place at the right time, was all part of what made safari so rewarding. Every time we set out on a game drive, we knew we'd see something remarkable. We just didn't know what it would be.

One day it was the baby giraffe on unsure legs trying to drink from a puddle and a zebra who farted loudly when something startled it. Another day it was the regal leopard nicknamed Marula who munched on the hindquarters of an impala she'd killed overnight, so close we could hear her ripping and chewing the flesh. We were treated to a rare sighting of wild dogs, sometimes called "painted dogs" for their distinct brown spots. We watched them wrestle and play while Al told us they were among the most endangered mammals on earth, only a few thousand left in the wild. One evening we stopped to skip stones in a watering hole, unaware that a trio of rhinos were hiding in a nearby bush, waiting for us to leave. As soon as we pulled away, we heard a snort and turned to see their big gray bottoms trotting out for a drink.

We turned a corner one afternoon to see a male lion sauntering along. When Al stopped the truck, Willa carefully slid under a blanket, only her eyes peeking out. "I'm not scared," she whispered. "I'm just more comfortable when he can't see me." The lion walked up alongside Willa and Teddy's side of the open jeep and paused. He turned his head and met their stare, as if to say, "I see you," then walked on his way, in no rush at all. James, worn down by so many Woody Woodpecker mornings, slept through the whole thing.

At dusk on our last night, we stopped in a dry riverbed. Willa had told Al and Sydney that she wanted to look for frogs, and the three of them wandered off together around a bend (hard to imagine us being okay with that just a few months earlier). James snored quietly under a blanket in the backseat. Teddy and I climbed nervously out of the truck to stretch our legs.

Within minutes, we heard the unmistakable sound of baboons barking in panic. They were close by, and it sounded like there were dozens of them, all frantic. Teddy and I leapt back in the truck and cowered, straining to see if Willa was coming back. Were we under baboon attack? Were those baboons under attack by something scarier? Why were we sitting here with no truck keys and no guides and no gun and no Willa?

After an eternity (seven minutes), Willa and the guys ambled back, kicking rocks and chatting as they walked. Yeah, they'd heard the baboons, they said when they got back to the truck. They'd also heard a leopard. Baboons were probably fending off an attack, they surmised. Willa was too disappointed about not finding any frogs to care ("We only found tracks!"). Teddy and I rode in silence the whole way home. James never woke up.

Durban

Arriving in city after city at times of the year when most people were busy with school and work was one of the obvious benefits of traveling when others couldn't. We had mostly empty security lines, hotels to ourselves, and easy access to tourist sights and restaurants. But after we left Timbavati (bear hugs from Al and stoic handshakes from Sydney) and flew to Durban, South Africa's third largest city, we realized it was Good Friday. We had not known it was a Friday at all, much less one that began a holiday weekend. Our hotel was packed.

Durban offered an entirely new perspective of South Africa, with a diverse population more racially and culturally mixed than anything we'd seen in the country so far. It had the world's largest Indian population outside of India, which was reflected in the crowds at our hotel and beyond. We tried Bunny Chow, a popular fast food dish created by the Indian migrant workers who'd come to the area decades before. As we scooped curried meat out of a hollowed-out cube of white bread, James delighted the restaurant's owner by declaring it "one of my favorite foods!"

A guide we found online walked us around a downtown market, where we saw hundreds of Zulu, Indian, and Muslim sellers hawking the full spectrum of Durban's necessities. At one point we crossed a footbridge over a busy highway. Our guide described how it had once been a danger zone.

"Muggers would rob the marketgoers and then throw them over the rails to their deaths," she said without emotion before moving on. If we hadn't been listening, we might have assumed by her nonchalance that she was sharing the date the bridge had been built or the engineer who erected it.

Teddy and I looked at each other, blind-sided yet again by a topic that would surely prompt endless Tough Questions. Sure enough, despite all the new and nifty things we'd encountered that afternoon—brightly colored pinafores! Bootlegged Jackie Chan movies! Traditional medicine men haggling over animal bones! Zulu butchers preparing cow head soup!—James had only one thing on his mind for the next two hours.

"Wait, *what* did she say about throwing people off the bridge?"

We drove out to the Midlands, an area of the KwaZulu Natal province about an hour and a half from Durban, to see the national Nelson Mandela Capture Site memorial. This was where, on August 5, 1962, after seventeen months in hiding, Mandela was pulled over by cops on an unremarkable farm country road and arrested, beginning his lengthy incarceration.

The Capture Site featured an extraordinary sculpture erected on the fiftieth anniversary of his arrest, an outdoor piece that has drawn millions of visitors. We followed a stone path symbolizing Mandela's long walk to freedom toward what looked from a distance like fifty jagged steel rods poking haphazardly out of the ground. As we approached, the towering rods began to fall into position, melding together into an optical illusion of Mandela's face.

Easter Sunday was cold and rainy. We went to a petting zoo with tractor rides and magic shows where the kids fed animals from paper bags of kibbles. A chalkboard sign with arrows directed people to the cafe, to the goats, and to a prayer room. The gray skies and chain-link animal enclosures gave the place a gloomy feel, but Willa and James thought it was incredible.

"Be honest," I said to Willa as she fed a rabbit. "What do you like more, this place or safari?" She stared at her shoes and tried not to smile. "Be honest!" I repeated, both of us laughing.

"This place," she finally muttered.

"I knew it!" I said, giving her shoulders a playful shake, thinking of the bazillion dollars we'd just spent.

Later, we walked to the barn and joined a dance party with other families led by a staffer wearing a moth-eaten Bugs Bunny costume. "This has got to be the strangest thing we've done all year," Teddy yelled to me over the repetitive beat of "Baby Shark" as we clapped along.

Our travel agent told us that a gated community nearby had a great Italian restaurant in its clubhouse. Picture a country club somewhere in suburban Tampa, say, and imagine a family of four from Bulgaria or Argentina appearing for Easter brunch, no reservation and smelling just a little bit like a petting zoo. That was us. The maitre d' sized up our stained t-shirts and raincoats, trying, I think, to make sense of our accents and lack of reservations. He found us a table in the back.

We warmed up inside, and our soggy clothes started to dry as we ate pizza and drank wine. "This is serious interloping," I told Teddy.

"Even more than the Baby Shark thing," he said. Long tables filled with well-to-do, mostly white families dressed up in cashmere sweaters and Easter dresses for the occasion, grandparents in their Sunday best, cousins running around and coloring. I watched the ones my age and wondered about their lives. Who had a work deadline the next day? What was on these people's minds? I loved seeing the world this way.

Johannesburg

When we landed in Johannesburg, the kids were bouncing off the walls. They'd just spent weeks cooped up while on safari and in drizzly Durban. They had to burn off this energy or we'd all go nuts, especially considering what lay ahead: two full days of guided tours. They wrestled at the baggage claim in Tambo Airport and ran circles around our hotel lobby as we tried to check in.

The receptionist suggested we take them to a trampoline facility at a nearby mall—the kind of place where rowdy kids could jump themselves ragged while parents watched from a peaceful distance. For three hours, Willa and James flung themselves around, springing into sunken pits of foam, leaping onto inflated mattress-like pads, and cracking heads with all the other tiny maniacs in there. It worked. When a private van rolled up to our hotel the next morning, "Sullivan" sign in the window, our kids were as ready as they were going to be.

Helpful was the fact that Willa and James thought our guide was cool. Bongani was an artist who wore an afro and a stylish green bomber jacket and fist bumped everyone we passed once the tour got underway. He seemed to know everyone in "Jozie" (as the locals called it). He and James held hands as we explored neighborhoods Bongani described as former "no go" zones, parts of the city once marked by abandoned buildings and high crime that now housed revitalized artists' lofts, music studios, cafes, and fashion designers, many of them Black-owned and operated. He introduced us to the founders of a photography collective, called "I Got Shot in Joburg," a name that asked people to reconsider the city's reputation as a hotbed of crime, and served up lore about the city, like how it was believed that people were always in a hurry because the city had been founded during a gold rush.

"Most guides do boring grownup talk," Willa said as Bongani fist-bumped a few more folks. "But Bongani is fun." More important, what Bongani showed us was different from anything we had seen after six weeks in Cape Town, across Afrikaner farmland, on safari, and in Durban. When I had a coffee later that day with Ayandi, a former work acquaintance from South Africa, she confirmed what I suspected: Joburg was indeed a more modern, diverse city—with more Black-owned businesses and restaurants—than others we had visited. In her opinion as a Black South African, Cape Town was still mired in the past. "I can't stand the place," she confided.

I told her about meeting Sydney, our anti-poaching guide—the one we had swooned over as a hero, his work lining up so nicely with our values: Poachers were heartless villains who deserved to die. What she said flipped my narrative. "There's a guy in my mother's neighborhood who is probably a poacher," she told me. One day he was living hand to mouth, the next he'd bought a car and house for his family. Everyone suspected the money had come from poaching, she said, but no one said anything. While she strongly condemned poaching, she pointed out that the money "lifts the desperate out of poverty."

I had never considered the poacher's human experience. Nor, come to think of it, the experience of someone in China or Vietnam who might be trying to cure a loved one's cancer. Sometime later that month, a friend in New York posted a news article to Facebook about a poacher who'd been eaten by a lion. "Couldn't have happened to a nicer fellow," he snarked. Before talking to Ayandi, I might have piled on. Now I found myself wondering what this poacher's story had been.

Bongani made sure our eyes would open even wider before we left. On our last full day, he took us to the Apartheid Museum, a place so appalling in its honesty that I openly wept the full two hours we spent inside. (Willa and James intuited that this was not a time to whine and tagged along quietly, listening to our kindergarten-level explanations of each exhibit.) Much like the Holocaust Museum in Washington, DC, the Apartheid Museum's permanent exhibit spared no detail as it put visitors through the emotional gauntlet, the aim to prevent such a brutal history of hate from repeating itself. We walked out with the last words of hanged freedom fighter Solomon Mahlangu ringing in our ears: "My blood will nourish the tree that will bear the fruits of freedom. Tell my people that I love them. They must continue the fight."

If we were hoping for levity after that, we were out of luck. We drove in silence to Soweto, the famous township where Nelson Mandela had once lived. We parked outside the Hector Pieterson Museum and Memorial, which honored the lives of hundreds of student protestors who were killed in a 1976 uprising against apartheid. A large black and white photo hung outside. We had seen the same image at the museum earlier and knew that it depicted a teenage boy named Mbuyisa Makhubu running down a dirt road in overalls, crying and carrying the body of twelve-year-old student Hector Pieterson in his arms. Hector had been shot by police during a protest, and his eyes were closed, his mouth bloody. Running alongside them was Hector's sister, a distressed fifteen-year-old girl named Antoinette Sithole. The disturbing photograph held an iconic place in South Africa's history: When it was published in 1976, it sparked a global outrage that would eventually help bring about the end of apartheid.

As we looked at it, a woman walked toward us. She was in her sixties with close cropped hair and a round face. She wore a blue cardigan and a knee-length skirt. "I want you to meet Antoinette Sithole," Bongani said to us as she approached our family. We were stunned. The teenager from the photograph. Sister of the slain boy whose death helped change history. We introduced ourselves, awed by her presence, then stood on a sidewalk outside the museum, listening as she told us the story of her brother's sacrifice.

Mozambique

Vilanculos

The more we traveled, the more comfortable we became arriving somewhere new with zero prep. We'd touch down in far-flung countries—the kind we had only heard about on the news or seen in an atlas—and ask the most basic questions. Like, "Wait, where are we?"

It's not that we got lazy, it's that our days took every ounce of energy and attention we had. This meant we were so focused on the present we were incapable of thinking about future destinations, even those just one day ahead. In a way, it was freeing. Our use of travel agents and booking everything in advance really had allowed us to relax once we got underway.

But our lack of focus did occasionally catch us flat-footed. When we landed in Vilanculos, Mozambique, from Johannesburg, we walked from the runway into a cinderblock airport. Every foreigner in front of us was quietly counting and arranging wads of American dollar bills as they approached the customs desk.

"Fifty American dollars cash, per person," the uniformed official grumbled when it was our turn.

We all looked at Teddy, Minister of Finance. If anyone was going to pull out $200 in cash, Teddy was our guy. But the look on his face said everything. Had he bothered to check the itinerary, he might have noticed the very clear, bolded instructions from our travel agent regarding cash due at customs: **"Reminder: Please be prepared to pay $50 CASH (USD accepted) PER PERSON at customs upon arrival in Vilanculos."**

Normally, we carried about $2,000 American dollars tucked away in some official envelope of Teddy's. It was a universally accepted currency that could get you out of a jam. After so much safari tipping, however, Teddy was down to just a few fives and tens. Flustered, he cobbled together $50 to get one passport back. But this border official wouldn't part with the others until we produced $150. Could we leave and go find the money and come back? "Do whatever you want," the official said. Our passports, however, were staying there.

The closest ATM was a 15-minute drive away and only let users take out 5,000 Mozambican Metical per transaction, or about $75 USD (a currency and exchange rate we only learned about four minutes before). We had a family meeting and decided Teddy would find our ride to the hotel and drive to the ATM while the kids and I waited at the airport for him to return with the cash. He headed out while we settled onto a bench. When he eventually returned to bail us out, there was no finger pointing. If anything, I found it amusing when Teddy got things like this wrong.

Vilanculos was one of our vacation stops, a do-nothing-just-relax beach stop without touring to cap nine weeks in Africa. When we'd suggested the Seychelles, Tamsyn, scoring yet another point for team travel agent, had come back with Vilanculos, which, she argued, was easier to get to and far less expensive. Vilanculos hadn't yet hit the travel magazines and Instagram feeds the way the Seychelles had.

Home that week was a villa overlooking white sand beaches hugging a twinkling Indian Ocean. It was the kind of place that delivered fresh-squeezed juice on trays at breakfast and stocked its tubs with fancy bath salts. The beach below us was an extraordinary bit of natural landscape. The difference between low and high tide was more than a mile of sand, and when the tide was out, ribbons of shallow pools ran almost to the horizon as bright painted wooden boats lay on their sides, waiting to be buoyed again. We could wander around examining exquisite shells and observing tide pool marine life like giant orange starfish, the only tourists out there.

But it was also a working beach. Every morning we awoke to the sound of local men, women, and children shouting as they hauled in fishing nets. On some mornings, we'd see the bounty, with teams divvying heaps of silver fish to sell at the market. On others, we watched them reel in empty nets. I'd look down at my bathrobe and wonder what we should be feeling.

Mozambique was the poorest country we would visit all year, with more than half of its population living on less than two dollars a day. Its economic development had been cratered by years of civil war and the subsequent mass displacement of millions of people. Now, excruciating images from Mozambique were in the news again. Weeks before, it had been devastated by two massive cyclones, which had struck the coastal nation back-to-back, ranking among the worst storms to hit the African continent in decades. Reports from their aftermath featured desperate images of flooding, famine, and cholera outbreaks. Our travel agents and the security firm we hired assured us that Vilanculos was far from the stricken regions and canceling our trip would be like avoiding Washington, DC, after a hurricane in South Carolina. There was no storm damage to speak of where we were.

But the poverty around us underscored our status as privileged people and the divide between us up here on the veranda—and everyone else. I could relate to a line from William Finnegan's memoir *Barbarian Days* about being "rich white Americans in dirt-poor places:" "We sucked, and we knew it, and humility was called for." At the same time I recalled a Ugandan speaker I'd heard at the conference in Tanzania, the anthropologist who challenged travelers to visit places like Mozambique just as they might France or Japan. With deference and curiosity—not with assumptions, and definitely not with pity.

On our second day, several local kids wandered down the beach toward us, curious about Willa, James, and their sand toys. Ranging in age from about five to twelve, each child wore t-shirts that were old and ripped. There was no common language. But who cared when there were towers to decorate with shells and water to fetch in buckets from tide pools? A sand city can't build itself! We watched as Willa and James played for hours, both of them seeming to savor the opportunity. The same group came back again and again during our stay to rebuild their structures and play pickup soccer.

MIDDLE EAST

Two weeks: Jordan (Amman, Dead Sea, Petra, Wadi Rum) →
Egypt (Cairo, Aswan, Luxor) → *United Arab Emirates (Dubai)*

Jordan

Amman

We included the Middle East as a pit-stop between Africa and Europe because an American travel agent insisted we would be fools not to. I'm glad we did. We saw significant sights—so many wonders of the world!—and, even better, shared excellent times with my parents, whom we convinced to join us.

When I think back on those two weeks, though, it's also difficult for me not to cringe a little. We flew from Johannesburg to Dubai on our second long-haul of the year only mildly aware that we were about to swap the peace and autonomy we'd enjoyed in Africa for a highly supervised two-week sightseeing marathon across Jordan, Egypt, and Dubai. Despite everything we'd learned so far, despite our commitment to not replicate the kind of ill-considered, carefully curated sightseeing experiences we had endured way back in Colombia, we would once again struggle to find the balance between touring and doing things our own way.

We stumbled off the plane into the Amman, Jordan sun asking each other the same questions—"What's the currency here?" "Do we need a visa?" (Not asked: Did we learn nothing in Mozambique?) A man in an official-looking blazer holding a "Sullivan" sign appeared. "Mr. and Mrs. Sullivan?" he asked. Yes, we did need visas, he said, and pulled the necessary paperwork, already completed, out of his folder. In our gratitude, we failed to see how this VIP treatment was a grim foreshadowing of our future.

The call to prayer projected from a mosque next door to our apartment-hotel as we unpacked. James, covering his ears, yelled, "What's that noise?" Willa and James knew nothing about Islam, and we hadn't provided any context. We were now in a Muslim country, we explained, and an official called the *muezzin* reminds Muslims by loudspeaker that they should pray five times a day—at dawn, noon, midafternoon, sunset, and nightfall. It was also the start of Ramadan, we added, a holy period when Muslims fast from sunrise to sunset to show devotion to their faith.

Willa and James would go on to have many more questions. *How come women wear veils? Are we allowed to eat during Ramadan? How come we are, and they aren't?* They had figured out there was more than one religion by now. The Zulu medicine men we had seen shopping for bones and feathers at the Durban market believed one thing, the Catholics across South America another. There had been that Shabbat dinner in Bogota and the Xhosa woman in South Africa who told us that burning *impepho* grass allowed her to communicate with her ancestors. Willa and James were curious to know which of the gods they'd learned about was the "real" one and if the rituals they observed really "worked." Islam, with its prayers and fasting, added more complexity.

We stepped out onto the roof of our building at sunset to reunite with my parents, Grammie and "Beepaw"—Beeps, for short—who were waiting with open arms and big smiles. "I feel like I'm making a cameo in a TV show I've been watching all year!" my dad said as he hugged us, referring to our daily blog and Instagram posts. We gazed out at Amman together in awe, the city a carpet of low-slung beige buildings stretching to the horizon in every direction. We pulled on sweaters as the sun went down.

My parents are low-key travelers, easygoing and fun to be with. My dad is a quiet intellectual who enjoys water coloring and cycling. My mother, from Memphis, is the chatty, opinionated one, a flirt with a self-described *Hee Haw* sense of humor. They're two very different people, but it works. We told them all about our slog of a travel day—from Mozambique to Johannesburg to Dubai to Amman—and they described their own journey, a drive from Israel that passed through seven armed checkpoints.

As we turned our attention to the weeks ahead, my mom raised an eyebrow and looked at me. "Seems like a lotta stuff on the itinerary," she said. As I crawled into bed that night, I pulled open the schedule and scrolled. And scrolled. And scrolled.

Uh oh.

⌣⟶

A guide named Hessan waited for us that first morning at 9 a.m. sharp, wearing a khaki vest and name tag, ready to usher us into a waiting van with "Sullivan" in the window. We had come to Jordan for Petra, that mysterious wonder of the world carved into towering cliff faces, but first we had a full day in Amman, Jordan's capital city, with stops at The Royal Automobile

Museum and the Amman Children's Museum. *Did we really need a private guide, driver, and leather-interior'd, air-conditioned van for these?* When we pulled up to the kids museum, we politely told Hessan that we did not need him to escort us around inside. He could relax in the van. Grammie, a contrarian prone to frugality, skipped this stop. "Why would I pay to walk around some children's museum?" she huffed, only half-joking.

Wandering through the museum's "Human Bodies" exhibit, Teddy spotted a speed pitch booth. Museum-goers were invited to test their strength by lobbing tennis balls against a target, their throwing speeds clocked by radar gun and displayed on a digital screen. This was irresistible—and Willa and James egged him on. He strolled over, picked up a few balls, and casually began slinging them against the bullseye.

Suddenly, a museum employee in a red staff vest appeared. He watched Teddy for a few tosses, curious, then seemed to get excited, trying to tell us something using gestures. Eventually we understood: He wanted to have a throwing contest with Teddy. Teddy gamely went first, no doubt assuming one pitch would put the matter to rest. But when the guy stepped up, he stripped off his red museum vest and gave a few proud stretches before taking a running start and letting rip a fireball of a pitch. Or bowl, I should say. He was a cricketer. And he'd just beaten Teddy's score.

"Oh Jesus," I heard Teddy say to himself. Then, smiling at me and my dad, he asked, "Is this really happening?" It was on. Just as our kids didn't need a shared language to play with kids all over the world, these two men apparently didn't need one to bro out in a speed-pitch booth. Around and around they went, upping the ante every time that ball smacked against the target. My dad and I looked on, amused, while Willa and James jumped up and down.

As Teddy would later tell a friend, "I was trying to find the velocity middle ground between beating his ass and a torn labrum." After about five back-and-forths, he apparently found it. At the risk of reopening that old minor league injury, Teddy put the contest to bed with an unbeatable speed. His opponent grinned and raised his hands in surrender as he put his red vest back on. The two men parted ways with sportsmanlike gestures.

"Nice work," my dad said to Teddy.

"I couldn't let that guy win," Teddy replied, massaging his shoulder. We joined the kids, who'd lost interest in the throwing contest and were playing a dung beetle game in which they maneuvered metal "poop balls" along a steep track, trying not to drop them.

That night we dined at the apartment of a local family, Omar, Resha, and their three children. We'd done plenty of these "blind friend dates" so far, but they'd always been set up by mutual friends and acquaintances. This one was of course arranged by travel agents and chaperoned by Hessan, whose presence, I admit, was helpful. Should we bring flowers? "No," he replied, "Jordanians don't give gifts you can't eat." We picked up a box of sweets instead. We also wanted to understand the etiquette of greeting and departing. Handshakes were appropriate, "but not between men and women."

The seven of us arrived at a nondescript four-story cement building on a residential side street, one of the thousands just like it we had seen from the roof of our hotel. A large folding table covered with platters of food filled the small entryway of the family's apartment, the smell of roasted meat with herbs and spices inviting us in. Omar and Resha hosted Americans for dinner as part of a USAID program that paired locals with tourists to promote cultural understanding between English-speaking Jordanians and Americans like us. When we described it later to a friend who works in the foreign aid world, he explained: "Diplomacy's cheaper than bombs."

As we passed around dishes like chicken *maklouba* and filled our cups with orange soda, we talked about Omar's favorite football team (Barcelona), their plans for Ramadan, and how Resha is a better typist than Omar. There was a lot of "kids these days" lamenting from both parents about their two teenagers, who, indeed, seemed more interested in Instagram than listening to their parents' Ramadan plans. We wrapped the meal with coffee in a small corner arranged with leather loveseats and a few folding chairs, while Willa and James disappeared into the kids' room to play with Legos and Barbies. After coffee, we were served tea.

"I felt a little stiff in there," I said in the van home afterward, feeling especially caffeinated. The conversation had flowed just fine—USAID had done its job well—but the greeting protocol when we arrived had me second guessing my handshake and every move thereafter. I felt I had spent the whole dinner trying to avoid breaching some other social norm I didn't know about. My mom reassured me. "You carried the conversation tonight," she said. "I keep forgetting you're a grownup!'"

Dead Sea

"I kind of regret that we aren't going to the Dead Sea," my dad said as our driver Adnan steered us along a highway.

"I think we *are*?" I replied, pulling open the itinerary. Sure enough, buried among dozens of other stops and outings on our schedule was a single line item: "Day pass to Holiday Inn Dead Sea."

Hessan lowered the plexiglass partition between us. "Everyone ready for the Dead Sea?" he asked from the passenger seat, before delivering facts, like how it was the lowest point on earth and bacteria was the only living thing that could survive its high salinity.

The Holiday Inn was a large resort with multiple pools and a gravel beach that recalled a kind of moonscape with no vegetation, just hazy grays and browns and grit. After changing into our suits, we marched down into the water, turned around, and plopped backward, instantly buoyed into comfortable reclining positions in the dense, cool water. My parents looked like they were sitting in gray Jello as they bobbed by on their backs. Willa squealed at the bizarre sensation—"It won't let me swim on my stomach!"—but James and his eczema bailed immediately. *Dead Sea: Great for Floating, Terrible for Paper Cuts.* When I absent-mindedly tried to remove a fleck of sand from my eyelash, it took ten minutes to recover.

We stretched our stay for hours to enjoy the calm. We swam and slathered ourselves with thick Dead Sea mud, and James, the only one on shore with dry hands, took a photo of us together posing on the shore, covered face to feet in brown muck, healed, more youthful looking, and whatever else we were supposed to be after scrubbing.

There may have been several stops and lectures between the Dead Sea and Petra, but what was most memorable about that three-hour ride was the plastic garbage out our window. We had already seen pollution on our trip and would eventually go on to see even more, but Jordan was a shock. While the Dead Sea itself had seemed clean, the desert highways were a different story. A wall of discarded plastic bottles and bags stretched alongside the pavement, uninterrupted, for hundreds of miles. I thought of all the bottles we had been drinking lately in the absence of potable tap water.

Hessan knew the trash was a bad look for tourism. He explained that he and his colleagues once met regularly to conduct roadside cleanups, but gave up when they realized it was futile. In the absence of laws and processes for waste management, he said, regard for keeping things clean went out the window, along with the litter. Hessan was growing on us. Having sensed we appreciated straight talk, he'd relaxed and started giving it to us—even gossiping about which tourists he found the most irritating. ("The French.")

Petra

The ancient jewel of Petra housed more than just the famous "Treasury" facade from our guidebooks. It felt more like a kind of *Indiana Jones* meets *Game of Thrones* movie set lined with roads and dotted with tombs and temples carved into dramatic rolling sandstone cliffs, all of it dating back more than 2,000 years. Mystery shrouded the place, Hessan explained, with historians still doing their best to hypothesize who once lived there. As we made our way through its narrow canyons, we tried to imagine what ancient life must have been like. The markets, the tradesmen, the smells and sounds.

Unlike pristine, regulated Machu Picchu, Petra teemed with selfie-stick hordes who poured out across the grounds from coach buses and, in the absence of ropes, climbed on ruins and scaled cliffs. There were trinket hawkers and men in buggies whipping donkeys unmercifully to shuttle tourists to and from the site in record time. Petra may have survived thousands of years, but at this rate, would it soon erode to dust? Somehow Teddy and I still fell under its spell.

Willa and James, however, lasted twenty minutes. Drained by the heat, the Boring Grownup Talk and the back-to-back, go-go-go tourist adventures that preceded our arrival, they wanted out of this crowded, chaotic place. "I don't like feeling so terrible!" Willa wailed. "The hotness! The hungriness! The boringness!" My mom agreed. The three of them gave the Treasury a look, posed for a few photos, then returned to the hotel for an afternoon of swimming.

Had Petra been our only destination, had we just spent the previous day or two wandering around, going to parks, playing Rat-a-Tat Cat—had our kids been given the kind of time to just, well, hang out—they might have appreciated it more. Yet nearly every hour in the Middle East up until then, and, it appeared, going forward, was scheduled with some guided tour or bespoke activity or transit. In one week in Jordan, we covered Amman, the Dead Sea, Petra, and Wadi Rum desert. During the next, in Egypt, the list included three different cities: Cairo, Aswan, and Luxor, and by the looks of it, more museums, cooking lessons, a monastery, lunches and dinners, and so, so many lectures.

Not only were we overloaded with outings, we had crews of hardworking guides, hosts, and drivers who sought to anticipate our every need, real or imagined. A guide was necessary, but this was more than that. Teams of handlers ordered for us in restaurants and hovered at the reception desk when we checked into hotels. It was tightly managed travel that might have been a welcome luxury for some, and certainly well-suited for foreign dignitaries, but it wasn't the experience we were after.

Of course, we had no one to blame but ourselves. When the travel agents had come to us with a proposal for these two weeks, had we pushed back? Suggested some tweaks? Asked for more downtime and fewer hand-holders? Nope. Back when we signed up, we still didn't know how we liked to travel. We had scanned their proposal, shrugged with a kind of blind faith, and said, "Sounds great, book it." After all, we were clear that we had a four- and six-year-old with us, right? By the time we knew how to spot red flags like these on an itinerary, we were already locked into nonrefundable plans. There was nothing to do but go along with it.

Egypt

Cairo

We wrapped Jordan in the bed of a pickup truck, taking a wide lap around the golden sands of Wadi Rum desert, a place where imposing cliffs and otherworldly rock formations served as the backdrop for Matt Damon's 2015 movie *The Martian*. When it was done, Willa and James begged to do the ride again, but we were headed to the Amman airport for our evening flight to Cairo.

The call to prayer echoed throughout the terminal as we waited to board, and on our flight, attendants placed red stickers on the headrests of anyone fasting for Ramadan to indicate that they should not be offered food or drinks. When we landed, these same passengers were handed to-go boxes of food to enjoy after sunset.

Egypt brought even more guides, vans, and lectures. We were offered *chilled* hand sanitizer in the van, not by our driver or our guide, but by a third helper—a "host" named Mohammed, a well-meaning man who wore a blazer and name tag and rode with us in the van just to make sure we had everything we needed throughout our stay. Thirsty? NO PROBLEM! Alas, what we needed most by then was to kind of just be left alone.

"Tomorrow we will go for a tour of a shopping mall," Mohammed told us from the front seat on our first ride together. Our agents had probably shared something about how we liked to see everyday life and this was his team's literal interpretation. Teddy and I looked at each other. "Thank you so much, Mohammed," I said. "But that's okay, we don't need to do that."

"We can take you for a tour of the mall," he repeated, emphatic, dabbing his forehead. He seemed to feel that if the Sullivans didn't get their tour of a shopping mall, they might complain to his bosses. He wanted us to be happy customers. It was inconceivable that this might mean that all we wanted to do was look out the window and watch Cairo go by, a fascinating city, ancient and modern, teeming with ten million inhabitants. Eventually we were able to convince him to skip the mall tour.

Fortunately, we were soon assigned Abeer, a no-nonsense guide in her fifties who spoke English with a Scottish lilt and walked with authority through the streets of old Cairo, swatting away hawkers and parting the seas for us from behind oversized designer sunglasses. She scolded and shooed, pointed and directed. We saw how male peers on the tourist circuit scattered in deference. I was grateful Willa and James met Abeer. There had been, and would be, few female role models on our travels, and Abeer offered a bracing dose of woman power in a world full of Men in Charge.

We suspected Abeer found the hand-holding and infantilizing just as tedious as we did. At lunch in Cairo's Khan El-Khalili bazaar, she read us aloud the English-language menu. She knew we understood how restaurants worked, yet this was her employer's protocol. We played along, telling her what we would like. She then turned to the English-speaking waiter at her elbow and repeated what we had said.

That afternoon, standing in the shadow of the Pyramids, that mother of all bucket list destinations, we stared up in awe. Even Willa and James, who by now absolutely loathed scheduled tours in the heat, bounced up and down in excitement. Willa in particular had been reading about Giza as part of homeschooling and was eager to explore the inside of Khofu's tomb, no doubt imagining something sinister with torches and mummies.

"It's not everyone's favorite thing," Abeer warned as she waved us inside. "Some people find it claustrophobic." Once I stepped through the door, I saw what she meant. If you wanted to explore the inside of this Great Pyramid, you had to crab-crawl up a makeshift wooden ramp through what was, in effect, an airless sphincter lit only by a few hanging bulbs. It disappeared into blackness.

"I can't do it," I said to Teddy.

"Not a chance," he replied, just as horrified.

"Wait," Willa said, a mix of disbelief and disgust coloring her face. "You mean we're not going up?"

My heart sank. Here she was expressing the first genuine enthusiasm about touring she had shown yet in the Middle East—and her parents were wussing out. But there was just no way I was going up there.

"I'll go with you," we heard a voice say, and, not for the first time, my mother saved the day. We watched as Willa and her 75-year-old grandmother shimmied up and out of sight. I was stunned. Not only at my mom's willingness (and agility!), but at *Willa*. Just months ago she'd been the kid who sobbed every day at school drop-off. Now she was scurrying around the bowels of the pyramids without her parents.

I looked down at James, who seemed just as shocked as we were. He couldn't believe his sister's bravery. But he had been undergoing a kind of transformation of his own. All that attention he started to receive from strangers back in Rio had continued unabated everywhere we traveled. Kind-hearted strangers, usually guys, would regularly ruffle his hair and pinch his cheeks.

They'd toss him toys and fruit from their street stalls. They'd hold out their fists while walking past in the street, giving him a bump and offering some kind of hey-hey-my-*man*-style greeting. Every time I wanted to look over my shoulder and ask, "Do you *know* that guy?"

James had always been the under-the-radar Sullivan, a second child Teddy described as "just happy to be in uniform." He didn't need to be the star—making the roster was good enough. But here he was, seemingly having a moment on some kind of bromance world tour. Guides and drivers took selfies with him and dialed up family members on video chat, just to show off—*look who I'm with!* He held hands with Boris at Machu Picchu and with Alberth in Lake Titicaca and arm-wrestled with Bongani at lunch in Soweto. Bongani would even go on to sketch a portrait of James and post it to Instagram with the caption, "One of my favorite humans."

My parents didn't believe this until they saw it for themselves: In Amman, James rode on Hessan's hip through the car museum, and in Cairo, an Egyptian tourist in his thirties stopped us and asked if he could shake James's hand. The two of them chatted—*how are you, what's your name*—then parted ways. This last encounter was something of a final straw for Willa, who turned to us with a look of exasperation on her face. "Why is James so ... so ... *famous*?"

All of this was having an effect on his confidence. Famous James—the nickname stuck—seemed to be embracing this man-of-the-world persona. Where he used to hide behind my legs when grownups spoke to him, there was a swagger there. In Petra, we overheard him chatting up an American tourist. "I went to a children's museum in Amman," he told her. When she expressed polite interest, he leaned in closer, ready with a joke. "It was a museum *for* children, *not* a museum with kids' skeletons in boxes."

Famous James wasn't about to go up in that pyramid hole, but when at last Willa and my mom emerged, triumphant, and we went for lunch at a nearby tourist restaurant, he was ready to reclaim the spotlight. James surveyed the lunch menu and turned to Abeer.

"Abeer?" he asked with a mischievous smile.

"Yes, James?"

"Do you want ... *a beer*?"

We all groaned and I offered an apology in the form of an eye roll her way. She was a devout Muslim observing Ramadan. Thankfully she was a funny woman and guffawed at his attempt at standup, but I made a note: Some of this newfound confidence needed a little dialing back.

On the way back to our hotel, we stopped at a red light and noticed the man riding on a motorcycle next to our van was wearing a dusty old Orioles baseball hat. We rapped on the glass to get his attention, then pointed at James's hat. As soon as he made the connection, he started beaming. As the light turned green and we started to pull away in separate directions, the man ripped off his hat and flapped it back and forth in the air at James, who returned the gesture.

Aswan and Luxor

Our family was mostly alone along Egypt's tourist circuit of temples and tombs. While these sites shared the furnace heat of Petra, they did not come with any of the same selfie-stick hordes. It was usually just us and a couple of stray dogs. This had its benefits. We could wander in peace and Teddy felt free to entertain us by moonwalking whenever we had to wear disposable shoe covers, which were required at some archeological sites.

But there was something off about these conspicuously thin crowds. Outside Aswan, a city in the south of Egypt, the 2,500-year-old Temple of Isis sat empty among palms on an island in the glassy Nile. A sprawling outdoor restaurant onsite could accommodate hundreds but appeared shuttered. When we asked about it, our guides said it was because we had arrived late in the season, or that it was too hot. It was hot—often 106 by noon—but that wasn't it. Sweltering Jordan had been packed.

"Ten years ago, this place was shoulder to shoulder," one guide eventually let slip. "You couldn't even see the temple because it was so crowded." The reason emerged: These empty destinations were the lingering effects of the 2011 "Arab Spring" uprising, when images of tens of thousands of passionate protesters broadcast around the world had ground the country's tourism industry to a halt overnight. Eight years later, it still hadn't recovered, especially among Americans. Yet again, negative news headlines scared off would-be visitors and collapsed economies.

That night at dinner in Aswan, a chatty five-year-old American boy with blond hair wandered over to our table in the empty hotel restaurant. He'd overheard Willa and James talking about a popular kids' nature show and wanted to share that he, too, loved that series. His parents, a bearded dad and a mom with a newborn strapped to her chest, made their way over.

They'd just moved to town from Iowa. *You moved here? From Iowa? Wow! Why Aswan?* The dad looked over his shoulder and lowered his voice before explaining how they intended to cross into Sudan to begin converting Muslims there to Christianity. Willa and James listened to this intently. Before we could ask any questions, though, the little boy began belting out an earnest rendition of the nature show's lengthy theme song.

The Middle East trip reminded us that the world is filled with complicated and difficult-to-explain realities, about religion and so much more. And while we had grown slightly more comfortable with answering the kids' Tough Questions, Teddy and I were still terrible at predicting when they might ambush us. In hindsight, it should have been obvious that a week immersed in ancient Egyptian history would mean near-constant discussion of death and dying. So much talk of the afterlife—and all those mummies with their freakishly intact eyelashes—amounted to a crash course in mortality.

But when the questions came flooding—"What happens when you die?" "When will you die?" "When will *I* die?" "Can you really take your boat/ toys/pets with you when you die?"—we were, once again, caught off guard. We defaulted to gentle bluntness when they asked us about death: *Everybody dies. Different people have different beliefs about what happens after you die.*

Do you need to go to the bathroom?

There's a video I took on Day 127 of our trip among some ruins. It was a scorching morning in Aswan, and the scene opens with an energetic guide in a polo shirt gesturing at a wall of hieroglyphics as he explains their meaning. I pan my phone to reveal his audience: some stray dogs, James digging in the dirt with a stick, Willa twirling like a ballerina, Teddy looking at a map on his phone and my parents drifting around out of earshot. We no longer knew where we were or what we were looking at.

As much as it pains me to admit, Willa and James actually spent much of our time in Egypt playing inside air-conditioned vans idling outside World Heritage sites people would kill to see before they died. When we tried to convince them to join us at the mega-ruin Karnak for our very last stop, James stomped his foot in protest.

"Why?" he asked. "We don't even *stand anything*!"

He was right. We had taken some of the most exciting chapters of human history for young learners—mummies! buried treasure! hieroglyphs!—and squeezed the educational energy, much less the fun, out of them. Just that day we had descended into the tombs of King Tut, Ramses III, *and* Ramses IV; Climbed the steps of Queen Hatshepsut's temple; Explored Queen Nefertari's exquisitely painted tomb and toured Luxor Temple. It was preposterous programming for a four-year-old. Add to it the lengthy drives between each and the exhaustive lectures from private guides ("As you can see…")—and we had blown it.

The grownups were sapped, too. My mom lay on a slab of stone near yet another ancient burial site and let her arms flop to the side, the sun beating down on her. "If I die," she gasped with a laugh, "just throw me in one of these tombs." Highlights for Willa and James had been the bribes they earned, like Coca-Colas—*so many Cokes*—and pieces of Bubble Yum Grammie had brought from home.

The Middle East had been educational, but not in the way we imagined. We would leave Egypt wiser not about pharaohs, but about how we liked to travel. We saw now that we could have made half the number of stops, even eliminated whole cities, and been happy. Guides are important in these parts, but we would have done better with those who fit more of a "knowledgeable peer" profile than teams of ever-so-professional luxury handlers.

Perhaps the most valuable lesson learned, though, was this: *From now on, view with ultimate skepticism anything deemed "kid-friendly."* It was a label so consistently misrepresentative across all venues (see: Cartagena chocolate-making experience) that we joked operators should produce photo evidence that an actual child James's age had enjoyed whatever tour or experience they were hawking. It seemed that "kid" was a stock image of a polite and curious eleven-year-old who skipped ahead of the group at Karnak asking keen questions about the Ptolemaic period. Nothing like James, who, while Famous, was also … *four*.

United Arab Emirates

Dubai

Despite warnings that it wasn't "worth it," we finished our Middle East sojourn in Dubai. "It's an exploitative soulless city for rich ex-pats!" was the basic message. But we were curious. We checked into the outrageously gaudy Atlantis Hotel, a place with not one but dozens of chocolate fountains at its many breakfast buffets, a two-story high aquarium, thirty-two restaurants, and the world's largest water park. It was perhaps the Dubai'iest Dubai hotel to ever Dubai. We had just one full day there before my parents headed home. It began at the deliciously late hour of 10:15 a.m. After two weeks of Woody Woodpecker wake-ups to sightsee, it felt incredible to sleep in.

While Teddy and the kids bobbed around the hotel's "lazy river" in innertubes, I took advantage of the city to run the kind of practical errands that big, modern interludes allowed us to take care of, like restocking toiletries, replacing grimy t-shirts, going to a gym, shipping home souvenirs, getting haircuts. I indulged in a spin class and told my dad to meet me at the Starbucks in the Dubai Mall afterward. We were going to grab a coffee before one last outing together: ascending the Burj Khalifa, which, at 2,716 feet and almost twice the height of the Empire State Building, was the tallest building in the world. ("Why would I go to the top of the *Burj Khalifa*?" Grammie opined, rolling her eyes from an innertube that morning. "I fly on *planes*. I know what the world looks like when you're up high.")

In any other mall in the world, meeting at "the Starbucks" would be a sensible arrangement. But in Dubai, a city with roughly seventy malls, the Dubai Mall was the second-largest in the world (the first was up the street), and featured thousands of stores and restaurants, a hotel, ice rink, movie theater, theme park, and aquarium. It had seven Starbucks. We wandered around looking for each other for an hour, texting unhelpful details, like "I'm at the one next to Gucci." Eventually, miraculously, we found each other and sat down to sip lattes behind a velvet curtain strung at the entrance to prevent Muslim mall-goers from having to see non-Muslims eating and drinking during fasting hours. Every food purveyor in the mall had them, which had made finding each other even more difficult.

We chatted happily about the last two weeks together, laughing at the over-the-top service we'd received and the sightseeing death march we'd endured. He commended the kids for being troupers and asked some questions about where in Europe we were headed next. He said he was thinking of maybe joining us in New Zealand in six months, a place he'd always wanted to see. I encouraged him to buy his ticket. We knew we should get going, but it felt so luxurious to just sit and talk.

Then he paused.

"I don't want to leave here without saying this," he said. "I'm proud of you. Not only for having the idea to do this trip, but for having the guts to go through with it." I looked up at him, feeling so touched and grateful.

"Aw, thanks," I replied. It was so inadequate to what I was feeling. But I think he understood.

EUROPE

Seven weeks: Spain (Madrid, Mijas) → France (Paris, Disney-land Paris, Bordeaux, Corsica, Vence) → Germany (Berlin) → Netherlands (Amsterdam) → Denmark (Copenhagen) → Norway (Fjordland) → Sweden (Stockholm)

Spain

Madrid

"We want to keep going with you!" my parents repeated. We were hugging them goodbye outside the Atlantis, our bags loaded into a cab. They were flying back home, and we were headed to yet another continent. As with so many visitors that year, my parents were glum about the prospect of returning to real life after getting a taste, however brief, of our year-long adventure. I knew they envied the fact that we got to continue traveling.

Our third long-haul flight of the year went more smoothly than our first two, partly because our tolerance had increased, but mostly because the non-stop from Dubai to Madrid was during the day—far less punishing than any red-eye. Instead of wrestling with pillows and fighting over blankets, we watched our shows and landed in time for dinner, relatively unscathed. The first text I received when I turned on my phone was from my dad, letting us know he and my mom had arrived home safely.

"Just pulled up to the house," he wrote. "Mohammed had a team here mowing the lawn."

If you played "One of These Things Is Not Like the Other" with our year's itinerary, the European leg would be the anomaly. From the moment we touched down in Madrid, things felt different: The lightning fast Wi-Fi, the drinkable tap water, the familiar culture—and soon the revolving door of visiting friends and family on their summer vacations.

We had tossed out dozens of casual, "You should *totally* come see us" invites back in New York, envisioning people showing up around the world the way our parents were doing. But everyone who accepted our offer picked Europe. France in June was easier for employed Americans with school-age children than, say, South Africa in March or New Zealand in November. This lent a kind of summer-vacation feel that set this stretch apart from the other places we went, as close to a return home as we were likely to experience all year.

We quickly settled for the week into an apartment in Madrid's charming *La Latina* neighborhood. Not one tour planned. Nowhere to be. Our own kitchen. Compared to the desert beige of Jordan and Egypt, and the gleaming air-conditioned skyscrapers of Dubai, Madrid's public rose gardens and lively outdoor cafes offered yet another drastically different change of scenery—and a shot in the arm.

I had lived and worked in Europe for three years after college and felt certain we could handle planning this stretch on our own with only minimal input from travel agents. We needed freedom from plans, still smarting from our heavy-handed experience in the Middle East. This apartment had come recommended from a former co-worker of Teddy's.

Teddy's high school Spanish, honed in minor league bullpens, was serviceable at best, but that was okay. The people we interacted with in those first few days were patient with us, just happy that summer had finally arrived. Adding to our excitement was that Lobsy was back and had convinced her five sisters and a few more extended family members to rent an apartment in town while we were there. The gaggle had their own plans, but we planned to see them a few times, including for Willa's seventh birthday, which was that week.

Almost immediately, we saw how scruffy we looked compared to others wandering Madrid's chic streets. Six months in, we were more or less still wearing the same traveling clothes we'd started with. We decided to freshen up with a little shopping. The day I donned a cosmopolitan upgrade of pants from the threadbare joggers I'd worn through jungles and deserts, James did multiple cartoonish double takes, disoriented by my change of uniform.

We appreciated that we didn't have to hurry through breakfast to be on time for any tour guide pacing the lobby. Our apartment featured an electric orange juicer, which quickly outranked the pyramids. Willa and James stood in their pajamas and bedheads, taking turns pressing halved oranges against the spinning machine, awed whenever it deposited fresh juice into their cups. Afterward we knocked out ninety minutes of journal writing and math games, glad to be back in our routine after skipping school work for most of the Middle East (there hadn't been time).

An elementary school across the street even provided ambient school sound effects, with shrieks and laughter from the blacktop floating up through our open balcony window. It was a warm and sunny late May and the playground cacophony drew a curious James outside one day to sit on the balcony, arms around his knees, taking in the panorama of fun below. Did he wish he had friends to play with? Did he want to go back to school? Our kids hadn't shown signs of loneliness, but James's teachers had said a kid his age needed peer socialization above all else.

I leaned over to James on the balcony and told him to grab his ball and meet me by the door. We had learned by now that if you were a kid and you had a soccer ball, you could make friends—which is why we kept replacing lost and shredded balls all year despite the impracticality of packing them.

The two of us set out into our neighborhood, ball under his arm, wandering up one cobblestoned street and down another, taking in the birdsong and quiet clink of cutlery from outdoor cafes. When we passed a walking tour, James looked at me and jabbed his thumb their way. "I'm so glad we're not with *them*." Instead, he was on a mission that had become familiar: Waiting for three o'clock, when school kids would empty from classrooms, ready to play. Famous James with a soccer ball wasn't shy about engaging strangers anymore.

Sure enough, by 3:15 the promise of his afternoon had been fulfilled as he passed the ball back and forth on some *plaza* with kids it seemed he'd known for years. It's doubtful any of them realized he was American—his buzzcut had by now grown out into a mop that matched the shaggy look preferred by every *Madrileño* boy. Also, kids don't talk to each other. They just play! When the ball got wedged high up between a brick church wall and a mounted floodlight, James and his new buddies spent forty-five minutes trying to knock it back down—throwing other balls at it and recruiting taller, older kids to help. Eventually some husky middle schooler got it dislodged, and it bounced back to the street to cheers.

Teddy and Willa missed the action that afternoon. Willa needed a nap after staying up late to watch a *flamenco* performance with Lobsy and her sisters, and poor Teddy had a bad cold. At first we thought all his sneezing was just more of the seasonal allergies that had dogged him and James practically all year; it hadn't occurred to us that "following the sun" also meant "following pollen season." But in Madrid, his fever and chills left no doubt: After nearly six months, one of us had finally gotten sick.

We assumed a year of constant airplanes, public bathrooms and unfamiliar food would wreak havoc on our systems, but they hadn't. We had spent the first half of the year fever-free. While I would go on to catch Teddy's cold a week later, Willa and James never did. In fact, those two colds in Spain would turn out to be the *only colds any of us* got the entire trip. Spending most of our days outside helped us stay healthy.

After Egypt and Jordan, Willa and James were not only reluctant but utterly unwilling to even *consider* that a museum or tour could be anything but torture. We had to compromise. When Teddy was able to crawl out of bed again, we went to the Prado, which was more of a surgical strike than cultural immersion: We circled eight paintings in the venerable museum's brochure—works by Velasquez, Bosch, Rubens, and Caravaggio that rang vague Art History 101 bells—and Map Guy trotted us to each one as if we had a buzzer to beat. Had we permanently ruined sightseeing for our children?

Most of our days in Madrid were spent outside, where it was not yet scorching, enjoying the kind of dazzling afternoons perfect for moseying around Retiro Park, the largest public green space in the city. The word that kept coming to mind: *glorious.* Sprawling gardens of lush rose bushes gave way to trees that looked like a cartoonist's bubbly drawings. Pristine gravel pathways meandered among gurgling fountains, playgrounds, and manicured lawns and hedges.

On one visit we spotted a group from a nearby nursing home on what appeared to be their daily morning outing. Dressed to impress, the men in suits with hair pomaded back, the ladies wearing dresses and lipstick, they were playing *petanca*, a Spanish version of boules. Smiling aides in scrubs played, too. When they left, they made their way out of the park slowly in distinguished, happy pairs, arm in arm, laughing and talking as they went.

Willa turned seven in Madrid, the second of our four birthdays that year. We surprised her with a trip to a big suburban "indoor skydiving" experience called MadridFLY on the outskirts of town, the kind of not-particularly-cultural, we-could-be-anywhere outing like the Johannesburg trampoline facility or the Cape Town bike park. Willa and James took turns getting blown around inside a giant vertical wind tunnel with the help of an instructor, their inflated, rippling cheeks cracking us up every time they whizzed past. "This place should be called Madrid FUN!" Willa told the English-speaking instructor when it was over, her hair wild.

In the Uber back to town, she read aloud a birthday email from my dad. "Have a great time," she read, nearing the end of the note. "I wish I could be there with you, and I hope—"

"—and I hope you have a pleasant flight," James said, cutting her off. He had flown on so many planes by now he was mindlessly reciting flight attendant scripts.

Birthday lunch was at an Italian spot where Lobsy and her sisters piled into seats along a long table for a wine-y, pizza-y celebration, the restaurant's large glass doors thrown open to the sunny sidewalk outside. Early in the meal, Willa disappeared to the bathroom and returned spinning and twirling in a red flamenco dress that James had picked out for her. The requisite oohs and aahs followed.

On our way to Retiro after lunch, Willa spied a nail salon and begged us to let her get her fingernails painted. Inside, we attempted to explain to the nice ladies what she was after—just color, not a full manicure. Willa picked something pink from a rack on the wall.

"I want this one," James said from behind us, holding up a bottle of blue polish. The mood in the salon got awkward. Patrons and the manicurists alike laughed nervously, unsure how to respond to this odd little boy who wanted polish. One woman tried to let him down easy in broken English. "Well, um, it's not…" she said, pausing. "Well, it's not *your* birthday."

As if that would deter him. He hopped up in a seat and splayed his fingers on the table, feet swinging in anticipation. She was at a loss, as were the salon ladies, who glanced sideways at one another, commenting under their breath in Vietnamese. But he got his polish.

When we said goodbye to the aunts and Lobsy, she confirmed that she would be back in a few weeks to see us in Copenhagen, Denmark. And this time she had convinced Teddy's dad to come! She was unstoppable. As for us, we were headed to southern Spain. Willa had three flamenco dresses zipped into her suitcase—one for her and two for her beloved cousins, who at that very moment were en route from Washington, DC, to meet us.

Mijas

The Madrid airport featured separate check-in and security lines for any-one traveling with small kids, and we welcomed the opportunity to sidestep the massive summer lines and breeze to our gate. We were on our way south to the small town of Mijas in the Andalucia region, where we had booked a house for a week with some good friends from New York and Teddy's sister, Claire, who was coming with her husband, Harlow, and two little girls, Crosby and Grace. (Lobsy, who had just touched down in DC from Madrid, was already babysitting Claire's youngest, a baby boy.)

The reunion of cousins could best be described as "shrieky," the kids overwhelmed with excitement at being together again. Within minutes, all three girls were dressed in flamenco dresses and watching James demonstrate proper operation of an electric citrus juicer. When our friends from New York arrived with their three-year-old, the kid chaos ratcheted up even higher. "Mama, do you like *this* headband?" four-year-old Grace asked her mother multiple times a day as she modeled various looks borrowed from Willa's suitcase, the contents of which, like James's, seemed to have exploded all over the house.

Our original plan had been to meet up with this crew in Paris. *Thank god we didn't do that*, I thought, as I watched the five of them tearing around the yard, a red blur of flamenco dresses and swim trunks. Instead, we'd declared the visit a "vacation" and spent the time catching up over glasses of Spanish wine while working on a thousand-piece puzzle I'd purchased at a Madrid puzzle shop (unaware until too late that it depicted tiny cartoon characters fornicating on a beach). Could we have been in the Catskills? The Great Lakes? Sure. But hosting this group in a vacation house seemed better than the alternative: touring Alhambra with five kids under seven.

Not that it stopped me from feeling a little guilty. Shouldn't we have been experiencing the beauty and history of the area's many Moorish towns? Weren't we squandering our time in this place by working an (x-rated) puzzle by the pool? My tortured relationship with how we "should" be traveling persisted.

After five days, our friends and Claire's family flew home, all of them returning to school and jobs. Teddy admitted he envied them just a little for going home. Maybe it was the seasonal allergies that continued to bother him; maybe the fact that our belongings were slung all over this big house, making packing feel daunting; maybe because we'd stayed up too late drinking wine. Whatever the reason, he was dragging.

"I'm tired, too," I told him, though I did not feel any desire to return home. If anything, I felt relieved our time *wasn't* yet up. Had we been heading back, I would have felt desperately sad. For me, traveling for a whole year was the right choice. I felt like we were just getting going.

When we landed in Paris and boarded a shuttle bus on the runway, Teddy's nerves were still frayed. He decided he really hated airport shuttle buses. They were crowded and inefficient! "I'd pay a *premium* for flights with a *guaranteed jetway*!" he said. I wondered if he had hit some kind of wall.

I spoke in French to direct a taxi driver toward our apartment rental, which seemed to surprise him. "You speak *French*?" he asked *en francais*. Willa and James stared at me, seeming to ask that same question. We inched closer toward the heart of the city, and as we rolled down our windows to watch the early evening Friday crowds, we could feel the summer weekend energy in the streets. People in short sleeves and summer dresses left work and headed out to meet friends, ready for the night ahead. I was reminded once again of the Bryson quote, the one about spending life arriving in a new city each evening.

Teddy's "exhaustion" dissolved. As it did, we learned an important lesson. The few times in our travels that we ever actually said the words, "I'm tired," were when we were *actually tired*. As in, we'd awakened too early that day or hadn't slept great the night before. Or had spent five days drinking Spanish reds in a house full of shrieking kids. Once we got a good night's rest, we'd always feel fine again. We vowed to remember this. Tired of your job? Tired of your workout routine? Tired of your relationship? Or are you just … *tired*? We now saw the distinction. Teddy never mentioned wanting to go home again.

France

Paris

We stayed in France for two weeks, checking boxes that represented a kind of trip down memory lane for me. I wanted to show the kids Paris, where I had lived in my twenties and where, now, two of their school buddies were joining us for a long weekend. We had plans to visit a family I knew on a vineyard near Bordeaux; a rental house on the island of Corsica, where I had spent an eighth-grade foreign exchange, awaited as well. Somewhere along the way I realized we would be in the country for the seventy-fifth anniversary of D-Day, but it was too late to add Normandy, where I had taught English for two years after college.

Paris in early June made Petra's crowds seem like Egyptian ones. The crush of human bodies swarmed the same "must-see" stops. The Luxembourg Gardens shoulder to shoulder, the Arc de Triomphe mobbed. Menacing hordes of tourists careened down streets on electric scooters and Ile St. Louis ice cream shops had lines thirty deep.

It was the first time we had to contend with tourists on this level. Were we just another American family with fanny packs and maps battling crowds for a glimpse of the Eiffel Tower? We sure looked like it, a reminder that as much as we wanted to sniff at tourists, we were, of course, part of the problem. The city of Rome had just banned sitting on the Spanish Steps. We didn't go to Rome, but after seeing what happened when local governments failed to protect their most treasured destinations, we understood its rationale in a way we might not have without our front-row seat to over-tourism.

We found ourselves taken aback by the diversity of Parisians. Had we come to Paris straight from New York, we probably wouldn't have noticed. It looked like home. But after so much time traveling in places where the people were fairly homogenous—or, when they weren't, didn't commingle much—it was striking.

The kids were oblivious but had their own object of fascination: the pullout sofa in our Airbnb. When we checked in and saw only one bed, Willa asked where she and James were going to sleep. "This is a sofa bed," I explained, pointing at a loveseat. "It turns into a bed." They thought I was serving up some mom joke about magical furniture. So, we demonstrated. You would have thought we had introduced them to a talking baguette. The shrieking! The delight!

"Just when we thought we had sophisticated world travelers on our hands," Teddy muttered to me as we watched them get on their hands and knees to inspect the underside.

Disneyland

Two nights in France were spent at one of Disneyland Paris' accommodations, more cowboy-themed dorm room than hotel, with a cattle-call breakfast "buffet" of paper plates, croissants wrapped in cellophane, and individual packets of Nutella. Some friends couldn't believe we were wasting travel days on something as commercial and silly as Disney. We reminded them that this was our real life, elsewhere. We had the time to fit in activities we'd do at home—arcades, movies, mini golf, and global fast-food chains—comfortable with the fact that not every outing needed to be "authentic." They could just be…authentic, no quotation marks necessary.

It was drizzling outside and chilly as we boarded a coach bus and rode to the park entrance. Teddy and I feigned excitement upon arrival, but the kids were more transparent in their skepticism. At least at first. "Coney Island has way more rides," Willa observed, puzzled. They neither knew nor recognized classic characters like Pinocchio or Donald Duck. When we walked by a crowd lined up to get the latter's autograph, Willa and James pointed and squealed with excitement—not at Donald, but at an *actual* duck, pecking in some nearby grass.

But then they discovered roller coasters and led the charge to ride Thunder Mountain again and again. They sang "It's a Small World" on repeat. Willa's face lit up as she cheered the parade each evening, waving to Mickey and the others, whoever they were. By the time we left two days later, we could tell our kids had indeed created magical memories—and would probably feel compelled, as we had, to continue the cycle of hell with their own kids someday.

St. Cibard

A high-speed train took us south toward Bordeaux, where we rented a car and drove even farther out into the rolling wine country to stay at the home of some old friends. "We're coming to France with the kids," I'd emailed my pal Jan. "Mind if we drop in for a few nights?" In a year of setting aside our introverted instincts, I had once again dug into my rolodex and pulled out a contact with whom I hadn't spoken in ten years. The answer, happily and enthusiastically, was yes!

Jan and his family owned a vineyard along a hillside dotted with Roman ruins and cherry trees in St. Cibard, a zero-stoplight town. When Willa and James weren't playing hide and seek with Jan's nieces and nephews, they were joined by a hound in picking and tossing back cherries for hours.

When we left Bordeaux for Paris a few days later to catch our flight to Corsica, it was pouring. We'd started to notice that, in a strange coincidence, it often drizzled or rained on "getaway day," a term Teddy borrowed from his minor league years on the road. We stood on the train platform, ready to board. In James's backpack were a few small toys he had received for his fifth birthday, which had been a very low-key affair. He was particularly proud of his new Kindle, a gift from Lobsy. He had started the year unable to read "the" and "that," and could now sit quietly with a chapter book—not to mention read airport signs and restaurant menus, which cut down on the number of questions he asked. "It's one of the greatest accomplishments of my life," his teacher Teddy would say. We also carried two hand-carved wooden crossbows that fired wine corks, gifts from Jan that would go home via DHL.

Sheets of rain came down at an angle as the doors to the train opened. Between the car and our platform, a gap yawned before us, slippery and precarious. Willa leapt into the train first, successfully clearing the abyss. I followed with a big step, crossbows in hand. I then stopped abruptly just inside the door because the person in front of me was putting bags on an overhead rack. Behind me, though, James did not notice that I had stopped. In his total concentration, eyes down at the gap, he leapt forward, expecting to land safely inside the train. Instead, he collided face-first with my backpack and tumbled backward into the chasm between platform and train.

The only thing stopping him from dropping all six feet down to the tracks was a foot he'd somehow snagged on the train ledge, giving Teddy just enough time to yank him back onto the platform. James screamed in terror, his lower lip bleeding and quickly fattening. Teddy carried him into the train just as the doors closed, concerned passengers asking if he was okay. Amazingly, he was.

Corsica

I had been looking forward to our next destination from the moment we started planning our trip: Corsica, the French island just south of Italy. Joanna, one of my best friends from New York, joined us with her husband Dave a day after we arrived. We had a small house among the pines overlooking a horse meadow, the beach just steps away. It was hot and the sea breeze brought notes of herbs and sunscreen.

"Wow, you're tan," she said after she walked in the door that first day and gave us all hugs. "You only get *that* dark when you've been in the sun all day for months." She confirmed what I had started to suspect. That despite all the hats and sunscreen, six months of "following the sun" had meant our skin was taking a beating. Even fair, Irish-blooded Teddy had a bronzed glow.

Joanna and Dave would turn out to be the easiest kind of visitors to host on a trip like ours. No kids of their own (yet), their own car and their own plans. I don't regret a single visitor we had, but hosting did have a way of altering the rhythm of our days and the feel of our adventure. We had grown accustomed to being just the four of us, perfecting an existence that had us nimble, in sync, on a program, and hadn't predicted how additional bodies —*beloved* additional bodies, but still, additional bodies—could bring their own opinions, family dynamics, not to mention dietary preferences and sleep schedules.

Of course, we were the ones who had insisted all these folks come see us, and they had shelled out money and taken time off to do so. As soon as we realized how our usual routine—school in the morning and afternoons wandering around neighborhoods in search of playgrounds—was hardly the stuff of visitors' European vacation dreams, we scrambled to play host in unfamiliar cities and deliver a great time, making reservations and researching activities in places where we'd only just arrived ourselves.

For now, though, things were easy. We hired Victor, a local skipper, to take all of us out to explore the area's many beaches and coves one day, boarding a twelve-person Zodiac—basically an oversized rubber raft with an outboard motor—for our first stop: Cavallo Island, a quiet spot where we had reserved a table for lunch.

Everything was going great at first. Sun glinting off the turquoise water, laughter in the air. *Isn't this fabulous! Look at us on a boat in the Mediterranean!* But soon we reached darker blue waters farther from shore, and when Victor pointed our speck of a raft toward a horizon dotted with white caps, the mood changed. I could only imagine what Teddy's father, an avid sailor who had covered tens of thousands of nautical miles on his sailboat and preached safety above all else, would have thought about the judgment of our captain (not to mention of his own son).

The farther we got from land, the more intense the swell grew. Before long, we were getting pummeled. The front of the vessel would rear up on waves then slap down again, jamming our vertebrae and soaking us with cold spray. The warm coastline, which had seemed within swimming distance just moments ago, was now a wisp of beige far, far away. The wind picked up and we moved Willa and James to the safety of the rear of the boat, where they crouched with Joanna and Dave.

After we crested a few particularly steep waves, slamming hard on the other side, I heard Teddy talking to himself. "This is really borderline, *this is really borderline*," all while white knuckling a rope with both hands to secure himself. The ride had gone from unpleasant to scary. I held on tight to another line, bracing my feet against the rubber edge of the boat to avoid being bounced into the sea.

"Well now!" we heard poor newly pregnant Joanna yell in a faux cheery voice to assure the kids. "Isn't *this* an adventure!" ("Yeah!!" they squealed in response, loving the rollercoaster).

"Just five more mee-noots!" the visibly shaken Victor yelled out over the pounding waves. But we could all see that Cavallo Island was still just a hazy strip in the distance. We were halfway there, and the sea churned in every direction. We tightened our grips, lowered our heads, and powered through with trembling hands. Would this next intimidating wave be the one that flips us all out? How could we be so dumb?

Mercifully, as we approached the island, the wind began to die down. As it did, we sat upright and unclenched, exhaling as we brushed the wet hair out of our faces. We could hear the kids giggling in the back with Joanna. The boat picked up speed over the calm homestretch and the sun warmed us. Cavallo Island beckoned just ahead.

As soon as we saw our table, perched on a deck overlooking a quiet cove of turquoise water, we forgot about the ride in. The kids joined an idle bus boy tossing bread to the fish; our meal was homemade seafood pasta and white wine. It was quiet and warm. The fear and anger drained away as we laughed and told stories. When a gust of wind sent James's Orioles hat off his head and into the water below, Teddy chucked his shirt and dove in off the restaurant's deck to fetch it back, no trouble at all. Afterward, a sheepish Victor steered us to various coves along the coast where the water was calm. Whenever he anchored we would jump in and swim to shore, warming our bodies on empty beaches of hot, smooth rocks.

The boat ride to Cavallo Island terrified us. So did the train slip in Bordeaux. But rather than fill us with anxiety, these and other brushes with peril only seemed to be making us more relaxed. We learned lessons from each, the most important of which might have been that we could recover quickly. I'm not saying we went full *laissez-faire*. We were still cautious. But we had to acknowledge that by this point our tolerance for risk had gone way up.

Germany

Berlin

Our forty-first flight of the year took us on a budget airline to Berlin from the south of France, where we had just splurged on a Father's Day weekend. Our grubby tees and fanny packs didn't fit in at the hotel we booked—one with jasmine growing up the walls and plush bathrobes in the closets—but our passports did: The hotel had one of the highest concentrations of Americans we would encounter all year.

Not that we encountered many. Why in a world with so many tourists did it seem like hardly any of them were American? There were 330 million of us! We were the world's third most-populous country! Where *was* everyone? When we did see Americans, it was as if they had all read the same guidebook with chapters exclusively on Petra, Cape Town, safari in South Africa, and the French Riviera. Later, we'd see the same for Sydney, Australia and Queenstown, New Zealand.

Most of the tourists we encountered were instead European and Chinese, and by far the most ubiquitous were Germans. German travelers were everywhere, all year round—a high-earning populace with abundant vacation days, a mega-hub airport and, apparently, a limitless desire to see the world. They had been in obscure places like Bob Marley's house and in Plettenberg Bay, South Africa. The Berliners we met back at that funny Brazilian resort had struck us as out of place at the time, but by now we understood that *of course* there would be Germans there.

Berlin was scorching when we landed, and we looked overheated and shipwrecked standing next to our bags as we waited for our host to let us into the apartment we'd call home for five nights. The flight had been crowded and loud, and I had sat wedged between two oversized strangers while a baby wailed. We hadn't had anything to eat since breakfast.

My phone buzzed. It was a text from Teddy's sister Claire. *Strange*, I thought. It was 7 a.m. on a Monday back home. Her message contained a row of green sick-face emojis. Her daughters Crosby and Grace, the beloved cousins we'd just hosted and shared headbands with in Spain, had *lice*. She wanted to know: *Do yours have it too?* I peered down at the part in Willa's hair for less than two seconds, all the time it took.

"They def have it," I typed back, my jaw tight.

I kept the discovery to myself as our host showed us around, but when she left, I announced the bad news to Teddy and the kids. Willa touched her head and looked at James, as if thinking about how to react. Gross? Sure. But … wanna play Rat-a-Tat-Cat? They did not care.

Their parents handled the infestation with less, um, equanimity. Five months removed from jobs and it was as though we had completely forgotten how to manage stress or problem-solve. Things deteriorated when we discovered our place had neither AC nor—much, much worse given the circumstances—a washing machine.

A follow up text arrived from Claire with urgent real-time advice: "Find someone to hire to come help you immediately. I'm sure there's a service in Berlin. We had someone at our house within the hour."

Right. Okay. Focus.

Teddy stuffed all our clothes into laundry bags and left to find coin-operated washing machines while I flipped open my laptop and used Google Translate to read every Berlin parenting listserv, call local pediatricians, and even, I'm mortified to admit looking back, phone the American embassy. Nothing. Berlin did not have a service that made lice-eliminating housecalls.

Meanwhile, Teddy's laundry mission failed spectacularly: When at last he found a laundromat, he didn't have enough Euros, enough machines, or enough time to do all the more-urgent-than-ever loads. He only realized that closing time was looming *after* frantically filling and starting a bunch of machines. He had to stop what he'd started and shovel soaking loads of clothes back into the bags, Willa's little pink underpants scattered on the floor as onlookers looked askance at him. He eventually got the hell out of there and took an Uber to the one drop-off laundry service he could find, off in some suburb.

There would be no clean clothes that night. No cavalry in the form of a service like Manhattan's "Hair Fairies" to show up "within the hour." No air-conditioning. Defeated, and hot, we bought lice shampoo and two nit combs from a pharmacy, sat down, took a deep breath, and began combing lice from Willa's and James's hair. We worked for three hours, squinting, our necks bent. Nobody spoke. Teddy worked on James on one side of the room, while I made my way through Willa's hair on the other. The kids zoned out on iPads.

Taking control of the situation mellowed our mood, the quiet, meditative work eventually calming us. We even started to feel less grossed out. The next morning, we awoke and did it again. And again—every morning for four days, each nit-picking session less of a big deal than the one before it.

After wrapping our sesh one morning, we befriended an American mom from Philadelphia at a playground. Her daughters played with Willa and James on the swings while she and I chatted. Just as we made plans to meet up at a biergarten later that week for an early family dinner, James walked up to me and asked, "Did you tell her about the bugs in my hair?" I wanted to disappear with embarrassment—but only, I realized, because she was American. No one in Germany seemed to think lice were a big deal. In fact, nowhere else we went that year cared a whit (or nit!) about lice. I learned to stop telling The Berlin Lice Story to non-Americans because it never really resonated. The more we traveled, the more we would spot parents casually pulling nits out of their kids' hair, and the more we noticed how in a lot of places, lice combs were as ubiquitous at checkout counters as lighters and gum.

What had felt like an Ebola-level emergency in Berlin got downgraded to something closer to athlete's foot by the time the lice resurfaced later in Norway. We groaned about having to nit-pick again, but didn't, notably, freak out the way we had in Germany. *The kids have lice. This happens to children. Everyone is going to be fine.*

Our five days in Berlin turned out to be a delightful respite from visitors and a return to the original vibe of the trip. We wandered random neighborhoods and made random friends. We rode a Hop On, Hop Off bus to get the lay of the land, but the kids snoozed most of the ride—perhaps the only way we managed to side-step Tough Questions about the city's World War II history. We had a blind friend-date picnic with an ex-pat couple from Brooklyn and followed through on that biergarten dinner with the Americans from Philly. We even took a commuter train out to Potsdam, where we were guests of honor at a barbecue hosted by Bjorn and Eva, the friends we made in Brazil.

We poked around leafy neighborhoods like Prenzlauer Berg, where families strolled to playgrounds and couples enjoyed lunch at sidewalk cafes on cobblestoned streets. Everytime I came across a neighborhood I liked that year, I'd say, half-jokingly, "Let's just move here!" and this place was no exception.

Prenzlauer Berg also confirmed a suspicion I'd had about the best way to use Airbnb in a big city. We thought we were being smart by booking places that were centrally located and accessible to all the tourist sights when the key was actually to stay in neighborhoods where we'd *move* if we were relocating to that city. Every metro area has its hipster/arty/rocker/preppy/posh/stroller-ish/etc. pockets, and we realized we'd missed out by not finding our residential niche.

Netherlands

Amsterdam

When New York City launched its Citi Bike bike-share program in 2013, we thought the world had gone mad. "How long until someone dies?" Teddy would ask. When Willa got a three-wheeled scooter for her second birthday and wanted to "ride" in our apartment building's carpeted hallway, we'd insisted she wear a helmet.

So, imagine my surprise when Willa and I rounded a corner in Amsterdam, cheese and salami in a grocery bag, ready for a picnic, to see Teddy and James riding toward us. On a shiny tandem bicycle. Without helmets.

"We rented it!" Teddy said with a proud grin, pulling up and putting his foot down to stop in front of us. "Isn't it sweet?"

It was. Cherry red and chrome, with a little seat and handlebars up front for James.

"The ride here was insane," he added, staring at the horizon as he ran a satisfied hand through his hair.

"You rode this thing through the streets?" I asked.

"Yeah!" James said, his eyes wild. They described busy intersections and streets with rush hour traffic.

We had landed in Amsterdam the day before. The five days ahead held three different sets of American visitors, including my sister and her husband, as well as outings with a few ex-pat friends who lived in town. We were only missing one thing: Our luggage. The flight from Berlin marked the first and only time all year that an airline lost our checked bags. On a normal vacation this would be very bad news. For us it hardly registered. We wore the same clothes all the time anyway! We just bought toothbrushes at a pharmacy and washed our undies in the sink and waited for the bags to show up, which they did two days later.

Wow. If Teddy's cool with riding bikes out here like this, then I am too, I thought. Willa and I rented our own bikes, and in the weeks that followed, our family biked together through cities again and again. Sometimes with the kids on a tandem, sometimes in a wheelbarrow-like cargo bucket, sometimes on their own bikes. We had our mishaps. Willa wiped out two different times that first day in Amsterdam. Twice, kind strangers ran to her aid, including a biker-type with handlebar mustache and leather vest who tightened her loose front wheel before walking off with a smile and a wave.

There was nothing more glorious than pedaling a bike through a beautiful city. Teddy was the first to admit we'd been missing out. One evening as the sun set, he pedaled James and me to dinner through the heart of Amsterdam on a single bike. I rode side-saddle over the rear wheel while James sat up front (Willa was off with a visiting friend and her mother on a bike of their own). I caught a photo of the three of us in the reflection of a shop window as we barreled by with wind-blown hair and billowing shirts. It sits framed on my desk today, a reminder of whizzing across Europe's busy bridges and neighborhoods on two wheels, wind in our faces, rapturous.

Denmark

Copenhagen

The first month of our European chapter was spent exploring just two countries: Spain and France. We had covered a lot of ground while in each, but it had felt manageable. For some reason, though, we decided it would be totally fine to knock out *five more countries* in the *three subsequent weeks*—a manic pace, even for us. After Germany (five days) and Netherlands (four days), we now faced Denmark (four days), Norway (four days), and Sweden (four days). These were our shortest country stays all year and, not surprisingly, what had sounded great on paper turned out to be much too much. By the time we landed in Copenhagen, it was getting hard to distinguish one country's quaint cobblestone streets from another's.

Unable to dive deep into a place, or even process what we were learning when we were there, we saw how country-hopping was different from region-hopping within a single country. Our nine different stops over two months in South Africa hadn't felt crazed, it had felt like immersion. So many different places to help us understand a single nation's many facets, cultural and physical. But now? We weren't even scratching the surface. We looked forward to Asia, when we would return to exploring single countries for several weeks at a stretch. For the first time, we appreciated how, for our family, travel agents—who would have gladly pointed out to us the flaws in our Europe itinerary had we used them this leg—fell in the "can't live with em, can't live without em" category.

Fortunately, Lobsy and "Beepaw Brendan" were in town and that made Copenhagen special. The only way Teddy had gotten his dad to Denmark, a place I suspect my father-in-law never thought he would see in his lifetime, was by finding the shared space on a Venn diagram between "Destinations Near Amsterdam" and "Destinations Easily Reached by Direct Flight From DC." Copenhagen it was. Brendan's travel agent booked a flight, a lovely hotel, and stocked our days with restaurant reservations and a guide. And a shiny private van with "Sullivan" in the window.

Naturally, Willa and James were skeptical of this last one. *Was this some kind of sightseeing sneak-attack?* We had cut back considerably in Europe and they wanted it to stay that way. I'd gotten a family photo in front of the Eiffel Tower but only in exchange for Orangina. We'd slipped in that Hop On Hop Off bus in Berlin, but only because a "convertible bus" looked fun. Amsterdam's Van Gogh Museum captivated Willa and James with a kid-focused scavenger hunt, but the Prado in Madrid had been a race against the clock. In Corsica, the mere mention one morning of going to "check out a town" triggered one of their whiniest days yet.

Thankfully, our Danish guide Sine was one of the gems, a reminder that a good guide can, and should, feel like an old friend—one with connections to in-the-know spots, a sense of when to keep it moving and a trove of juicy stories bordering on gossip. She took us on foot through off-the-beaten-path neighborhoods, ordering us herring sandwiches and cinnamon buns as we went. She helped decode some of the mysteries we encountered, like the many open-air flatbed trucks we'd seen crawling the city, decorated with homemade banners and balloons, blasting dance music from mega speakers and transporting teenagers, all hooting, hollering, dancing, waving, and drinking champagne. This, Sine explained, was a time-honored Danish tradition: high school graduation party trucks.

Brendan might have disliked the hassle of flying somewhere far away, but once there, he peppered Sine with questions and always listened intently to her answers. He was especially intrigued by the Danish concept of *hygge*, pronounced something close to HYOO-gah, defined by the Oxford Dictionary as "a quality of coziness and comfortable conviviality that engenders a feeling of contentment or well-being." I always took the concept to mean sheepskin blankets and fireplaces on snowy days, but Sine clarified that *hygge* was more a state of mind, a habit of slowing down to enjoy a small indulgence. Brewing the perfect cup of coffee, say, then sitting down to savor it.

In a year free of distractions, the concept of *hygge* meant more to me than it had when it was the subject of a popular coffee table book back home. Just the other day, Willa had told us her "top three favorite feelings" were, "Drinking hot chocolate inside the overnight Peru train when it was cold outside," "the feeling of a butterfly landing on my arm," and "riding in a safari truck with the wind on my face." I had some too: Warming up on Corsican rocks after a swim in the Mediterranean. Riding a bike through Amsterdam. Making dinner in our Cape Town kitchen.

In fact, the more we talked to Sine, the more it seemed that many of the awakenings we'd experienced so far that year were just the Danish approach to life. Prioritizing time with loved ones above everything else, for instance, and spending as much time outdoors as possible ("There's no such thing as bad weather, only bad clothing!" Sine said). The idea that you could transport multiple children or heavy pieces of furniture—even a fridge—on a single bicycle; or that you could create and consume with intention, not abandon. We saw how the Danes made the most of their personal time, calling Thursday "little Friday" to add a touch of leisure to the work week. Simple pleasures were essential in life.

Of course, so much leisure could only exist in a culture where the people were financially secure—which, in this Scandinavian socialist country, they were. Brendan was on it: "Tell me again about the socialist system?" he asked Sine. He wondered, if all colleges were paid for, and the state is taking care of everyone's medical needs, even offering them extensive paid family leaves and at least one month of vacation per year, what's the motivation to work? To innovate and make change? How does anyone learn ambition? You could argue for our system or theirs, but that wasn't the point—and he didn't. He only listened. Conversations like these helped all of us see there was more than one way to do things, not just "right" or "wrong" or "good" or "bad — just … ways.

Ready to plunge deeper into Scandinavia, we bid Lobsy and Brendan tearful goodbyes. Lobsy had already booked her ticket to see us in China in six weeks, but Brendan confirmed with a smile that this was the end of the road for him. He gave us the usual: a firm hug, an affectionate nod, and a reminder to be safe.

Norway

Fjordland

Every time we attempted to map out a road trip to see the Norwegian fjords we became overwhelmed. Which fjords to see? Take a train? Drive? Camp? All the guidebooks and travel blogs seemed to push the same "untouched" and "pristine" areas "best" for taking in the view, which we knew could be code for "tourist trap." We decided to try something we'd only done in Brazil: find a local agent to book us something in our budget. A few weeks before we arrived, a friend connected us to a low-cost local agent named (yes, really) Thor, to whom we paid a small fee to suggest and book a four-day itinerary.

He booked us at a cozier, not-creepy Norwegian version of *The Shining* hotel, a grand nineteenth-century spot with water views on the Bjørnefjorden and rooms that featured bunk beds built into the walls for the kids and a queen bed outfitted with one bottom sheet and *two twin top sheets and comforters*, one for each sleeper—the most ingenious solution to co-sleeping we'd ever seen.

A day trip to Bergen validated our decision to use a travel agent. Without Thor's input, we probably would have stayed there—and regretted it. Bergen is lovely, but it was also crowded with tour groups and buses, proof that internet travel research roads often led to the same popular places. The fish market was packed with foreigners lining up to sample pricey king crab claws and "whale burgers," while the main drag featured little else than shops selling snow globes and hoodies with the Norwegian flag.

Back at our place, far from the fray, the landscape was dramatic—sparkling water, a sky constantly changing. Walking along the shore, we saw dozens of orange jellyfish beneath the surface of frigid water and, on the beach, smooth dark stones perfect for skipping. It was sunny and rainy at the same time. Where had we seen this light before? Lake Titicaca in Peru, I thought. The Western Cape of South Africa, Teddy suggested.

We drove each day along Thor's routes, in and out of steep mountainsides covered in colossal storybook pines, forest floors coated in electric green moss, white cumulus clouds that came and went, glacier ice atop peaks in the distance—and, always, that twinkling expanse of blue water.

All of this should have been fun and relaxing. But there were distractions in Norway. For starters, the lice had returned, and we were back to nitpicking, this time with a more potent Norwegian shampoo that would eventually put an end to the ordeal, but which required us to sleep in shower caps. Teddy and I hadn't found any lice on our heads, but did the treatments anyway, cracking up at how ridiculous we looked in our plastic headwear at bedtime. One night we posed for a selfie—never to be shown to anyone, ever—to commemorate the absurdity.

Far, far worse, though, was how Willa and James decided it was time to abandon their great behavior and start misbehaving. We will always remember Norway for a regressive spell of naughtiness made worse because they seemed to be getting a special thrill out of pissing us off.

Having so many visitors in Europe had allowed us to view our kids through the eyes of others, especially people who hadn't seen them in a while: Willa and James dialed up the napkins-in-laps and regaled people with stories that left everyone in stitches. "They've matured so much!" people exclaimed. "They act like little grownups!" The trip had helped them become more self-aware and courteous members of society thanks to so much time spent in adult orbits—restaurants, yes, but also museums, performances, shops, hotel lobbies, and airplanes. It was one big crash course in *How to Behave*.

But, it turned out, having kids who knew *how* to behave was different from having kids who chose to behave. Willa and James could turn the charm on and off at will. Around visitors, they were good. But as soon as it was just the four of us, as it was in Norway, they dropped the act. James would irritate Willa by swatting her Kindle to the ground or karate chopping her back, in response to which Willa would shriek "James!" When our multiple demands for order went ignored, we'd break through their resistance by employing that time-honored strategy known as "yelling." Both kids would then collapse in tears, Teddy and I would feel like failures—and we'd all be worse off than before.

One afternoon, in an attempt to break the cycle, we went down to the hotel's spa area, which included a circuit of ice pools and hot tubs filled with weekenders from Oslo trying to enjoy a quiet retreat. But our kids were out to get us. James did cannonballs into lanes of quiet lap swimmers and Willa zig-zagged at a sprint from the pool to the jacuzzi to the ice bath, over and over as we scurried behind both of them, whisper-yelling at them to stop. We were the quintessence of the pathetic amateur American family abroad and returned to our room even more dispirited than when we had left.

Why this sudden unraveling? We weren't sure, but our best hunch was that the late European sunsets had profoundly disrupted their sleep schedules. By the time we reached Scandinavia, where the sun actually never set at all, they were a wreck. And as a result, so were we. It was one of those seemingly innocuous details—the sun sets late in European summers—that wound up affecting us in a major way. With just ten days left before we took off for Asia, we did our best to make do, tightening the drapes and putting them to bed earlier.

More important, their behavior motivated us to formalize a discipline system we'd been testing called "Minutes," which was built around screen time. Typically, the kids were only allowed to watch their iPads at airport gates and on airplanes. We'd arrive at our gate, the screens and headphones would come out, and they'd zone out on unlimited shows until we landed somewhere else. For better or worse, they lived for this (and so did we).

Now, it was under threat. In the Minutes system, if the kids misbehaved, we'd dock minutes off their screen time on the next flight. Having seen how incentives worked with homeschooling, it seemed likely that disincentives might also carry some weight. First there was a warning—"I'm about to give Minutes!"—which was usually enough to stop them in their tracks. But if their bad behavior persisted, we'd start docking. One minute off for every whine and complaint, two minutes off for not listening when grownups asked them to do something, five minutes off for punching, hitting, or shoving. A whopping ten for the rare sibling biting attack.

The Minutes would pile up on an invisible ledger we kept in our heads, and when we'd get to an airport gate for the next flight, we'd set a timer for the total number each kid had accrued. They'd wait out their punishment in agony, watching iPad timers tick down.

The good news was they could always get an eleventh-hour reprieve for good behavior. Things like "having a calm body in line at the airport" could get them as many as five or even ten Minutes knocked off their sentences. They were so desperate to get those screens they complied, every time, which made airports more pleasant overnight. After six months, we finally found a system that worked. We kept it the remainder of our year.

Sweden

Stockholm

Social media continued serving its stated, well-intentioned purpose: to foster connections and bring people closer. With its help, we were able to stay in regular touch with people like Stina and Erick, the Swedish couple we'd met on that Cape Town township tour hosted by Mhinti and Mama Miriam. They had been following our travels ever since and made sure to reach out when they saw we were Stockholm-bound. "I cannot believe you've been traveling since we last saw you," Erick said with a smile as he greeted us at the playground, a paper bag filled with Swedish gummies outstretched to the kids. Walking alongside them was daughter Ines, which startled us. She'd been a baby in a chest carrier the last time we'd seen her. It was a funny marker of time that reminded us just how long our trip really was.

For a city we'd never visited before, we had a lot of people to see, even after we said goodbye to Stina and Erick. Our appetite for socializing had expanded to include not just new pals like them, but anyone, really, we could excavate from the depths of our personal rolodexes. People like Cape Town Luke and Vineyard Jan, whom we hadn't seen in years, even decades. "Remember us?" we'd email. "We're coming to town!" It always stunned us when people replied with full-throated invitations to barbecues and picnics.

I'd met Henrik and Maria more than twenty years before as a high schooler studying French and hadn't seen either since. But when I shot them one of my out-of-left-field emails, they replied immediately with an invitation to a pool party. As in Berlin, we caught a commuter train out to the burbs to be guests of honor at a barbecue of friends and neighbors. This Swedish crowd's crisp linen pants and beachy blond blowouts offered a stark contrast to Teddy's backpack and my limp ponytail, but we didn't care. There were glasses of white wine to drink and questions about Swedish life to ask.

And then, seven weeks had passed. It was not only our last night in Stockholm but also our last night in Europe. We ordered room service (Swedish meatballs) and played music (ABBA) as we culled the things from our suitcases that we no longer needed and packed up the ones we did, including fresh t-shirts and deodorant.

I'd begun to view our transition from Comfortable European Break to Asian Adventure as falling off a kind of cliff. We would suddenly be so far away. So very *without* cobblestones or visitors from home. Things were about to get real, it seemed. But rather than feel anxious, we welcomed the chance to "get back" to the adventure and forge ahead into unfamiliar territory—see what was what and return to life just the four of us. We needed to keep moving.

ASIA

Three months: Mongolia (Ulaanbaatar, Gobi Desert) → China (Hong Kong, Beijing, Xi'an, Chengdu, Lijiang, Shanghai) → Vietnam (Hanoi, Ninh Binh, Halong Bay, Hoi An, Hue, Saigon) → Cambodia (Siem Reap) → Singapore → Indonesia (Amed, Ubud, Manggis, Sideman, Flores)

Mongolia

Ulaanbaatar

I have a friend who once cycled from New York to San Francisco. By the time she reached the Rockies, she said, she'd grown physically fit enough to cross them. I more fully understood what she meant when we arrived in Asia, our most challenging continent, after six months of travel. All that had preceded it had been our training—we had gained endurance, flexibility and efficiency. We'd also developed a capacity for not sweating the small, or even medium stuff. Plus a capacity for just, you know, sweating. We were ready to spend three months immersed in cultures with completely alien social norms, alphabets that contained not a familiar fragment and, sometimes, accommodations that, shall we say, *deepened* our relationship with critters.

When we left Sweden, we were about to travel for twenty hours across twelve time zones, including a four-hour layover in Moscow (where we ate lukewarm "quesadillas" at a TGI Fridays and spotted a vending machine that sold only deodorant). No one slept on the six-hour flight from Moscow to Mongolia. We arrived early in the morning, glassy-eyed and half dead, at the Chinggis Khaan International Airport in the capital city, Ulaanbaatar.

Welcome to Mongolia, a vast but sparsely populated country situated at high altitude between Russia to the north and China to the south. *Mongolia.* We had not thought of coming here ourselves, having left much of our Asia planning to the imagination and expertise of travel agents. They were the ones who insisted this place was a can't-miss. Especially because they could get us there in time for the Naadam Festival, an event we had never heard of, but naturally had to attend.

We were settling back into life at the mercy and warm embrace of travel agents. Though Teddy had once been to China and Japan for a business school trip, and the two of us had spent our honeymoon in Thailand and Cambodia, we were pretty new to Asia. And while we may have disliked tightly programmed itineraries and guides, we were glad someone else was back in charge of logistics and decision-making after Europe. Sure enough, in Ulaanbaatar, an official with a "Sullivan" sign fast-tracked us through airport immigration lines, and our hotel room was made available at 9 a.m. on the morning we landed because someone—not us—had thought to secure an early check-in.

Our guide Gansukh greeted us at the baggage claim and announced he would be at our side for the next *two weeks*. Seemed like a lot, but the kids sized him up and liked what they saw: A fit and handsome young father who had two mischievous boys of his own. There were high fives and jokes between the three of them as we headed to our hotel, a new tower taller than most of the skyline. Where other cities like Amman and Bogota had extended to the horizon, the view from our hotel room showed how Ulaanbaatar stopped abruptly at the city limit, nothing beyond but grassland.

We knew what we needed to do: unpack and power through that first day, drinking lots of water and making sure to stay awake until sunset—no matter what. Here's what we seasoned travelers did instead: closed the drapes and took a five-hour nap.

Was it worth it? Definitely not! We were messed up for days! My first memories of our first afternoon in the city, which locals called "UB," are hazy. I seem to recall stumbling around a sparse Soviet-era amusement park near our hotel, Mongolian pop music piped through tinny speakers, couples holding parasols pedaling buggies along an elevated track, Willa and James seesawing in a daze. It was overcast and muggy. There was a crumbling cement slide once tiled to look like a dragon and a rollercoaster that ran only when enough people came along to fill all the cars.

Inside the city limits there was more of a boomtown feel. When Gansukh retrieved us that afternoon, we inched together through rush hour traffic, passing low, crumbling buildings topped with jumbles of telephone wires, which stood alongside gleaming glass malls and office parks. Though few buildings stood much taller than twelve stories, there were construction sites on every block, signaling towering changes ahead.

We headed to a department store, where Gansukh said we needed to buy traditional Mongolian apparel for the festival. I wasn't so sure about this errand. Were visiting Americans supposed to wear traditional Mongolian clothes? Were we going to offend people? Wasn't this … *cultural appropriation*? No, a friend back home reassured me by text. The context mattered. "You're not wearing the clothes as a joke or a costume," she said. "It would be like wearing a sari to an Indian wedding—a sign of respect."

Willa, unable to believe her good luck at this surprise shopping trip, bounded into the store and began modeling one colorful caftan after another.

"You're going to be a movie star!" Gansukh told her.

"No, I'm going to be an engineer," Willa replied over her shoulder as she admired herself in the mirror. Famous James pulled a blue and gold hat with a pointed tip off the rack and said he was done shopping, more interested in entertaining the shop ladies with "funny" stories (they did not speak English, but laughed anyway). I bought a caftan in robin's egg blue with a narrow collar, sash and capped sleeves, while Teddy walked out with a long-sleeved shirt embroidered in gold.

On our way home, we passed a Buddhist temple. Gansukh pointed to rows of golden cylindrical prayer wheels outside the building and explained how the faithful spun them to make wishes and seek good fortune. James, still trying to make sense of all the religions he was encountering—and, probably grateful we weren't going for a tour—pointed to a pigeon sitting atop one of them. "That bird," he said, "is prolly wishing for all the crumbs in the world."

When our van pulled up to the Naadam Festival fairgrounds the next morning, we joined thousands of spectators filing into the stadium, all of them dressed to the nines, including Gansukh, who looked sharp in a maroon tunic and wide-brimmed felt hat. We were glad we had dressed up. We were also glad Gansukh was there to translate, explain what was happening, and help us navigate the throngs of people to our seats, which we reached just as the president of Mongolia began his welcome speech.

The "festiball," as James called it, was Mongolia's most important annual event, an epic celebration of Mongolian culture that showcased, among other things, its three most "manly" sports: archery, wrestling, and horseback riding. Wrestling was the most important of the three and matches played out without weight classes or time limits because, as Gansukh pointed out, warriors needed to be prepared to fight adversaries of every size for as long as it took. The wrestling event was for men only, and they wore bolero-style jackets over bare chests because at the turn of the century, a woman disguised as a man famously kicked everyone's ass. These revealing tops were designed to keep that from ever happening again.

Naadam's athletic traditions, rooted in war, dated back to the days of Genghis Khan, a figure I'd always associated with brutality, but whom Mongolians revered as a symbol of religious and political freedom. He was a hero who brought innovation and trade from east to west. The climax of the opening ceremonies portrayed a reenactment of Khan's life, with an actor in a fur robe and hat ascending a podium with his arms wide, war music blasting from stadium speakers as the crowd cheered.

Between events, we wandered the fairgrounds, eating *khuushuur*—mutton dumplings fried with garlic and chives—and watched people fill to-go cups with ladles of fermented camel's milk, a mildly alcoholic drink favored by locals. To our surprise, we rounded a corner to find a man wearing a royal blue t-shirt printed with "#RandomTravelingBlackGuy" in large block letters. He was American, we learned when we said hi, and indeed, he was Black. He told me the shirt was a light-hearted attempt to normalize the sight of a Black American man touring the world, which he felt was too rare. We followed each other on Instagram.

Willa and James begged to stop at a homemade game booth where festivalgoers paid to throw darts at a large wooden panel of balloons. A man in his seventies with an inch of ash dangling off the cigarette in his mouth handed them darts. *Pop! Pop!* The same guy returned to deliver prizes: tattered, second-hand stuffed animals—a beige teddy bear with matted fur and a pink bow tie hanging by a string for Willa, and for James, an unappealing blue cartoon character with a downturned mouth. Six months ago, when our kids had a toy closet brimming with plastic toys, these threadbare friends wouldn't have gotten a second look. They may have even inspired a wrinkled nose. These days, however, Willa's and James's whole relationship with toys had been recalibrated, and they were dazzled. They doted on these stuffies, tucking them into bed, carrying them everywhere.

On the second day of the festival, we drove out toward Ulaanbaatar's flat, grassy surrounding countryside, our vehicle just one in a mile-long line of cars on the two-lane highway, each crammed with families, many with babies riding in the driver's lap. "How come *they* get to sit in the front seat?" Willa asked with a pout.

"No fair," James added. Everyone in this gridlock, including us, was headed to catch the most exciting event of the festival: a horse race.

Gansukh timed our arrival perfectly. We parked in the grassland and trudged toward the crowds, reaching our reserved tourist section just as a tiny puff of dust appeared on the horizon about a mile away. It was the first-place rider closing in. There was no track out here, just a windswept plain lined with tens of thousands of people, now on their feet and roaring. I got goosebumps as the bareback racers closed in. These were not just any jockeys, Gansukh told us. They were *children*—boys and girls as young as six.

We squinted to get a better look, amazed at the idea of such brave little riders. A few minutes later, a boy in a red helmet and dusty trousers, who couldn't have been more than ten, came into focus and streaked across the finish line, his horse's mane whipping in the wind. I can't ever remember feeling prouder of anyone in my life. It reminded me of marathon day in New York, when bearing witness to strangers' perseverance always makes me cry. Except in this case, the stranger, poised and tough, was a child just a few years older than my own. When he won, press and organizers swarmed him at the finish line.

"This is my favorite part of Mongolia!" Willa said, jumping up and down and speaking for all of us. We were transfixed and stayed to cheer on the next seventy riders, each impossibly young, hunched over their horses in determination as they thundered by. Those who had to scramble down and pull at horses eating grass mere feet from the finish line earned extra whoops of encouragement from the crowd.

These hundreds of riders had set out in the predawn darkness and galloped for thirteen miles across a steppe landscape unchanged from the days of Genghis Khan, and they had done so alone. Watching it unfold—the triumphs, the failures, the bravery, and the danger—Teddy and I shared the same thought: *There's not a single parent we knew back home who'd let their six-year-old do anything like this. Including us.*

Starting with Sophia, who had played unchaperoned back at the Santiago playground, we had encountered small children around the world exhibiting an independence that, where we lived, was inconceivable. Kids commuting alone on foot along busy highways, stirring boiling pots, babysitting groups of babies. A toddler in Salvador, Brazil, had passed us on the street taking purposeful strides, wearing nothing but a diaper and flip flops—with a pacifier in his mouth. Where was he going, all by himself? Answer: Somewhere!

A few days later when we flew south with Gansukh into the Gobi Desert on a prop plane, we landed at the one-room Dalanzadgad Airport, a concrete building plopped on an otherwise empty expanse, and drove an hour to our lodge in a four-by-four caked in dirt, bouncing along the dusty tracks that criss-crossed the landscape in all directions. Mongolia is roughly the size of Alaska, but most of its three million citizens lived in UB, not out here in this desolate landscape.

After about half an hour, we spotted a herd of 300 goats and sheep trailed by a nomadic girl trotting behind on horseback. James watched her for a moment as we slowed to a stop. "Why is she chasing those animals?" he asked. I explained the concept of a shepherd. When Gansukh rolled down his window to greet her—he told us he knew her family—she caught him up on weather conditions and the latest news from her parents. Willa and James stared at her out the window, jaws slack. So did I. She was about eleven, alone for miles, charged with watching over her families' wealth during the summer school break. She did not seem distressed or bored or scared. She was hard at work! In charge!

Gobi Desert

Before we got there, I thought the Gobi would have rolling dunes akin to what we'd seen in Jordan's Wadi Rum. But actually, only 5 percent of the Gobi is sand. Most of it is flat and coated in rocks and yellow-brown grass. I understood why it was called "Land of the Eternal Blue Sky," and got a chill imagining Genghis Khan and his army charging toward us in a cloud of dust from miles away on the horizon.

We were glamping in a *ger*, or traditional Mongolian yurt, that week. We had indoor plumbing and power outlets, but no Wi-Fi. And in the absence of roads or even a single chirping bird, it was very, very quiet. The lodge had a small common area with leather couches where guests could gather to read and play games between excursions. On our first afternoon there, we were surprised to hear American voices. We had already befriended an American couple staying at this place, retirees from Philadelphia named Alan and Carol. Now there were more? Gansukh explained that the Mongolian owner of the lodge now lived in New Jersey and targeted the American market almost exclusively.

James wandered over to the group, a couple in their fifties with three college-aged children. We watched from afar as he introduced himself and asked about the game they were playing. It was anklebone, a traditional Mongolian pastime played with sheep bones. But James already knew that. He and Gansukh had been playing it for days. This was just his warm-up act. Based on the few words we heard from across the room—"piranha," "elephant"—Famous James had pivoted to telling stories about our travels, holding court and earning peals of laughter. "How *old* are you?" someone asked.

New people had become a permanent fixture in our children's lives, not to mention a valuable way to break the monotony of being together. Both kids had refined their small talk, having developed easy responses to the same questions they were asked in new places every day: "What's your name?" "How old are you?" "Where are you from?" "What countries have you already visited?" And the most frequently asked of all, the one impossible to answer: "What has been your favorite place?"

Gansukh helped us find a few kids their age to play with in the Gobi. One afternoon he took us to visit a nomadic family at their *ger*, the first of a few such home visits with locals. Just as we had in Jordan, we asked for a pre-visit etiquette briefing and arrived bearing oranges and boxes of cookies we'd purchased at a grocery store in UB. Within the first five seconds I breached protocol by pointing at something of interest inside the *ger*, and an alert Willa lowered my hand. "No pointing, remember?" she whispered.

Our host was a warm and friendly woman in her thirties with four kids. The oldest was out herding goats while the little ones watched cartoons on a small satellite TV. Willa and James joined them on the rug. One of the boys, about seven years old, wore a Steph Curry Golden State Warriors jersey; we hadn't seen many American tourists out in the world, but our country's *culture* was everywhere. Mongolians in particular loved the NBA. That and KFC, according to Gansukh. (Indeed, KFC would turn out to be the most ubiquitous brand we'd see all year after Yankees hats.)

When lunch was served, all five kids threw back bowls of stew made from dried beef, black tea, salt, and mare's milk, their eyes glued to the TV. I wondered if Willa and James were too zoned out on Mongolian cartoons to realize what they were gulping, but then Willa stood up and asked for seconds, which delighted our host. We grownups sat on low benches and talked about daily life, raising kids, cooking, and school. Gansukh translated and offered helpful context. When at last it was time to leave, our hostess ruffled James's hair and asked if she could keep him.

At dusk that evening, Gansukh recruited three little girls Willa's and James's age—daughters of the lodge's cook—to play hide and seek outside on the grass. After weeks in busy cities, on tours, and among deadly predators, our kids relished the chance to run free outside. There were no cars or leopards here, just space and time. The kids played rounds of tag together as the sun set in that vast sky and competed to throw rocks the farthest distance, that night and every night thereafter.

Punctuality, Gansukh explained, was not part of Mongolian culture. People in his nomadic country moved on "Mongolian Time," which meant they got there when they got there. When logistics were at the mercy of animals and weather and terrain, it was hard to be "on time." In the absence of Wi-Fi, our days in the Gobi slowed to an easy rhythm, even as Gansukh filled them with activities and excursions. We wandered the Yol Valley, a verdant swath cutting between steep rocky cliffs. We rode horses, James with Gansukh on one horse, and Willa on another with a boy about nine whose father ran the horse operation. We borrowed dune buggies from the lodge and took them out across the steppe to explore, amused anytime we encountered a herd of sheep because it always sounded like they were calling Teddy's name: "T-E-E-E-E-E-E-D!" Packs of wild horses dotted the land, too, but not much else.

The Flaming Cliffs is a region of the Gobi known for its dinosaur fossils. The morning of our visit, Gansukh told us he had an exciting surprise: He had arranged for a paleontologist to come to the lodge and talk to us about dinosaur fossils! The kids thought this was amazing. A real live paleontologist? Someone to tell stories about adventure and Velociraptors and T-rexes? They couldn't wait. But when the scientist turned on a projector and began clicking through charts and graphs about the Cretaceous period, their eyes glazed over. James did not know what a graph or chart was and had no idea what "Cretaceous" meant. They had been tricked once again into "Boring Grownup Talk," which they had begun referring to simply as "BGT." James fidgeted and looked out the window, while Willa daydreamed about something, perhaps beef stew and Mongolian cartoons, which was way more fun than this.

At the end, James raised his hand.

"Yes?" the paleontologist said, as if seeing James for the first time. "You have a question?"

"Yes," James said with confidence, his chubby legs straight out in front of him on the seat. "What came first ... dinosaurs or Genghis Khan?"

We thanked the paleontologist for his time. "I used to want to be a paleontologist," Willa told him as she shook his hand goodbye. "But I don't want to anymore."

We should have just gone straight to the cliffs, which are called "flaming" because the dirt is high in copper and at sunset, the land appears neon orange. It's a major attraction for the Gobi, which meant there were about a half-dozen four-by-fours in the parking area and a handful of German tourists wandering up and over the peaks.

Our driver took us to an empty stretch he said was covered in dinosaur fossils. Sure enough, we immediately spotted something white in the ground and after dusting it off, realized it was a fossil. Then another, and another. They looked like white rocks and practically littered the ground around us. When we picked them up they crumbled in our hands like chalk. Willa and James were fascinated. Real dinosaur "bones!" They began gathering them in piles.

We shared their excitement. I had never seen anything like it. But something about picking them up and playing with them felt wrong. Here were fossils that had survived hundreds of millions of years, and now we were just letting them disintegrate in our hands? Where were the guards? The signs that said "Do not touch fossils?" How many years left before the selfie-stick masses arrived and destroyed them all?

We stopped touching the fossils and told the kids to do the same. Before we could explain why, Gansukh leaped out from behind the jeep dressed in a Tyrannosaurus rex costume and started chasing James and Willa, who squealed and set off running and laughing.

On our last day in the Gobi, Willa and James helped stuff dumplings with the kitchen staff. When they saw their handiwork come out of the steamer, the kids were astonished and ran to offer some to new friends Alan and Carol, the retired couple from Philly, who declared them delicious. Willa and James beamed.

"Maybe we can meet up again sometime?" Willa asked, gazing into Carol's kind eyes with a bit of longing. "Like, when we're back home?" Her desire for human connection was adorable but also sad in a way. Were we doing everything we could to get them the socialization they needed?

That night a group of students aged eleven to sixteen from a nearby music school came to the lodge to perform traditional Mongolian music and dance. A half dozen of us gathered on a hill at sunset, where a rug had been laid out across the desert floor, and watched the children sing, dance, and play their instruments. It had rained earlier in the day, and an electric gold sunset exploded against cumulus clouds tinged with purple. The performers' colorful robes swirled and glinted in the fading light.

Before their last song, the students turned to Willa and James. *Want to join us?* My instinct was to speak up and make excuses on their behalf—*they're shy, dancing's not their thing, they need to warm up to new people,* that kind of thing. But before I could say anything, our kids scrambled over to the group as if they thought they'd never ask. They all joined hands, and as the music started, began moving in a circle, James in white tube socks pulled to his knees and Willa wearing the same blue dress she'd worn piranha fishing in the Amazon. When someone asked me later if anything in our travels had moved us to tears, the memory of that moment came flooding back.

We had one final night in Mongolia before flying to China, and we spent it dining out in UB with a British-Russian family we had befriended at our hotel before going to the Gobi. Wayne worked for a major Australian mining company whose interest in Mongolia's gold and copper had contributed to UB's recent growth. Their six-year-old daughter went to a British school in town. This was our second dinner with them. At one point the topic turned to Scandinavia.

"Norway is at the top of our travel wish list," Wayne's wife Alionna said. "Where did you stay?"

We told her all about Thor and the great driving itinerary he'd created for us. It was hard to believe we had been there just three weeks before.

"Here," I said, handing them my phone to scroll through photos. The two of them huddled over my screen, their eyes growing wider as they swiped at image after image of crystalline water and pine forests. Suddenly they stopped. Wayne turned red and Alionna handed back my phone. I looked down at the screen. To my horror, they had stopped on a forgotten photo: that selfie Teddy and I had taken in our Norway hotel room, he in his underwear, I in a nightgown and glasses—both of us wearing lice shampoo shower caps.

On our last morning, Gansukh wore a suit and tie to see us off at the airport. "Goodbye, Fruit Boy," he said, hugging James. *Jimce* in Mongolian meant fruit, and Gansukh had given him the affectionate nickname on day one. We would miss Gansukh, one of those special guides who showed us the soul of a place and helped us fall in love with it. We waved goodbye to him through the glass and walked away to our gate, bound for Hong Kong.

China

Hong Kong

"Is it still okay for us to be going to Hong Kong?" we'd asked our security firm and travel agent the night before taking off. Pro-democracy protests had grown in intensity over the last few weeks, and the news showed activists raging in the streets, battling pepper-spray and violent police arrests. They told us it was safe, and we landed at night into a suffocating humidity.

There was an email from Gansukh waiting for Teddy, one thanking us again for a great visit—and, for some reason, offering the kids unsolicited advice about their eating habits:

> *James, i bit concerned about your diet. U should eat bit more son. There is Mongol saying if you wanna be a strong Mongol wrestler, you gotta eat large portion. I would not reccomend Willa to eat big portion because we never advice girls to have big portion. Girls should keep the figure.*

Sigh.

In Hong Kong we did not use guides. We knew enough people who had lived and worked in the city to know that it was easy enough for tourists to navigate, and we spent five days back in our comfortable rhythm: Breakfast buffet, homeschool, wandering new neighborhoods, and meeting up with friends old and new.

"Hong Kong is a lot," Teddy said after our first day. After a week on the endless and empty Mongolian steppe, Hong Kong's crowds, towering skyscrapers, traffic, smells good and bad hit us in the face. "It feels like New York!" Willa said as she skipped across a busy intersection.

Everything in our suitcases smelled "farm-y," as Willa put it. After a week among the Gobi's camels, horses, and goats, we were ready for a laundry mission. Teddy set out with our bags while I took the kids to a playground. It was Sunday, and an elderly church group sat nearby singing hymns, their eyes closed, hands swaying above their heads. At the other end of the playground, a little girl and her brother amused themselves by pushing their goldendoodle in a baby swing. It felt good to be back on a park bench somewhere out in the world, observing what was what.

I had begun keeping lists of the things we did and saw, all organized by category—"bodies of water swum in," "dogs met," "friends made," that kind of thing. I maintained them in a Google doc and added as we went. One of our favorite lists so far was "modes of transport taken," which by now included everything from tandem bikes and bullet trains to camels and funiculars. In Hong Kong, we added the Central-Mid-Levels, the world's longest outdoor covered escalator, which commuters used to reach neighborhoods stacked up the sides of the city's impossibly steep hills.

As walkers, Willa and James had improved their stamina and speed considerably, but they still hated to walk uphill in the heat. Who doesn't? Hong Kong's suffocating heat wilted our hair and sapped our energy. ("Your face is so shiny," Willa regularly pointed out to me.) The appearance of a magical moving staircase, therefore, right in the middle of a busy city, ready to sweep us skyward, seemed too good to be true—the kind of "invention" Willa might sketch in her notebook. We used it to explore neighborhoods and find air-conditioning and snack breaks.

One of our AC escapes took us into an empty French bistro in the Central neighborhood. We cooled off with lemonades and played a game of Mastermind we bought at the mall. Our server was from the Philippines and curious about us. "You're really brave," she told us as she set down another round of lemonades. We asked what she meant. "Out here? In public? With your kids?" She was referring to the political unrest we'd seen in the news and told us she only went outside to get to and from work. Even so, her mother was worried sick about her all day.

What she was saying didn't match our experience. We covered a lot of ground in Hong Kong and witnessed a city of millions of people going about their daily life. We didn't see any unrest. I was reminded of New York's Occupy Wall Street protest in 2011. TV news footage at the time made it seem as though tens of thousands of angry rioters were swarming Manhattan, when in fact Occupy was really about 200 people in tents in a small park. We lived four blocks away at the time and would never have noticed them had it not been for the news.

Once again, dangers that generated frightening international headlines did not affect us or many of the people who lived there. There had been a car bombing in Bogota during our stay that had killed twenty people; a terrorist bus bomb at the Great Pyramids a week after we'd left that injured sixteen and, of course, those cyclones in Mozambique that had devastated tens of thousands of people. But just because we went to these places did not mean we were in the line of fire.

The world *was* a dangerous place—with scary weather episodes and explosive politics. There were cities like Rio and Bogota and Johannesburg known for being filled with peril, but there was also just the garden variety danger from driving or walking or being alive. There was the lurking danger of illness and the existential danger of climate change. We appreciated more than ever how we were both safe and vulnerable no matter where we went.

Most of the time, our family of four stuck together—all day, all week, all month, all year. If I hadn't lived this experience, I might ask: Why not split up? Why not give each other alone time? Get a sitter? But not only had we adapted to the togetherness, we had come to prefer it. If only the Cartagena versions of Margaret and Teddy could have understood this.

Every once in a while, though, Teddy or I peeled off for a few hours of solo time. In Hong Kong, I planned a whole morning to myself after Teddy encouraged me to sign up for a spin class I'd found online. "Get breakfast by yourself afterward!" he said. *Wow.* This was going to be amazing.

At 8:15 a.m., I said bye to my family, who was on their way to the breakfast buffet. Their plan was to do school, then meet me after lunch on the other side of the Victoria Harbour. I left with my fanny pack, a change of clothes in my backpack, and a few HK$ bills for the subway, which didn't take credit cards. I hopped a packed rush hour train, happy not to be going to an office. By 10 a.m., I had completed the class and showered in the locker room. I couldn't wait to enjoy a few glorious hours of Margaret Time. Maybe a lovely little cafe somewhere? I hadn't eaten yet and after a tough workout, I was ready to chow down, have a coffee, and relax with my book! I was nearing the finish of an excellent biography about Genghis Khan and could already taste the latte I'd soon be sipping as I paged through those final chapters.

But in the locker room I noticed something missing from my bag: I had forgotten to pack a bra. *That's annoying,* I thought. *But, hey, no problem. This is a city! I'll just pop into a store, buy a cheap bra, and get back to my morning.*

I tried on a bra at a nearby women's department store and leaned out the fitting room door. "May I wear this out?" I asked the woman who worked there. (English is one of the official languages in Hong Kong.) "Yes, but no exchanges or returns after I cut this tag," she told me, holding a pair of scissors mid-air. "No problem," I replied. *Snip!*

I dressed and walked out to the register wearing my new bra, eager to get breakfast underway. The lady rang me up and I reached to pay.

Now, those who know me well know that I can sometimes be absent-minded. It's a trait that has its upsides—I'm not particularly anxious—but one that can really ruin a day. A day you didn't realize you needed. A day you had been looking forward to all week. When I reached into my fanny pack to pay for the bra, I did not have my wallet. My mind raced before I remembered: I had taken it out the night before and must not have put it back. It was sitting there at the hotel. Right next to my bra.

The lady waited, and I remembered the tags she had just snipped. I counted out just enough bills to cover the total. (Google Pay on mobile phones wouldn't be available for another year.) It was all the money I had on me. And now it was gone. I walked out of the shop into the steamy Hong Kong morning, far from the hotel, with no money for the "Margaret Time" breakfast I had been so excited about. I didn't even have enough for a cup of coffee from a cart. I had no way to take the subway back to the hotel and Uber, which would have been a perfect solution, wasn't a thing there. I considered taking a cab back and having Teddy meet me with cash, but frankly, I couldn't bear the look on his face.

I just needed to wait until they came to our designated meeting point, the Peak Tram ticket station. I sat on a bench for two and a half hours by myself to serve my sentence for being forgetful. I had a phone, a book—and a bra!—but no food, no water, no coffee, no AC.

When Teddy and the kids finally showed up, I felt like one of the mummies we'd seen back in Egypt. I suppressed the urge to whine as we rode the tram up to Hong Kong's highest point, Victoria Peak. We'd already ascended funiculars, gondolas, and skyscrapers to see the view in so many other cities—Bogota, Santiago, Rio, Cape Town, Valparaiso, Dubai, Bergen—did we really need to see another? Teddy and the kids told me it was great. But I have to take their word for it. I was too dehydrated to notice.

We had been eating well in Hong Kong—I still dream about the soup dumplings we ordered from this one sidewalk stall—but we knew there was so much more unsampled street food out there yet to try. In the interest of time, we booked an afternoon food tour in the Prince Edward neighborhood with Ronald, a twenty-something student from Hong Kong we found online. Along with us were Jeff and Pete, travel buddies from Auckland, who laughed at all of Willa's and James's stories despite blistering hangovers from a big night out in Macau.

We showed up hungry and spent the afternoon sampling food from a dozen different street stalls, hole-in-the-wall restaurants, and non-descript teahouses. We ate stinky tofu, fish skin dumplings, and fish balls on sticks. There were sweet pineapple buns, octopus, and egg waffles. Willa and James loved the mango mochis but skipped the paper plate of pig ovaries. "Those are quite nice, actually," Pete said between bites. I found mine to be chewy and cold but ate them anyway.

Food tours like this were becoming our favorite ways to learn about a city. They usually took place in neighborhoods off the beaten path, allowing us to sample small bites of area specialities and chat with locals. We also loved the chance to meet like-minded travelers like Pete and Jeff. We were already making plans to reunite with them in New Zealand.

Beijing

Hong Kong was something of a gentle introduction to our three weeks in China. People spoke English and "The Great China Firewall," which restricted access to the internet—no Google, no Instagram, no YouTube—didn't apply there in 2019. We had found it easy to navigate the east-meets-west way of life. We knew that was all about to change as we flew north into mainland China.

We were greeted at the Beijing Capital International Airport by a van and driver and Nancy, a thirty-three-year-old tour guide and lifelong Beijinger. Our existence over the next two weeks—across Beijing, Xi'an, Chengdu, and Shanghai—would be filled with private guided sightseeing tours reminiscent of our time in the Middle East. It wasn't ideal, but we also suspected, correctly, that we would need all the help we could get.

Nancy was immediately concerned: Is it true Teddy's *mother* had flown to *China* from the *United States* all by *herself*? Lobsy had landed in Beijing two hours earlier and was waiting for us at the hotel. "This would never happen in China," Nancy said, her hand on her chest. I'm sure she was picturing some frightened granny with a shawl and a cane, confused and alone. Lila had flown fourteen hours across eleven time zones, and, sure enough, when she greeted us at the hotel, looked like a woman fresh off a spa day.

"Hi guys!" she said, hugging Willa and James to her legs. This was her fifth visit to see us that year and her first time ever to Asia. She had always wanted to see the Great Wall.

Somehow it was even hotter and more humid in Beijing than it had been in Hong Kong, or maybe it just felt that way because of the smog, which lent the place an overcast, dreary feel. Nancy told us Beijingers joked that money could buy everything except blue sky. Right away we noticed how men beat the heat by wearing their t-shirts scrunched up high to expose prodigious bare bellies, a look we learned was called "the Beijing Bikini." Fortunately, our small hotel, tucked away in the narrow *hutong* alleyways of the city's old quarter, had air-conditioning. The kids wasted little time catching Lobsy up on all things Mongolia—the wrestling matches, the dinosaur fossils, and Gansukh. They taught her how to play anklebone, and Willa modeled her dress from the Naadam Festival.

The next morning en route to Tiananmen Square, Nancy told us about her honeymoon, which she took in New York. She was amazed that we lived there, especially with young children. She had felt unsafe around so many people with tattoos and piercings. "So many gang members!" She demonstrated how she had clutched her purse tightly to her chest everywhere she went. Even more stunning to her was how we had spent nine weeks in Africa. "People here don't go to Africa," she said. "They think you will be killed!"

When we pulled up, I took one look at Tiananmen Square and knew the lollipops I'd packed as bribes weren't going to be enough. At 8:45 a.m. it was already ninety degrees, and the place was mobbed with tourists. By 9:15 a.m. the lollipops had been consumed and whining set in every time Nancy started a sentence with, "As you can see…"

Then, someone walking past us did a double take as if they recognized us. They began speaking to us in Mandarin. Nancy translated: "They want to know if their group can take a picture with you." *What?* We were among the few non-Chinese tourists in a sea of thousands, and Nancy explained how most of the crowd hailed from rural provinces where they had never seen "Westerners" in real life. A novelty more interesting than the Forbidden

Palace, we wound up posing with a half dozen different school groups. Willa forgot all about the heat and reveled in the attention.

"I don't feel great," Teddy said to me, his hand on his stomach as we walked back to the van. We were headed off to a series of home visits with real Beijingers, which Nancy told us had all been government-approved. We knew from a trip to Cuba years before what that meant: they had been handpicked to share only the most wonderful things about Chinese culture. My stomach didn't feel great either. I thought back to the pig ovaries.

One of these home visits was to Mr. Liu's, an elderly Chinese Dr. Doolittle of sorts, whose tiny house brimmed with birds in cages, tortoises, lizards, multiple aquariums filled with fish, and a small white dog with a Bam Bam Flintstone ponytail. His African Gray parrot squawked "Ni hao!" as we took seats around the living room, and Mr. Liu pulled out a binder of faded press clippings from his illustrious career as a champion cricket fighter. He beamed as he pointed at each article.

Cricket fighter? Nancy explained that cricket fighting was a popular hobby and sport in China that dated back more than a thousand years. As if on cue, Mr. Liu left and reappeared from another room grinning ear to ear, holding a bowl of prized crickets. Nancy translated that he had trained the crickets not only to fight, but also to not jump out.

Show-and-tell moved on to larger insects and lizards that he pulled out one by one from various tanks and enclosures, turning to the kids each time with a smile and shouting, "Hello!" at them, his only English word, to indicate that they should come hold the creatures. When it was time to go, and we stepped back outside his tiny rowhouse into the courtyard, Mr. Liu noticed that a large tortoise was missing from a pen and ran off to find it before we could say goodbye.

After that there was a calligraphy lesson and dumpling-making! A kung fu show *and* a kung fu lesson! More and more temples! But before we could get to the main event—the Great Wall, that wonder of the world we had all come to see—our go-go-go itinerary came to a screeching halt. Despite all the hand sanitizer (or "sand hanitizer" as James called it) and handwashing, despite all the bottled water we used to brush our teeth, those early rumblings of stomach pain Teddy and I felt back at the Forbidden City turned into a full-blown gastrointestinal nightmare. We managed to get back to the hotel and retreat to our dark room, where we curled into the fetal position, barely able to stand or talk. For the next twenty-four hours, we only peeled ourselves off the sheets to use the bathroom. That small air-conditioner did its best, but the heat felt especially oppressive.

Just as they hadn't in Peru's high altitude, back when Teddy and I had been hooked to an oxygen tank, neither Lobsy nor the kids got sick. They spent the day visiting a local park with Nancy, where Willa and James played hacky sack with some locals and ate lunch. Back at the hotel, there were rounds of card games and a movie in Lobsy's room. I'm not sure what we would have done if she hadn't been there.

Fortunately, we awoke the next morning feeling better and set out Woody Woodpecker early to fit in the Great Wall before our bullet train to Xi'an. It was so early that the place was nearly empty, just us and a low hum of cicadas. Our photos look as though we stumbled across a remote stretch of ancient ruins. We took our time climbing up and down the undulating sections of wall between towers, nothing beyond the stones but mist. Lobsy took it all in, savoring this latest feather in her travel cap. By the time we descended, the crowds were rolling in, and we saw how the place would soon fill with bodies, changing the feel from "otherworldly" to "Times Square." Three different families asked to take pictures with us on the way out. Willa flashed peace signs in each.

Xi'an

We rode a bullet train south, covering the same distance as Washington, DC, to Atlanta in just four hours, arriving in Xi'an that afternoon. The city is one of China's most popular tourist destinations, famous for its ancient history and home to one of the most important archeological discoveries of the last hundred years, the famed Terracotta Army.

By the next morning, a guide had us ticketed and entering the site. On view were more than 7,000 life-sized pottery soldiers, horses, and chariots dating back more than two thousand years. A structure akin to an airport hangar with a network of elevated catwalks overhead had been constructed around the archeological dig to accommodate both the ongoing research as well as the estimated one million tourists who visited annually.

As we inched along the walkways, I wondered if all one million visitors were there that day. We had seen major crowds in China, but nothing like this. The sheer density of human bodies jostling ten-deep to get a peek of the statues was overwhelming, people so packed they turned their heads sideways to avoid flattening their noses against the tourist in front of them.

Fortunately, I had recently perfected an important new coping skill: elbowing people. After Tiananmen Square, the Beijing train station and a half dozen other jam-packed stops we made in China, I saw how my American idea of How to Act in a Crowd—saying "excuse me" and stepping aside to give others space—got me nowhere. The Chinese tourists around us took a forceful "I'm coming through" approach that involved shoving with impunity. As soon as I observed how effective it was, I adopted the tactic with gusto.

"When in Rome!" I called over my shoulder to Teddy as I plowed my way through thousands of people, elbowing as I went, never apologizing once. Getting to shed the niceties and physically bulldoze people the way I had always fantasized about doing in Penn Station or at the DMV was one of the most therapeutic exercises of my life. I showed no mercy. No one batted an eye.

Chengdu

If Xi'an checked the "Terracotta Warriors" box off our China list, then Chengdu in the Sichuan province checked "pandas." As we sped southwest on a second bullet train, James caught up in his journal. "I was squished," he wrote in big capital letters about seeing the Terracotta Warriors. Lobsy read an English-language Chinese newspaper that explained how America was the sinister influence behind Hong Kong's student protests. I was deep into a bestselling novel banned in mainland China for its devastating depiction of the country's communist history.

Out our window, we passed 400 miles of non-stop apartment buildings, many still under construction. It was impossible to comprehend China's population, but hundreds of miles of nondescript suburban housing towers helped. Xi'an numbered as many people as New York City, yet wasn't ranked among the top ten most populated cities in China. With nearly eleven million inhabitants, Chengdu was more populous than some U.S. states.

Willa overheard Teddy tell his mom we were staying at a hotel called Temple House. "What did you say about temples?" she asked, on high alert. "Temple" had become a trigger word. "It's just the name of the hotel," I reassured her. "We're not going to an actual temple." She didn't seem convinced.

We did have a relatively flexible itinerary in Chengdu, with an opportunity for interloping—first at a giant wet market then at a city park—that had eluded us thus far in China. Our guide Carol had an easygoing manner we appreciated, with a casual sense of humor and snappy, digestible explanations. She never started a sentence with "as you can see." When, for some reason, James derailed our tour to catch her up on the rules of Hungry, Hungry Hippos, she listened and asked earnest follow up questions.

We went to the Dujiangyan Giant Panda Research Center, a sanctuary and protective facility for rescued pandas located an hour outside of town. When we arrived, we donned green shirts and work gloves to volunteer for the day, cleaning enclosures, making "panda cakes" (eggs, soybean powder, salt, and sugar) and feeding the animals, who, though they look like bears, have the fine motor skills of apes, lending them a hilarious human-in-a-panda-costume quality. The kids loved reading aloud the awkwardly translated signs—"Do not feed the pandas, they have their own recipes!" and "I am responsible for being cute, you are responsible for being quiet!"—while Teddy and I loved seeing our kids, accustomed to hotel housekeeping, mop up panda poop.

After our day with the pandas, serious interloping could begin, and what better place than at one of the enormous wet markets? This one featured long rows of purveyors selling their fresh produce and other perishables under a high roof with open windows, more warehouse than grocer. One cabbage seller wore a t-shirt that read "Punch me in the face so I feel alive," yet another English-language head-scratcher. There were also pig snouts and other pork parts, and fishmongers, with the usual tanks of fish and crabs, but also mesh bags filled with live toads the size of softballs and open-topped bins writhing and splashing with snakes and eels. One vendor haggled with a shopper while disemboweling a giant frog-like creature that was very much still alive and kicking.

In the hundred-year-old People's Park, a popular gathering place for locals, every corner held some new curiosity. There was a live digital readout display of the park's decibel level—like those signs that show your speed as you drive by—a measure to keep noise levels down. In the "Matchmakers'" section, flyers in plastic sleeves fluttered from fence posts. These, Carol said, were one-page descriptions of single, marriage-age sons and daughters hung by mothers and grandmothers, with relevant details like looks, height, weight, career, alma maters as well as a phone number where potential love connections could reach mom or grandma. "People don't usually know their moms are putting these up," Carol laughed, rolling her eyes.

We saw dozens of middle-aged and elderly women lined up in rows doing Guang Chang Wu, a form of line dancing, their boombox music turned low to comply with the decibel monitor. Each participant held something that looked like a small racket and balanced a ball on the netting as they danced. As we watched them move in synchronized steps, getting in their daily exercise, a man in his thirties walked over with a smile and showed Teddy his phone screen. It displayed a translation from Chinese to English: "Where are you from?" Six months ago this might have struck us as sketchy, but Teddy just typed back a translation—"New York City"—and a question of his own. The guy was excited about this and sat down next to Teddy to answer and ask more.

"Do you like China?" he passed back. For the next twenty minutes, the two of them typed and traded the phone, each curious about the other. "What foods have you tried?" "Is it hot like this where you live?" Meanwhile, Willa and James had by now borrowed rackets and joined the group in balancing balls and dancing.

At an outdoor tea house, Carol rented a *mahjong* board and taught us the game's basics as we sipped. Bridge-playing Lobsy picked it up right away. James preferred to build towers out of the tiles. Willa took a lemon wedge and put it in her mouth to eat. Seeing this, Carol's eyes went wide. "What are you doing?" she asked, covering her mouth and pointing to her arm to show how the sight of such a thing had given her goosebumps. Willa explained that she loved eating lemons and limes. Carol found this stomach-turning, which made us laugh. What pig snout was to me, Willa eating a lemon was to Carol.

Lijiang

The scene outside the hotel on our last morning in Chengdu was a familiar one: Lobsy boarding a foreign taxi, Willa and James in tears. "See you in Sydney!" she called out through the window as her driver pulled away. Despite a grueling, nearly twenty-hour trip home, Lobsy was already booked to fly *back* to see us *again* in Australia, which would require yet another nearly full-day trip. Her hot streak of long-haul flights put ours to shame. "Remember when we thought she'd be upset about this trip?" Teddy said as he waved goodbye.

Lijiang in China's Yunnan Province landed on our itinerary when we heard that Willa's school friend would be there for the summer. Her American dad and Chinese mom ran an artists' retreat on a farm twenty minutes outside Lijiang, a historic town of cobblestone streets and bridges over gurgling canals that was popular with trendy Chinese weekenders. It also seemed to be a popular destination for couples sitting for professional wedding portraits. Photographers and assistants carrying refractor panels trailed brides, some in white gowns and others in traditional embroidered robes, from location to location.

The farm our friends rented for the retreat featured several ancient buildings arranged around courtyards, creating peaceful places to sit and chat or read. It had been weeks since Willa and James had been free to run around outside in a rural setting, and they relished the chance to play pickup soccer with new friends who lived nearby. We ate apples off a tree, fed scraps to pigs, and Teddy and I toasted homemade liquor with Grandfather, the owner of the property, while our friends answered our many questions about modern China. I worried the sight of a glistening pig turning on a spit would upset Willa and James, especially after we'd just been feeding his buddies, but at dinnertime they grabbed their chopsticks and chanted, "Pork! Pork! Pork!"

Shanghai

I turned forty in Shanghai, our last stop in China, and we celebrated with a walk along the city's riverside promenade, the Bund. As if planted by our travel agency, a group of preteen Chinese tourists stopped me and asked for a photo. "They think you look like a Hollywood star," translated our guide Joyce. We ate dinner on a rooftop overlooking the Huangpu River and, beyond it, the twinkling lights of the Pudong district's skyline. Shanghai had a population of twenty-three million people, making it one of the biggest cities in the world. Its skyline at night was beautiful and the Content Intern took birthday portraits of his wife when the sun went down.

In the taxi back to our hotel, we chatted with a friendly driver who had just enough English to make a simple conversation possible. Shanghai was different this way—far more international, making it easier to navigate and explore on our own. Until then, we'd been walking into restaurants and shops across China and asking, "Do you speak English?" only to get blank stares in return.

We had come prepared with downloaded VPNs that allowed us to skirt firewalls to update our blog and download shows, but the country's heavy internet restrictions meant our Google phones could not access much—no maps, translation apps, or email—nor could we use WhatsApp or Instagram. Instead, we downloaded WeChat, the all-purpose Chinese messaging and payment app, and used it to communicate with our many guides, whose nonstop sightseeing itineraries may have exhausted us, but whose hand-holding we appreciated.

In Shanghai, we could chat with the cab driver. His eyes bulged when we explained our trip. Like a lot of the people we'd met, he initially expressed shock not at the scope or expense, but at the fact that we'd willingly left good jobs. Telling people we'd walked away from job security was like saying we'd given up electricity or had all our teeth pulled out. As the breadth of our experience sank in, he eyed Willa and James in the rearview mirror and shook his head. "Wow," he said. "So many food ... so many language ... *so many danger.*"

⌣⟩

Traveling light was easy thanks in part to a general rule for consumption: *One in, one out.* Fresh t-shirt? Toss a grubby one. When we got rid of things, we usually put them in bags and placed them by the trash bin in hotel rooms and apartments when we checked out, careful to label them "giveaway" or "rubbish" after a few hotels called to say we'd forgotten our belongings. We jettisoned everything from clothes and workbooks to bigger items like a folding stroller, brought and barely used, which we gifted to an Airbnb house-keeper in Paris.

After souvenirs got shipped home, Teddy would celebrate the return to our "fighting weight." I visualized our freedom from stuff in terms of an infomercial: In the black and white "before" depiction, our family groans under the weight of heavy suitcases and laptop bags, shaking our fists at jobs, obligations, and schedules. But in the color "after" clip, we stroll along, laughing, swinging just a few tiny bags, light as air, with no jobs or clutter to weigh us down.

But Asia was a challenge: Custom dictated that hotel staff and tour operators welcome us with physical gifts—traditional scarves and textiles, toys and games for the kids, a chess set, special chopsticks for each of us, monogrammed hand towels and, in one case, packaged in a large box filled with styrofoam peanuts, a faux wood carving the size of a toaster that depicted mountain goats climbing a craggy cliff. We worried about the risk of our hosts possibly finding these gifts in a pile marked "rubbish."

After a few weeks of such generosity across Mongolia and China, we improvised a new system. We'd pack the gifts up in a shoulder bag and make a big show of gratitude as we waved goodbye. Then, once safely inside the airport or train station, we'd offer the gifts to people who worked there. Our last stop in China was no different. We waved goodbye to our guide Joyce and headed inside Shanghai's modern terminal to catch a flight to Hanoi, Vietnam. I found an airport staffer pushing a janitorial cart and gestured to her. She took a look at the bag's contents, then held out her hands to accept them—and we headed off, back to our fighting weight.

Vietnam

Hanoi

On our 215th day, we landed in Hanoi, Vietnam's capital, the first of six stops in the country over the next three weeks. It was so muggy you could almost drink the air, and at ninety-six degrees, so hot that seven minutes after a sudden downpour the pavement was as dry as a bone. Welcome to August in Vietnam. The sweat marks on my clothes, not only under my arms but also, charmingly, under my butt cheeks, were here to stay, which greatly amused Willa and James. Plus, Teddy and I had run out of deodorant in Mongolia and had been unable to find any in all our weeks in China. Sweating is seen as healthy in China, we learned—a natural way to detox—and according to biologists, Chinese people sweat less than the Sullivans. We were finally able to restock in Hanoi.

While the heat might have been familiar, the traffic situation was not. Nearly everywhere we had traveled followed the same fundamental "rules of the road" we had back home. Green means go, red means stop, stay in your lane, use your blinker. In Hanoi, though, most vehicles were Vespa-type scooters with riders who heeded neither stop signals nor lane dividers, resulting in an erratic flow of noisy mopeds weaving in and out in all directions. "The only traffic rule in Vietnam is that there are no rules," our guide Khan joked as he steered into the fray, allowing the bikes to swerve around our van and pass us on the left and right.

Khan was one of many guides who had been assigned to us by our tour operator in Vietnam and Cambodia. While this kind of attention had proven invaluable in Mongolia and China—not for the temple tours but for the basic cultural orientation—it became clear almost immediately that such hand-holding would not be necessary in Vietnam, a country where English was widely spoken and Americans and Europeans had been living and visiting for decades.

On Fridays and Saturdays, the city closed miles of downtown streets for pedestrians, bringing out thousands of families and couples to wander together among the vendors and musicians, buying plastic light-up toys for their kids. We stopped to watch two shirtless men in their sixties kick shuttlecocks back and forth to one another from a hundred feet away, never letting them touch the ground. When they saw James, they did what every other man around the world had done: tousled his hair and brought him in for a round. James wasn't any good, but they loved showing him their tricks and sent him off with two of their birdies.

Local youth groups learning English would stop us on the street to practice their conversation skills, asking questions like, "Why did you decide to come to Vietnam?" "Have you tried the food?" and "Do you have any festivals you like to celebrate back home?" They would diligently jot their notes, then ask for a group selfie. Willa loved the chance to interact with them and ask questions of her own.

In the beginning of the year, Willa and James would shrug in confusion when addressed in not-so-fluent English. The tour guide Andres in Colombia was invisible to them, partly because they couldn't understand what he was saying. But over time, Willa and James both became more attentive and worked harder to understand what was being said. We recognized it as a small but important daily exercise in patience and empathy. Maybe they could imagine a day when they themselves might try to speak in a foreign language and appreciate some kindness.

We were about to call it a night one evening after a tasty dinner, when we saw a fleet of battery-operated kiddie cars lined up at the curb outside our small hotel. They reminded us of a miniature version of the fleet of Lamborghinis displayed outside the Atlantis in Dubai. To Willa's and James's delight, they were available for rent for $5. We paid the guy who looked in charge, judging by the wad of cash in his fist and cigarette dangling from his mouth. For the next thirty minutes, Willa and James careened around the street on pint-sized motorcycles with everyone else. Even though it was nine o'clock at night—even though I was doing nothing more than standing alongside other Hanoi parents watching the kids—I sweat through the seat of my pants.

Ninh Binh

Our guide Khan and a driver took us in an air-conditioned van to the Hanoi train station to catch a two-hour local train to the countryside near Ninh Binh, a mountainous part of the country known for rice paddies and deep caves. Along the way we made a quick stop at an outdoor market, where we noticed a vinyl sign featuring an image of a rhino. Khan translated: "Rhino horns are not magical. Do not buy them."

When we pulled up to the train station and walked around to the back of the van to collect our luggage, Khan stopped us. "You don't need to take the bags," he said without further explanation.

"I guess he's putting them in a luggage car or something?" I said to Teddy, who shrugged.

When we went to say thank you to Khan and goodbye, he replied, "I'm coming with you!" Again, we were surprised. We had slipped back into relying on travel agents' itineraries without reviewing them closely. When the five of us boarded, the train was packed with locals and a few European backpackers. We were the only grownups traveling with a chaperone.

The old train car wasn't air-conditioned, and the windows didn't open. Not a breath of air passed among the passengers as the ride got underway and we rumbled along. We all quickly sweat through our clothes. Eventually someone got up and used a food cart of hot corn on the cob to prop open a door, providing a little relief. The seat of my pants were, of course, soaked.

Teddy and I never complained about the heat. We were in awe of it, even as it sometimes defeated us, but we were careful not to whine because we knew the only way to have made a trip around the world work on our schedule was to visit Southeast Asia during its most stifling time of year.

When we pulled into the Ninh Binh station, I spotted a familiar van idling in the parking lot. Wasn't that the same van we had just left behind in Hanoi two hours ago? Khan led us out of the train, strode directly to the lot, and opened the van door for us. Our driver—the same guy from before—waved hello, the AC blowing his hair back.

"What is happening?" I whispered to Teddy.

"Is this the same van and driver we just had?" Teddy asked Khan as we got in.

"Yes," he said. "Drove here from Hanoi. Takes about … twenty minutes?"

Teddy and I looked at each other and started laughing.

"Sooo … then why did we take a train?" Teddy asked him, flapping the front of his t-shirt back and forth to air out the sweat.

Khan looked at him, surprised. "So you can have the experience!"

When Khan registered our shock, he burst out laughing. "You thought—ahahaha!—you thought … you were *actually taking that train somewhere?* Bahahaha!" As I recalled the many backpackers who had been doing just that, I started laughing, too, albeit for different reasons. The whole train ride had just been just some faux "roughing it" bullshit we had unwittingly paid a travel agent to book for us. The situation was not only farcical, it marked a new low in travel operators—beating even the proposed tour of a Cairo shopping mall.

To his credit, Khan did seem to be breaking personal tour guide speed records on behalf of our family. After blowing through Ninh Binh's Temple of King Le Dai Hanh and speed-walking through its manicured grounds, taking quick note of details—ancient horse sculpture, large carved Buddha, red and yellow flags—we got back in the van.

"Are these the fastest tours you've ever given, Khan?" I asked.

"Yes!" he replied. "Your family want lots of time for relax!"

A friend in New York once told me how she'd found a live cricket in her Brooklyn bed. It had escaped from her daughter's lizard tank and somehow made its way onto her pillow, where it stood, inches from her face, when she awoke. "No!" I had gasped at the time, both hands covering my face in horror.

What a joke. By this point, we were picking the ants out of our toothbrushes each morning and rather than spraying giant bathroom spiders to death, we were giving them funny accents and personalities. We shrugged at the sight of rats, even those scurrying inside homes and restaurants. Cricket in the bed? Ha! Try dozens of black beetles scuttling under our blankets at night the way they had in the Gobi.

Somewhere along the way, we realized that paying for a room or a restaurant meal did not entitle us to an experience free from the critters who called the place home. An incident in Ninh Binh would highlight just how far we had come. We stayed three nights among the rice paddies in a small inn, with rooms that had thatched roofs. On our first two nights, we heard the unmistakable *scritch scritch* of critters over our heads in the quiet. "What is that?" I asked Teddy, staring up into the blackness.

"I don't know, but whatever they are, they're busy."

The next morning, I asked a nice lady who worked there—the one who loved our kids and, in her accent, called them "Willy" and "Germs"—about the noise.

"This is rats!" she explained, giggling.

Rats? Wow! Okay! Hadn't been expecting that, but if they didn't bother her, then they wouldn't bother us. Willa and I had been writing limericks in homeschool, and that day I penned this one:

There once was a rat on the roof.
In daylight he's very aloof.
But after the heat,
He gets restless feet,
And dances at night like a goof.

Rats over our heads were cause for silly poems, not freaking out. We went to bed that night unperturbed and when, sure enough, we awoke to the same little sounds, we only noted them and rolled over to go back to sleep.

The next morning, Teddy had an epiphany while exercising. "I think I figured out the rat thing," he said, laughing. "They aren't rats at all—they're *bats*."

Suddenly everything made sense—the little roosting sounds, the nocturnal activity, the living in rafters, the staff nonchalance. When I asked again, the same woman replied, "Yes, this is bats!" I couldn't stop laughing. Of course this is bats and not rats. The fact that we were *so okay* with the idea that F***KING RATS would be scurrying over our heads all night made it that much funnier.

"I think we need to rethink our plans for the final week of this year," I said to Teddy. We'd had two days of downtime in Ninh Binh, and I did something we hadn't done much of that year: think ahead to future destinations. We were scheduled to go skiing in Japan on our last seven days of the year. It had been one of the first stops Teddy had lobbied for.

Now, though, it struck me as a bad idea. Was it possible that, at the end of so much moving around, we might want to do something slightly less intense than schlepping tons of equipment and wearing ourselves ragged on ski slopes where we couldn't communicate with anyone? Especially since we were not really ... skiers? We knew by then downtime mattered—breaks in the action allowed for reflection and bonding. We would likely appreciate having a "soft landing" before returning home.

"You're probably right," Teddy said. So, sitting under our thatched roof in the air-conditioning away from Ninh Binh's midday heat, we brainstormed. How and where should we wrap the year? A new plan emerged within a few hours: We got online, canceled the Japan ski trip, and booked a house on Kauai instead. It was the kind of major travel decision that would have taken months to finalize in another lifetime.

Ha Long Bay

A van drove us four hours south toward Ha Long Bay for a few nights on a boat. Teddy liked to listen to podcasts and audiobooks on these long drives, and so did the kids (we didn't allow screens on car rides to avoid car sickness). I preferred to look out the window in silence, especially in Vietnam, which provided some of the most fascinating scenery we'd driven through yet: small town life with chickens, uniformed children walking to school, and family-run businesses like bike repair shops and stalls selling brooms and plastic clogs. We passed motorbikes hauling dogs, trash, cartons of eggs, bags of plastic children's toys. Some of the loads were so enormous you could scarcely see the bike or driver at all, making it look as if two thousand cans of Pringles in clear plastic bags were just driving themselves down the road.

The photos we had seen of Ha Long Bay showed jade seas punctuated by conical mountains jutting skyward out of the water, the kind of dreamy landscape most of us only ever see on a computer screensaver. Apparently these photos were a magnet, because when we arrived, there were thousands of other sunburned cruising tourists, everyone docking in the same places, hiking the same slopes, descending into the same caves. We longed to return to the rustic quiet and bats of Ninh Binh's rice paddies.

Those emerald waters from the photos? Littered with plastic. Same with the caves and trails. One night we leaned over the side of our boat to fish for squid, a practice that involved shining a bright light into the water and waiting for squid who think it's daylight to surface. The only thing that bobbed by were squid-like plastic bags. When we took a tour of a nearby floating fishing village built atop barrel pontoons, we looked on as elders fished out every passing bottle and bag with long poles, as if cleaning leaves from a pool. The pollution was bad for tourism and worse for fishing.

The locals blamed Chinese tourists, which was a tired line we'd heard many times before. They were "everywhere" and "ruined" destinations with their buses and litter. Indeed, the Chinese did seem to prefer traveling in numbers (the medieval town of Toledo, Spain, had thousands). But the highest concentrations of Chinese tourists we saw all year were in … China. And the more we traveled, the more we understood how pollution had little to do with people and almost everything to do with government regulations (or lack thereof). We weren't surprised to hear this line, though. While most of the tourists in Ha Long Bay were Vietnamese, the Chinese, as in so many other places we visited, were tourism's preferred scapegoats.

Hoi An

Located outside picturesque Hoi An on Vietnam's central coast, An Bang Beach was a hamlet for Western backpackers, its sandy roads lined with banana-leaf palms and tiki bars decorated with hand-painted signs. We rented a small house there for five nights.

On our first day, I stopped a housekeeper on her way out. "Do you have children?" I asked. James's soccer ball still inspired the occasional match, but for the most part, heavy sightseeing and language barriers in Asia had stalled Willa and James's opportunities to interact with other kids. It was time to get creative. The housekeeper had just enough English to understand and nodded with a smile, showing us pictures. We made a plan.

The next morning at 7 a.m. when Teddy stepped into the living room for his workout, he was startled to see a boy about six years old standing outside our house wearing swim trunks and a towel around his neck, cupping his hands to see inside, his nose squished against the glass. He was our housekeeper's nephew, and he was ready for the big playdate. At his side was his cousin, the housekeeper's seven-year-old daughter, also in a bathing suit. Teddy let them in and woke up our kids, who jumped to action getting dressed. Kids! At our own house! To play with! Homeschooling could be skipped for this.

The group played all morning and came by several days in a row after that for coloring, drawing, jumping on rafts in our tiny lap pool, and playing barefoot soccer in the dirt road out front of our house, careful to avoid the chickens.

Soul is something Teddy and I talked about a lot as we traveled. It means different things to different people, but we knew it when we felt it. Some places, like Kingston and Rio and Valparaiso, had it in spades, but in others, it was conspicuously missing. Vietnam helped us pinpoint our criteria. To us, a place with soul seemed to combine the following, in no particular order: Natural beauty that inspired awe; the crumbling vestiges of past eras, not yet paved over or rendered "authentic" by the travel industry; evidence of resilience in the wake of a recent painful history; bright bursts of joy and passion in the form of music, textiles or food; warm, welcoming people; just the right amount of chaos.

Vietnam turned out to be one of the most soulful places we'd been to yet, and we fell hard for the place, in love with the kind people we met, the vibrant cities, and the varying topographies that sprawled between them. And the food! All those platters exploding with cilantro, citrus, and spice, the baguette *banh mi* sandwiches, the *pho* with fresh herbs and tangy sauces, all washed down with cold bottles of 333 beer.

But temple tours had crept back into our lives and even the fast ones were wearying in the most familiar way: guides who talked too much and didn't take the kids into account, expounding on this or that emperor in the minutest of detail, as if the audience were rapt PhDs, not little kids poking an ant mound.

Hoi An was a jewel of a city we would have preferred to explore on our own. Instead, we found ourselves standing on its ancient bridge one day as a guide described at length how carved wooden turtles represented longevity and dogs represented loyalty. It was well past lunchtime and he, like us, had sweat through his hat.

"Willa? James?" he asked. "What do you think this carved monkey represents?"

Both kids jerked up at the sound of their names. Neither knew what "longevity," "loyalty," or "represents" meant. Hearing a question about monkeys, though, James wagered a guess.

"Bananas?"

The life drained out of us as shiny vans across the country hauled us from enamel painting to lantern-making to boat excursions to a water-puppet demonstration to salt rice tasting to body-painting to rice farming to spring roll making to tai chi to water buffalo-riding to singing performances to the inevitable temples. Some of these outings were memorable, but most felt like artificial stops on some tourism conveyor belt.

Hue

Our renewed but fragile patience for touring ran out for good in Hue (pronounced "HWAY"), near the middle of the country, where our itinerary was so egregious that it eventually imploded—freeing us from organized sightseeing forever.

It began with a "responsible tourism" outing.

We thought we knew what responsible tourism meant. We'd known to pass on things like the "pet a cheetah" farms in Zambia and "whale burgers" in Norway. We'd declined to stay at a hotel on stilts in Indonesia where elephants carried room service to guests, as well as opportunities around the world to "dine with lions" or "swim with dolphins."

Tourism activities actually *labeled* "responsible" were trickier. We had seen the orphanage on our itinerary and cringed, but figured that no matter how bad it looked on paper, it must have been carefully considered. *Right*?

The Buddhist nun in charge greeted us with a warm smile when we arrived at the rural facility. She was a respected local figure who accepted our gifts of school supplies and food, which we'd picked up at a local market. While the children were still at school, we toured the place. It was old, but bright and clean. In a nursery, cribs lined the walls, all of them filled. Nuns tended the babies lovingly, including a newborn boy with Down syndrome who'd been left on the doorstep just a few days before. In a special needs classroom, Willa and James sat and colored happily for thirty minutes alongside students with severe physical and mental disabilities, while Teddy and I helped the teacher serve snacks. She was a kind woman who seemed to know and care deeply for each of these children.

Soon, a bus of elementary school-age residents pulled up, all of them in uniforms and neat, matching haircuts. They were curious about us, especially Willa and James. As they gathered in the outdoor courtyard, our guide and the nuns tried to herd us all together for the requisite group photo, which we declined. Instead, James joined a group for pickup soccer, while Willa had fun asking and fielding questions from a group of girls her age, using our guide as a translator. They smiled as they discovered common ground on favorite animals (dogs) and colors (blue).

Teddy and I felt uneasy about being there, not to mention self-conscious about being healthy, living parents. At least Willa and James were having genuine interactions with the children, which we couldn't say for other visitors passing through. We witnessed two separate coach buses of wealthy Vietnamese tourists from Saigon unload, fawn over the kids, take selfies with them, pinch cheeks, and give conspicuous cash donations (photo opp!)—before leaving again in a whirl of perfume and air kisses.

James got swept up in one of these flurries—a group wanted him in their selfie with some orphans—and he burst into fearful tears at the commotion, which still makes me sad. I'd failed to shield him from the manhandling, and worse, I witnessed how exposed the other kids were; they hadn't consented to photos or cheek-pinching either, but didn't have parents to protect or comfort them.

When we got back in our van at the end of the visit, I cried. Those kids were well cared for, clean and educated, and the women who watched over them were some of the most selfless, loving people I had ever encountered. But our visit felt indecent. We were silent the entire drive back to our hotel. "Responsible tourism" was a label we would treat with extreme caution from now on. It might describe well-intentioned experiences that make wealthy tourists feel good about themselves, but they can be harmful.

Our shame would be cemented a few weeks later in Cambodia, where we stepped off the plane to a barrage of government-sponsored billboards encouraging tourists to speak up if they saw Westerners bringing local kids to hotels and discouraging tourists from taking photos of poor or homeless children. But the most ubiquitous sign stopped me in my tracks: "Children are not tourist destinations. Think before you visit an orphanage."

With emotions about the orphanage still running high, we endured a second day in Hue known in our family simply as The Hue Day.

We boarded a colorful wooden tour boat for a private thirty-minute ride with our guide at 9 a.m.—exactly the kind of "experience" we could do on our own but wouldn't because it was a souvenir trap. As I tried to sit by the window and enjoy the view, our boat driver put on the hard sell for her pile of trinkets, holding up a sign in English that said something like "Buy some of this stuff so I can support my family" and pointing to a photograph of three adorable children, presumably hers.

We disembarked at a Buddhist pagoda where our guide, bless him, tried his darnedest to make things interesting for the kids. I appreciated the effort, but by this point, he was wasting his time. James needed just seven seconds to identify, and bow out of, any historical sightseeing visit. Old building with crowds? Guide spewing dates in accented English? *I'll be over here poking dirt with a stick.*

Next up: A Vietnamese kung fu school where students showed us their skills, and after that, a basket-weaving demonstration on a farm. When James wanted to try weaving, our guide mocked him—"You don't want to do women's work!"—before Teddy insisted he sit down and give it a shot.

We stopped at the Royal Tombs, a mausoleum decorated with intricate mosaics that sat atop 200 steps. "MA! MA! Can we pleeeeeeeease leeeeeeeave," James whined just as our guide began his "As you can see" preamble.

From there, butt sweat in full force, we arrived at a master kite-maker's house. Just like Mr. Liu the Chinese cricket fighter, this man showed us faded press clippings from his illustrious career. We faced a table heaped with parts for traditional Vietnamese kites and spent more than two hours "making" four of them, aka, assembling pre-made pieces with rubber cement. It was well past lunch and we were ravenous, Teddy and I cranking through an assembly line of "kid-friendly" kite parts as rapidly as possible so we could just eat some food already. Willa and James rolled around on the floor and moaned about how hungry they were.

By 1 p.m., we turned to our guide. "This has been great," I told him. "But I think we're going to need to cancel the rest of the day's activities."

What I meant was: *We need to cancel touring and experiences like these for the rest of our lives.*

It had taken eight months, 231 days, but we finally had the confidence to make big changes. Over lunch that day, we vowed, *for real this time*, to put an end to the struggle between doing what we loved—interloping on our own schedule—and relying on professionals. We now knew, without a doubt, what we liked, what we didn't, and what we were capable of handling ourselves.

Here's what we liked: Travel agents who solved our destination decision paralysis. We'd said "Southeast Asia" and they'd turned it into "Vietnam, Cambodia, Singapore, and Indonesia." Ones who managed all our flight and accommodation logistics; who made suggestions—rather than nonrefundable bookings—for things to do and see in places; who set us up with guides for the Machu Picchus and the Petras and the Great Walls of the world but spared us the rest of the canned tours and experiences. No more pricey, unnecessary filler like private cooking lessons, calligraphy demonstrations, or basket weaving. No more fake train rides. I cannot even mention the orphanages, which occupy a special category of toxicity.

From now on, if we decided to take a tour or hire a guide, it would need to be a local artist, student, teacher, or mom who offered low-cost group tours of their hometowns as a side hustle. Like Mhinti who showed us around her Cape Town township, or Ronald the college kid who led that food tour in Hong Kong. Give us the competent but casual types who served straight talk, who told jokes and ate meals with us without seeming nervous about our satisfaction. Whose small group tours allowed us to meet similar-minded travelers and make friends.

We had spent an embarrassing amount of money on long-winded guides we couldn't understand as they took us to sights and activities we didn't care about—all while our kids whined and begged for us to please make it stop. We had erred on the side of efficiency, safety, and some misguided sense of obligation. We were done with all that.

Saigon

We landed in Ho Chi Minh City, still widely known as Saigon by tourists and locals alike, reborn. This might be our last stop in Vietnam but it was the first day of the rest of our trip! We were in control of our own time! Our own *destinies*, dammit! We descended the stairs of our VietJet plane and boarded an airport shuttle bus that would take us from the runway to the terminal. We hated these buses, but that day? Nothing was going to get us down!

We crammed in, shoulder to shoulder with about sixty other passengers, ready to enjoy this place on our own terms. When the bus doors squeezed shut, we lurched forward on a swerving path toward the airport. It got very hot. There was no air-conditioning, and within one minute I could already feel the familiar seep of sweat through my clothes. We rode in suffocated silence. I looked down at James, whose wardrobe these days consisted mostly of short-sleeve button down shirts and matching shorts decorated in flowers or bright fruit patterns, a look he had picked up in Hanoi.

He seemed so tiny amid the crush of grownups around him. He also looked dazed. Wait, was he kind of green? Before I could finish the thought, he projectile-vomited onto his family, the floor, and the people around us, all of whom shrieked and dodged. I stared at the mess in disbelief as he did it again, this time with even more force.

Thankfully, Teddy snapped out of his shock and seized the tote off my shoulder. He dumped four kites to the floor and held the empty bag against James's mouth, just in time to catch a third wave. The driver, oblivious, careened along, forcing Teddy to bend his knees and sink his butt into a feat of athleticism he would later describe as an offensive lineman pass-blocking stance, simultaneously holding the bag at James's mouth and not slipping into the puddle at their feet.

I spun in circles, gasping, "Oh my god, I'm so sorry," to the people around us who were wiping goo off their pants and shoes. Willa clung to my leg. The smell was putrid. The ride seemed to go on forever. *How big is this airport?*

When at last the bus braked to a stop and the doors opened, all but six passengers ran for their lives. Who could blame them? Those who held back were all women, including a Buddhist nun. Each stopped to utter what sounded like compassionate words in Vietnamese as they pressed packs of wet wipes into my hands, and left. I started crying in gratitude.

The driver eventually walked back to see what the holdup was and kicked us out, waving his arms and yelling as if to say he'd handle the cleanup (or "get the hell outta here!" It was hard to tell). We ushered James into the airport and got him cleaned up in a bathroom before heading to our hotel, where he quickly fell asleep in the air-conditioning.

"That was quite an arrival," Teddy said as we unpacked and got ready for bed. Before we turned out the lights, though, we had one last matter to attend to. We emailed our travel agent and confirmed that we wanted to cancel virtually every tour ahead, refundable or not.

The next morning, James awoke feeling better, but still needed to rest. Teddy volunteered to hang back while Willa and I headed downtown to explore. The two of us buzzed down the muddy Saigon River in a water taxi, fascinated by the fishing huts interspersed with McMansion subdivisions, signs of a city in boomtown transition. Already that morning we had spent thirty minutes inside a convenience store looking at Vietnamese school supplies and junk food, loving the fact that we were on foot, free to walk where we liked, chat by ourselves, and pop into such "uninteresting" places as we pleased. "I love looking at people and wondering where they're going and what they're doing today," Willa said as we strolled. "I try to make guesses by looking at their clothes."

We got off the boat and followed signs pointing to the city center, which sat just across a major roadway. We were on our way to see a cathedral and the tower where the famous last evacuation helicopter took off at the end of the Vietnam War—or the "American War," as it was known here. All we needed to do was cross the street.

When the light changed and the "walk" symbol began blinking, we prepared to cross. But stopped. Three lanes in both directions continued to course with cars and scooters, none of them even pretending to acknowledge the red light in front of them. *The only traffic rule in Vietnam is that there are no rules.* What was amusing color commentary back in Hanoi was now a frightening reality here in Saigon.

How was anyone supposed to cross if no one stopped at red lights? Did the cars ever let pedestrians go? Wasn't someone going to see us and take pity? My mood darkened, my hopes for exploring downtown fading fast. I looked behind me, seriously contemplating just getting back on the ferry and calling it a day. "I don't know how to get across," I said to Willa.

This was neither the first nor last time Willa would see me as someone less than the totally in-control parent she and James had known back in New York, the one with a big job and sleek work clothes. Unleashed in the world, Teddy and I were just a couple of doofuses, stumbling around someone else's turf, unable to speak the local language, at least one of us wearing a fanny pack. Every day, the kids observed us lost, confused, or having to ask for help. It was Vulnerability 101. *Grownups get lost. Grownups don't know everything. Grownups ask for help.*

Suddenly, a local guy appeared next to us at the curb. Without breaking stride—without even looking left or right—he waded into the street, one arm straight up in the air. We watched, amazed, as he took steady, deliberate steps across all six lanes, the cars slowing to flow around him the way water might around a boulder. He arrived unscathed on the other side, and kept walking into downtown.

I looked down at Willa and knew I had to show her that we could try something new and scary, even when I really, really didn't want to do what that guy had just done. I took a deep breath. Stepping off that damn curb went against every instinct in my body, the most literal "leap of faith" I've ever taken. But when we did, sure enough, motorists began to slow and curve around us.

"Omigodomigodomigodomigodomigod," I said aloud as we inched along, our ponytails blowing with each passing vehicle. I clutched Willa with one hand and held my other high in the air, resisting the urge to dart out of the way when I saw cars and trucks barreling toward us. They knew the rules and even though I didn't, I wasn't about to do anything except imitate the other guy. In about fifty careful steps, we arrived safely on the other side. Before we could keep walking, we had to acknowledge this astounding feat. In a fit of pride and adrenaline, Willa and I jumped up and down as if we'd just crossed the finish line at the Naadam horse race.

When we used to go on vacation without kids, Teddy would shut off his phone for days as a way for the High-Functioning Entrepreneur to relax. It always transformed him into an alter-ego so chill he seemed like another person—one who took naps, read his book, and never knew what time it was. He was fifteen minutes late to everything and when he did show up, his hair was mussed, his shirt barely buttoned. I dubbed this person "Island Ted." As in, "Is your husband stoned?"

"Oh him? No, that's just Island Ted!"

I'd seen more of Island Ted on our trip than I had in our entire marriage. He'd sipped *caipirinhas* in Rio and moonwalked across Egypt. He'd doffed his shirt and jumped into the Copenhagen River with the other sunbathing Danes. He'd flaked on those Mozambique visas. And now, after the elimination of tightly controlled touring, the alter ego seemed to take over completely. This man, who once kept detailed project management lists for our family life—"research new vacuum cleaner," "get car inspected"—was now sunburned, eating spicy food with a beer at lunch, and happier than I'd ever seen him.

One day, we visited the farm of an elderly Vietnamese couple nestled among lush banana leaves in the Mekong Delta, a few hours outside town. We had canceled just about every tour and experience by then but had opted to keep this one on the schedule because we loved home visits. We arrived on the backs of Yamaha motorcycles, Willa and James doubled up in ill-fitting helmets, their arms wrapped around the waist of a guide named Chuong. Teddy might have been appalled at the idea of his kids riding on a motorcycle, but Island Ted was fine with it.

We got to know the farmer with Chuong's translation help and watched as he peeled large green pomelos for us, the Asian grapefruit-like fruit he grew on his property. We took our wedges and dipped them in a spicy rock salt mixture. Also on the welcome menu were fried crickets, which James declined but which Willa popped in her mouth like M&Ms. When Teddy and I opted to wrap ours in lettuce and add sauce, she teased us for being wimps.

Then Chuong translated that our host would now begin teaching us an ancient technique for harvesting our lunch by hand. I pictured vegetables. Maybe some more pomelos?

"Why did I think this was a fish farm?" I asked Chuong as we headed toward a field.

"Because it is!" he replied.

I looked up and saw several man-made ponds spanning the property. A queasiness took hold.

Teddy, the kids, and their new farmer buddy got to work using buckets to sling water out of one of the shallow ponds. Their repetitive motion removed so much water that eventually there were just a few inches left. And there, exposed and wriggling in the mud, were three fish. "These are snakefish!" Chuong translated to my horror. Snakefish are exactly what they sound like: fish that look like snakes. Each a foot long and about as fat around as a wine bottle. They were black and slimy as they burrowed in the mud.

The piranha incident in Brazil may have been transformative for me, but it had not changed me into the kind of people Willa and James had become. The kind of people who saw these repulsive creatures and thought, "I can't wait to catch one with my bare hands!" They leapt into the pit like kids at a candy store, flinging themselves around chasing the fish.

The farmer watched Willa and James with approval, then gestured to Teddy as if to say, "You're up." I took several big steps away. With his back to me, Teddy waded in and planted his bare feet in the mud, which rose to his calves. He put his hands up in preparation and swiveled his head to survey the ground in front of him. When he spotted thrashing, he lunged in its direction, missing. He continued stalking. It didn't take long. With a triumphant yell, he seized one of the thrashing fish in his grip. Willa and James were beside themselves, jumping and cheering for their hero (I choked back a scream). He dropped the fish in a bucket—then went back for two more. When at last he emerged from the pit covered in mud, he was wide-eyed and grinning.

Our host cleaned the three fish and put them on a spit, where they blackened over an open flame. Teddy rinsed off his hands with a hose and changed his t-shirt while the farmer poured us shots of cloudy homemade liquor from a plastic water bottle. We threw them back after a quick toast, our throats burning. When the fish was ready, he lay it flat on a platter and used two forks to shred its bright white meat off the bone. The five of us served ourselves with chopsticks, wrapping the steaming fish with fresh mint in rice paper and dipping the rolls in a spicy sauce. Island Ted closed his eyes with each bite.

Cambodia

Siem Reap

When it came to getting from point A to point B, especially via airports, we had come a very long way. Our systems worked better than ever. The kids had "done airports" so many times that they would quietly read their Kindles in most lines and had stopped touching those damn retractable belts long ago. If they noticed other kids playing with them—what is it with those things?— they'd shoot me a knowing glance. *Amateurs.*

One afternoon at a hotel we even overheard Willa and James in the other room playing "airport." They created makeshift stations for security, immigration, and even duty-free—"a place where you can buy makeup and gin at the same time," Willa explained. There was air traffic control waving in planes and overhead announcements about last calls and gate changes.

When we flew to Cambodia from Vietnam, however, I suffered a setback. On our 236th day, we boarded a twin-engine turboprop en route from Saigon to Siem Reap, where we planned to spend a week. The flight was at night, and after we took off, a nasty thunderstorm kicked up. I put down my Kindle when the plane started jouncing and grew increasingly freaked out as the turbulence turned violent.

Suddenly, a bang jolted the plane—was that lightning?—and sent us into a freefall. We stabilized with a bounce only to have it happen again moments later with even more force. As others around us screamed, I white-knuckled Teddy's arm and squeezed my eyes shut. The turbulence lasted the entire hour-and-fifteen-minute flight. The few times I peeked at my family, they appeared calm. Island Ted had tilted his baseball hat over his face for a snooze while the kids watched cartoons across the aisle.

When we landed—*hallelujah*—Willa took off her headphones and yelled, "That was fun!" Meanwhile, I wobbled out onto that Cambodian tarmac a different person. I had never been afraid of flying before, but that was all over now. We had about twenty-five more flights left in the year, and I would not relax on a single one, unable to read or watch shows. I'd just sit, jaw clenched, counting down the minutes on the flight map.

Siem Reap, Cambodia, is best known for its nearly one hundred ancient temples. Naturally, we wondered why we were still going. Willa and James's disdain for all things temples ran so deep that when Willa overheard me telling Teddy about a friend who'd gone to Temple University in Philadelphia, she was incredulous. "Who would ever go to a *temple university*?"

We loved our week there, assisted intermittently by a sweet guide named Virak, who had gotten the memo and mostly left us to explore on our own. One temple remained on the schedule: Ta Prohm, a thirteenth century Buddhist monastery best known for its depiction in Angelina Jolie's movie *Tomb Raider*. Teddy and I had fallen in love with the site on our honeymoon ten years before and wanted to see it again. Unlike the manicured Angkor Wats of the area, Ta Prohm had been left by the government to be devoured by the jungle. Enormous tree roots slid down and across carved facades like pythons, knocking over bits of the ancient walls in slow motion. I wondered what Manhattan would look like if all the humans disappeared and it was reclaimed by trees and animals.

Even if Willa and James were intrigued by Ta Prohm, I doubt they would give us that satisfaction. They immediately found sticks and started digging in the dirt. Our guide, a French archeologist, laughed when we grumbled about their indifference. "Please. My parents made me go to hundreds of temples when I was little," he said. "I hated them all."

A much better option was a temple-themed mini golf course Teddy found online. We rode there one morning in a tuk tuk, a two-wheeled carriage pulled by a motorbike. As we made our way out of town toward the place, we passed miles of country roads and farmhouses, a landscape reminiscent of Louisiana's bayous or the Florida Keys. It smelled tropical and swampy in the aftermath of a morning shower, its muddy roads lined with wooden houses on stilts, chickens pecking and kids playing out front among the palms.

We were the only customers at the homemade course a local farmer had built into a rice paddy like a Cambodian Ray Kinsella. "I'm so glad I'm not tiny," Willa said as she inspected a model of Angkor Wat that decorated the eighth hole. "I won't have to tour that tiny temple." On the tenth hole, Teddy made a hole-in-one and the owner rewarded him with an ice cold can of beer. Island Ted cracked it open and drank it on the spot—at 10:30 in the morning. When we tallied our scores, the kids begged to start all over again. Unlike any of the actual temples we visited in our travels, Willa and James still talk about the temple-themed mini-golf.

Most days in Cambodia we returned to our cherished routine: leisurely mornings of schoolwork after breakfast, afternoons out exploring on our own. We dropped our laundry at a wash 'n' fold that charged $5.50 to clean everything we owned—a dollar more and they'd iron it, too. We ate lunch in town, strolled, and rode around with our tuk tuk guy from the mini-golf day, who we'd put on our WhatsApp speed dial. He didn't speak English but understood whenever Map Guy pointed to a destination on his phone.

One day we hopped on the back of four Vespas to explore back roads with a small company that specialized in scooter tours. The Vespa guys didn't have name tags or polo shirts. When it poured, they tossed us some ponchos, unconcerned whether the Sullivans were dry and satisfied. We pressed on in the rain, stopping for home visits and roadside noodle stands.

One outdoor market sold, among other things, dog meat. Skinned canines lined a low table for purchase alongside a few boiled heads, their noses and teeth unmistakably dog. Unfazed, Willa and James inspected. I don't believe we ate dog that year, but if we did, I'm not sure the kids would have cared. Parenting experts always talked about how if you didn't indulge fussy eaters, they'd eventually eat a wider variety of stuff. Now I could see how right they were. Willa and James were eating what was served these days, their chopstick skills improving with each bite.

Of course, they still loved pizza and pasta, and when it was available, we let them have it. A waiter in Vietnam affectionately called Willa and James "Spaghetti and Pizza" after we returned to the same restaurant twice for these items. When he said it, it came out "Spaghetti and PEE-zer." "I think you guys have new nicknames," I said when he walked away. "You're 'Spaghetti' and you're 'Peezer.'"

James didn't miss a beat. "Then *you're* 'Gin' and *you're* 'Tonic,'" he said, pointing at me and Teddy.

Virak took us out to an open-air weekend market popular with families and couples who came in the evenings to sample snacks like dried fruit and reptiles and insects sold from dozens of carts and open-air grills. Locals bought paper bags of tiny fried frogs and tossed them back like potato chips. We inspected the various heaps, asking Virak what everything was. Willa popped a few crickets while the rest of us ate spears of green mango dusted with chili powder.

"What are these?" I asked, pointing to the brown eggs I saw people buying. "Oh, this is *balut*! My favorite!" Virak said, lighting up. He bought one of the eggs and brought it over to a table to demonstrate. It turned out to be a steamed duck egg. A steamed *fertilized* duck egg. He cracked it into a bowl, and out came a gooey embryo with webbed feet and duckbill. Virak added salt, pepper, and a squeeze of lime, mixed it up with a spoon, then devoured the delicacy in two bites. I thought of our guide Carol in Chengdu, China, the one who shuddered when Willa ate the lemon slice.

As Virak polished off the duck, James turned to me. He looked sheepish, like he had something on his mind. *Oh no*, I thought. *The duck egg was too much for him.*

"Mama, I want one of those cocoon things," he whispered. It took me a second to understand what he meant. Ten minutes before, we had stopped at a cart selling heaping trays of grilled silkworms, which Virak had been snacking on ever since, telling James how delicious they were. Now, James wanted one. He wore his signature look: dusty Orioles hat, floral print short-sleeved shirt, and matching shorts. His hair had grown long and shaggy, "like a Uruguayan soccer star," as one Instagram follower put it. He had on nail polish leftover from a Saigon salon.

"Do you mean a *grilled silkworm*?" I asked, trying to hide my shock. He did indeed. Teddy and I met eyes with a combination of apprehension and admiration as Virak passed James a jumbo crispy browned silkworm. He took it in a chubby hand and tossed it in his mouth, crunching a few times before gulping it back. Willa looked on. She had already eaten one and was impressed that her brother was now joining the club.

"Well?" we asked. He gave us two nonchalant thumbs up, then kept walking.

James was emerging as the trip's Most Transformed Sullivan, going from stroller to swagger in just eight months. "Who *is* he?" I asked Teddy under my breath. James had been "picky" and Willa "tentative" their whole lives. How often did our kids need to prove us wrong before we quit labeling them? These were clearly people who were still learning who they were and that included being silkworm eaters. We needed to get out of their way.

In retrospect we shouldn't have been surprised that places like Vietnam and Cambodia would provoke a lot of Tough Questions, specifically about war and its atrocities. But, as always, we were. Somehow we had skirted Tough Questions about WWII and the Holocaust in Germany, but we couldn't avoid them in Vietnam and Cambodia.

In Saigon, we had toured the Cu Chi tunnels, a vast underground system built and used by Viet Cong guerillas to devastating effect against U.S. troops during the war. Just as Robben Island in South Africa employed former political prisoners as its guides, Cu Chi tapped aging Viet Cong veterans to host tourists. We got Mr. Nam, a former guerilla who'd lost an arm at sixteen to American machine gun fire ("*Americans* did that to him? How come?"). He told us about the twelve years he spent living underground and fighting from the tunnels, and we hung on the translator's every word.

I thought of Lobsy's brother Byrne, who had fought in the war, and asked Mr. Nam what it was like to host the growing number of American veterans who visited this place. He said most of them were emotional, some offering apologies, "There is peace now," he said, "And that is all that matters." He felt no anger or bitterness toward the American vets. "They did not choose to fight this war," he explained.

When the visit took us past a display of replica Viet Cong booby traps, each accompanied by life-sized illustrations detailing how they maimed and killed American GIs, no amount of "let's keep walking, guys" on our part was going to prevent Willa and James from planting their feet in front of the gruesome images and demanding to understand what they were looking at. We took deep breaths. "Here you can see how the soldier steps on a pile of leaves covering a deep hole so that he will fall and land on giant metal spikes. And here…")

Now, it continued in Cambodia. We visited a nonprofit that trained large pouch rats dubbed "hero rats" to safely sniff out the deadly Khmer Rouge-era landmines that still littered the countryside and stayed for a live demonstration. Teddy and I were amazed at such ingenuity, but the kids had several details they needed to clarify first. *What is a landmine? Who would do that to other people? Why?*

Singapore

I nursed a midday beer to steady my nerves as I prepared for our first flight since the terrifying one. The two-hour trip south to Singapore was smooth and uneventful (not that I was calm). Singapore is a city-state located at the tip of Malaysia. We had heard it was a pristine metropolis, but still, we were taken aback by its glimmering skyscrapers, spotless streets, orderly traffic, and drinkable tap water. Did a place like this really exist so close to Cambodia's muddy roads and tuk tuks?

The city reminded us of Dubai, Hong Kong, and Shanghai, each an ultra-modern cultural crossroads with unique mashups of food, people, and architecture. We were staying seven nights at an apartment complex in town called Treetops, which had a tagline— "We Call it Treetops"—that confused and amused us. We had friends, as well as major housekeeping, to attend to. Once again, we were glad we had punctuated the itinerary with cities where getting haircuts and replenishing toothpaste was easy.

We had an urgent new addition to our to-do list: Get to a dermatologist. No one warned us that all this "following the sun" would wreak such havoc on our skin. Even with the hats and vats of sunscreen, our farmers' tans were impressive. We were freckled, spotted, often burned, and definitely wrinkling. Asia was especially rough. For me, the long days outside in humid, smoggy air had led to teenager-level breakouts, and for Teddy, showering twice daily to beat the heat had left him dried out and cracked. James's eczema had kicked into high gear.

Willa developed a stubborn rash on her chin somewhere at the tail end of China that had sent us in and out of local pharmacies across the region testing ointments and creams marked in languages I couldn't read. One of them, though we're not sure which, cleared up whatever it was. At some point I had walked into a Cambodian pharmacy, pointed at all the zits on my face, and made a "What do I do?" gesture to the lady behind the counter. She sold me a tube of something only mildly effective. Now, in Singapore, a dermatologist solved all of our issues once and for all.

At a mall dedicated to children, the kids went to a trampoline park and we bought new workbooks and some jump ropes. The place featured studios for piano and ballet lessons, and, by my count, four different kid barbers; there were dozens of high-end clothing shops and several stores specializing in math and science games. It catered to a demographic of parents ready to invest big money in their kids having, and being, the best.

We had a few friends in Singapore, an expat American as well as a Singaporean classmate of Teddy's from business school. We got together for meals, home visits, a trip to the National Gallery—and even a grownups' night out courtesy of a Treetops-recommended babysitter. "Your kids are really comfortable with strangers," she said when we came home that night.

I went on a blind-friend-date with a hilarious Brooklyn mom who'd relocated with her husband and three children. While our kids played together upstairs, she showed me how she faked good role modeling by hiding her Instagram scrolling habit behind a hardback book. And we had a visitor! Our buddy Phil came for the weekend. *From Boston.* For anyone else, flying twenty hours across twelve time zones for such a short trip would seem preposterous, but Phil was both a Singapore fan as well as a hardcore miles geek. For him, finagling first-class flights and luxury hotel stays all on points was the real thrill. We were impressed.

After shipping home a few souvenirs, our bags were very light. We wore the same three outfits. We'd given away all our gifts in Asia. We didn't buy much at the Singapore kids' mall. We were more extreme minimalists than ever by this point.

We were also smug about it.

Look how enlightened we are! We have renounced possessions! "Things" are unimportant to us!

Naturally, it was time for the universe to call our bluff. One sunny Sunday we set out in the morning to meet friends for breakfast. "When you visit Singapore," our Singaporean friend Jeremy told us, "it's not about what you *see*, it's about what you *eat*." The city had one of the most famous food scenes in the world, a head-spinning variety of options influenced by cuisines from China, Malaysia, Indonesia, and India. With Phil, we joined Jeremy and his family at some food stalls on the ground level of a nondescript public housing development on Sing Ming Road, where we lined up for strong iced coffees, soft-boiled eggs dressed in tangy sauce, marinated okra, chicken curry, and Indian-style crepes filled with spices. We ate the sublime food off paper plates around one of dozens of crowded outdoor tables.

Our bellies full, we said goodbye to everyone, including Phil, who was flying back to Boston that morning, and jumped in a Grab, Southeast Asia's equivalent of Uber, to return to Treetops for some homeschooling. Several hours later, it dawned on us: James's Orioles hat was missing. No one had seen it. We started removing couch cushions and tearing into backpacks. Had he left it at breakfast? In the back of the Grab? Where was it?

Forgetting how "stuff" didn't matter to us anymore, Teddy and I lost our minds.

That dusty black, white and orange O's hat was James. He'd worn it every day of the trip; it was his brand, iconic, a lucky charm. We had photos of him in that hat on top of Machu Picchu, in front of the Sphinx, beneath the Eiffel Tower, running along the Great Wall of China. And now it was gone.

Teddy and I went into a code red, lice-in-Berlin-level frenzy, retracing every step, analyzing our photos to pinpoint the timeframe when it had disappeared, calling, messaging, and emailing Grab customer service. Teddy found our receipt and googled every variation of the driver's name, even sending a Facebook message to one of the matches—some Malaysian man who, you won't be surprised to hear, never wrote back. We offered a cash reward not once but twice.

There was no sign of it anywhere.

Our Instagram followers, accustomed to seeing the hat in all our posts, filled our comments with heartbreak and crying emojis. "Noooo!" they wrote. "I'm flying to Singapore tomorrow to look for James's hat," my dad texted from Washington, only half kidding.

I was glum, Teddy despondent. (Willa thought we were both "crazy.") The only person who didn't seem to care about any of this was James. He'd already put on a yellow cap from Vietnam covered in a loud banana print and moved on with his life. Maybe he intuited what one of our Instagram followers commented: "On the bright side, bananas have a better chance of winning than the Orioles these days." More likely was that James's utter lack of attachment or sentimentality for physical things meant a five-year-old was actually living the ethos we'd only claimed to embrace.

When Phil landed back in Boston, he offered to ship us a replacement hat. Sheepishly, we accepted, forced to admit that, fine, some stuff mattered.

Indonesia

Amed

I might be the only woman with my profile who never dreamed of going to Bali—*the* paradise to visit if you were serious about satisfying wanderlust and "discovering yourself" in the process. I'm not sure I could have found the place on a map. I knew it was part of Indonesia, but was it some autonomous region? An island-state? Why were there so many Hindu traditions when Indonesia had the world's largest Muslim population? I wasn't sure.

But here we were, in Bali with a three-week itinerary covering four areas of the island, all plotted by an Australian travel agent. After Bali we would spend a week on the neighboring island of Flores. A month in these parts seemed like a long time, but maybe Bali *did* need to figure prominently in a year of travel like this? Everyone else seemed to think so.

We landed from Singapore at Denpasar airport (in-flight nerve-calming beer: *check!*) and drove three hours to a small town called Amed on the island's east coast. When we turned onto a road that led up a steep incline toward our place, I coaxed the driver along in my head: "That's it, bud, keep heading up." We'd passed dozens of tsunami evacuation signs along the route that depicted a figure sprinting away from a towering wave. I tried not to think about the 2004 tsunami that killed more than 200,000 people across southern Asia.

On Day 250 of our trip, we arrived at our hilltop cottage with a small pool and a patio overlooking the ocean in the distance. After two months in Mongolia, China, Vietnam, Cambodia, and Singapore—a stretch that had included sixteen different stops and nearly as many flights—we were ready to take the first "vacation from our vacation" since Corsica. For the next week, it would be just the four of us, the pool, an empty schedule, books, and sun.

We woke up when we wanted, did school without headaches, then spent the rest of the day in a state of half-coma bliss. Willa and James were less needy. There was still plenty of "Daddy, watch this jump!" but very little "Daddy, where's my bathing suit?" Better yet, Willa and James entertained themselves and each other. They played in the pool and when they got tired of that, they practiced jump-roping, a new hobby since Singapore. James could curl up with his Kindle for increasingly longer stretches of reading.

On days when we were feeling motivated, we descended the hill to the beach, where the sand was black with volcanic deposits and the waters alive with colorful marine life. There were a few tourists, many of them European, but the scene was quiet and rustic. We'd eat lunch at one of the seafood shacks, most of which were also backpacker homestays, and rented gear to snorkel the reefs, where Teddy had a transcendent encounter with a sea turtle. Maybe Bali really was an untrodden locale, free from t-shirt shops and selfie-sticks? Could my indifference have been unfair?

Ubud

When we first considered a year of travel, we envisioned staying almost exclusively in apartments and houses, Airbnb'ing around the world, "living like locals." House-hopping sounded great in theory, but given how frequently we moved, it made no sense. Stocking an empty kitchen every couple of days was impractical, plus eating at home meant we weren't out trying local food or meeting new people.

Staying in hotels didn't make travel any less "authentic." Having local experiences was about befriending strangers and taking their recommendations, not, it turned out, about where we slept. After a long string of hotels, we were always thrilled to move back into a house or apartment rental where we could eat at "home," on our own time, at our own pace, in our pajamas if we wanted, but the novelty was typically short-lived.

Travel agents usually picked the places where we stayed, using their connections to vet and book independently owned accommodations off the beaten path. About three-quarters of our stays wound up being hotels or hotel-like apartments, especially in Asia. Willa and James, who hadn't known what to do with that welcome hand towel back in Cartagena, now flipped the Do Not Disturb sign, filled out How Was Your Stay questionnaires, and regularly reminded us to tip the housekeepers.

In Ubud, the inland town popular with tourists for its famous steep rice paddies and holy shrines, we checked into a hotel unlike any we had seen before. "I think we've finally found our dream hotel room," I joked as we stepped inside. It was a concrete box with glass as its fourth wall, the only furniture a bed. Sparse perhaps, but a welcome change from the usual: Rooms with welcome binders, bowls of fruit, decor, trinkets, radio alarm clocks, and other superfluous items stacked on every surface that we always had to tuck away into a closet to make room for our own stuff. Here, we merely unzipped our packing cubes, put toothbrushes on the sink, and headed back out the door.

At reception we befriended a young staffer named Billy, who spoke English with a strong American accent despite never having left his home of Bali. We assumed he must watch a lot of American television, but he said he didn't watch TV at all. Later that afternoon, while driving to town with a driver arranged by our travel agent, Teddy and I chatted in the backseat about how good Billy's accent was. Our driver, who'd interacted with Billy in the hotel driveway, interrupted us. "That guy is not Balinese."

I looked up, surprised.

"Oh! Actually, he is! He—"

"No," he cut me off, meeting my eye in the rearview mirror with a frown. "He is a lady boy—have many boyfriends."

I made some cheery comment about how pillow talk was indeed a great way to learn a new language, then changed the subject as we approached town.

Ubud was an upmarket, Australian-ized vacation spot, a close cousin to what Mexico's Tulum has become for trendy Americans. There were surf shops and vegan restaurants with green juice and "brekkie bowls" on offer in places decorated with statement wallpaper and neon cursive signs like "Love is in the kitchen." Perfect for selfies. You could be forgiven for forgetting you were in Indonesia, the only reminder the Balinese people working behind the counters. "We haven't seen this many white people since Europe," Teddy said.

Ubud was a magnet for a specific kind of social media "influencer." When we arrived to hike the Tegalalang rice paddies, an elaborate system of ancient, cascading rice terraces of bright green, we expected to see other tourists like us, in comfortable walking shoes and backpacks. Instead, at 7 a.m., dozens of men and women had assembled, dressed for photo shoots, with full faces of makeup and hair curled into beachy waves just so. Some couples had hired local photographers to capture them holding hands and gazing into each other's eyes, while pairs of girlfriends took turns snapping photos of each other twirling in outfits pulled from a rolling suitcase. There was a drone overhead capturing someone's establishing shot. A bewildered rice farmer rested on a hoe, watching the flurry of action.

While amusing at first, it soon became depressing. All over town, foreign female visitors in skimpy looks struck identical poses: walking tip-toe while clutching a sun hat and looking downward; draping their bodies on the edge of an infinity pool; lying with their backs arched on a raft; flipping their hair when emerging from the water; and, of course, sitting, eyes closed, in the inevitable lotus yoga pose. They'd take the phone, examine the results, and start all over again. Teddy wondered what people hoped to accomplish. Was anyone here to enjoy the place or had they just come here to, as a friend back home liked to say, "live for the 'gram?"

We explored Ubud. We hiked the terraces, we went to the shrines. We toured exquisite bamboo structures by American architect Elora Hardy, and we shopped. I went to a spin class taught by an Australian expat. We even got a beer with Virak, who was in town from Cambodia with some other tour guide buddies to visit temples together.

But when it came to leave, we were ready.

Manggis

We had two more weeks in Bali and, fortunately, spent them far from the 'gramming masses in Ubud. I'm glad we did. While staying at the beach in Manggis, a town on the southeastern coast, we could walk for three hours among rice terraces that turned golden in the morning light and not cross paths with a single other tourist. We could ride bikes and eat lunch and meet locals and never see an Australian coffee house or watch someone pose. A whole agrarian and quiet island was out there. I was reading *A Brief History of Bali*, which helped me better understand how the island was a time capsule of sixteenth century Hinduism mixed with Chinese traditions and southeast Asian Buddhism, an improbable hybrid situated at the heart of the world's largest Muslim population.

We went for lunch at a cooking school run by Penny, an Australian-born chef who had lived in Bali for twelve years and spoke fluent Balinese Indonesian. The visit began at a vast outdoor market in the town of Amlapura, where Penny knew her way around the stalls and vendors. We spent over an hour sniffing produce and learning about new spices and veggies.

As with everywhere we had been so far in Bali, *gamelan* music—wooden hammers played on gong chimes—poured all day from nearby lavastone temples, and every home and shop displayed *canang sari* on their stoops, palm leaf incense offerings prepared and refreshed by women several times a day. Penny taught us how to properly make these *canang*, pronounced "cha-NANG," by creating a small palm-leaf basket tray and filling it with bits of flowers, rice soaked in holy water, and incense. Willa, more mystified than ever about religion, stared at hers when she finished and asked, "Does it work?" Across Asia, she and James had seen temples and met Buddhist nuns and monks; they had inspected shrines to deceased relatives inside people's homes. They liked China's beliefs about fortune and superstition, its concepts of lucky numbers and symbols.

Penny exuded a confident chill, her voice soothing. As we prepared lunch, her black dog Zorro snoozing at our feet, she told us how she had come to Bali after burning out at work in London and wound up staying permanently. She saved enough to buy a piece of land, eventually turning it into this cooking school and restaurant. She only served lunch because she liked her nights off; only cooked food she liked to eat, nothing else; and she taught classes because she liked to teach classes. Everything, down to the design of the building, was her vision.

Penny was an inspiration. Teddy and I had spent some of our more relaxed Bali days talking about creating the future we wanted, it having sunk in by now that we didn't have to experience life the way we had always been told to. Penny was proof that if you weren't afraid to try—if you were willing to resist the slide toward something familiar, something you were "supposed" to do—you could design a life you actually wanted to live.

Somehow this wisdom made an already delicious lunch even tastier. We stuffed ourselves with *nasi goreng* (fried rice), fish baked in banana leaves, bean salad, chicken with peanut sauce, and *sumping waluh* steamed pumpkin for dessert.

Sideman

Our last stay in Bali was our most remote, a house near the village of Sideman (pronounced SEED-uh-min) in the southeast. This was deeply rural rice paddy territory, surrounded for miles by beautiful, tiered farms. Our house wasn't fancy, but it had a large yard perfect for pickup soccer, which Willa and James played every day with the housekeeper's children, two girls and a boy, and their dog, Popo. After schoolwork, we'd hike through the paddies and find lunch down the road, usually at some family-run operation offering comfort staples like *nasi goreng* on the second floor of a convenience store. We may as well have been on a different planet from the Instagrammers in Ubud.

Not that it was totally relaxing. In the absence of development, this part of the island boasted critters of the National Geographic variety—the kind you see in photos and are relieved to learn live far away in remote, rural Indonesia. On our walks, spiders the size of my hand ruled over webs as large as refrigerators. At our house, foot-long tokay geckos with heads like golf balls stared down at us from the rafters. A sign in the bathroom read: "The geckos are particularly large in this house." *No kidding.* They rained droppings onto the same spot every day, including the straw floor mat on Teddy's side of the bed. He awoke each morning to fresh pellets at his feet, impressed by, as he put it, "The aim and consistency."

Our dining area was an open-air porch, and during dinner, the nocturnal tokays would appear in the rafters overhead as we ate, ready to start their day. Their "chirp" was more "mutant squeaky toy," and I flinched every time it echoed off the tiles. At bedtime the action really heated up. Tokays hunted birds, snakes, bugs, and other lizards in the thatched roof over our beds, one battle royale so loud I could have sworn James was banging on our bedroom door trying to get in (I actually got up to check).

During homeschooling one morning on the porch, Willa and I heard a splat. To the left of my bare foot lay a small, dead gecko. We looked up—right into the eyes of a tokay on the ceiling. He did not look happy about having dropped his breakfast. That made two of us. A few inches to the right and the dead lizard would've landed in my coffee.

The horrified-by-a-Brooklyn-cricket Margaret would have booked a direct flight home. This new and improved version simply began tucking her bed's mosquito net into the mattress. All the way around. Using tape on the head-board to secure it in place.

Flores

For our final week in Indonesia, we flew farther east to another island called Flores. To get there we took a budget Indonesian airline with a safety record I wish we hadn't googled.

Flores wasn't Hindu. Despite the fact that minaret towers sounded the call to prayer in the main town of Labuan Bajo, the island was actually predominantly Catholic, yet another reminder of just how many cultures, religions, and peoples had criss-crossed this trade-heavy archipelago over the centuries.

Labuan Bajo showed early signs of development—plenty of hotels and restaurants under construction on the coast—but still seemed decades away from reaching anything close to Bali's tourism infrastructure. Our travel agent had hired a local he knew named Marino to accompany us for the week, ensuring we would visit must-see stops like Komodo Island and some crater lakes at Kelimutu National Park, but also the lesser-known beaches and restaurants Marino and his buddies frequented.

We liked Marino immediately. He had not gone to a hospitality school. This was a guy who couldn't be obsequious if he tried. A Bob Marley fan with long dreads, a great sense of humor, and small kids of his own, he happily goofed off with James and Willa, kicking their ball with them and hoisting them up into tree branches. To our delight, he drank beers with us on empty, locals-only beaches and told off-color jokes. But he steered us safely. Having someone like him in an undeveloped place like Flores would offer our family yet another appealing option for traveling: a friendly "fixer" of sorts, able to give us as close to a local experience as possible.

On our first full day, we walked down to the port and Marino chartered a small wooden boat with peeling paint. He wanted to take us to some undeveloped islands for snorkeling and a visit to Komodo Island to see their famed dragons. Our boat puttered low in the turquoise waters, trailing a haze of diesel exhaust, a skipper at the helm and two crew on board, none of whom spoke English but all of whom wore jean cutoffs. Marino sat on the bow, his dreads blowing in the wind. We confirmed there were life jackets somewhere on board but didn't see anything like radio or communication equipment. There weren't any other boats around, either.

After about an hour, we pulled up to a small island and tied our boat to a dilapidated pier, its planks weathered and, in some spots, long gone. The pier was especially high, its spindly legs stretching far down into the water, where schools of fish glinted in the low tide. It did not have any railings.

We were there to snorkel, but the jury was still out on snorkeling for our family. Teddy seemed to rank it somewhere around "pretty neat," while my fear of fish made it more a version of exposure therapy than pleasure. The kids still didn't "get" how to breathe while wearing a snorkel mask despite prior outings in Brazil and Mozambique. They mostly sat on the sidelines waiting for us to finish. Indeed, Willa announced she and James wanted to stay with Marino on the pier, thrilled at the idea of having his undivided attention.

Teddy climbed down the ladder first and swam away, perhaps hoping for another sea turtle sighting. I went in next with a cringe and hovered within fifty feet of the pier, surfacing occasionally to see Willa and James chatting with Marino, swinging their legs over the water.

After about twenty minutes, I kicked my way back. I could only handle so many fish in one day. I grabbed hold of the wooden ladder with one hand and began peeling off my gear with the other. I could hear Willa and James giggling and telling stories somewhere high above me. All of a sudden, the talking stopped. In the silence, I heard only one sound—Marino saying something like "Oh!"—before a two-ton anvil, or something like it, came crashing into the water next to me, launching a geyser of white water into the air.

I stared at the cloud of bubbles, trying to understand what had fallen. Then I spotted it. *A yellow banana hat.*

"James!"

I lunged over with one arm and yanked him to me. He seized my neck, coughing up water then shrieking. I tried to comfort him while also making sure there was no blood. He had fallen from six feet overhead, wearing all his clothes and no lifejacket. I checked his head and body, relieved to see that, while rattled, he was not injured. I shuddered at the what-ifs: One foot to the right and he might have hit his head on the bow of a wooden boat. One hour earlier and he would've landed on coral exposed by low tide.

No one had seen what had gone down, so to speak, except Willa, who vaguely explained that James had been trying to navigate from point A to point B and lost his balance. As for James, he would later describe his point-of-no-return feeling in simple terms we could all relate to: "I knew I was going to fall in." Marino just chuckled, a reminder that where he was from, a kid falling off a dock was no reason to get all crazy. I followed his lead. By the time Teddy swam back and heard about the drama ("Whoa"), James was back in his usual good spirits. Marino hung his little banana hat on a boat line to dry, and we pulled away for our next destination, an hour-long ride during which we shared a lunch of rice, potato balls, barbecued tuna, and watermelon.

Eventually we spotted land, and our boat slowed as we got closer to the shore. "Are those … deer?" I asked. There were dozens of brown deer standing on a white sand beach, ankle deep in turquoise surf. I thought I was hallucinating, but Marino confirmed. I squinted harder at them. "Are they … drinking the ocean water?" Turns out they were. Marino said they drank sea water the same way they might enjoy a salt lick. I wondered if these improbable tropical deer knew they lived on Komodo Island, home to lumbering reptiles the size of St. Bernards whose poisonous bite could easily end their sea-drinking fun forever.

We stepped off the boat and spent an hour hiking the habitat of more than 1,000 dragons, observing as the creatures lumbered around flicking their forked tongues. The only thing between us and them was a skinny guide with a wooden staff—a level of protection that somehow didn't inspire as much confidence as rifle-bearing safari guides Thando, David, and Almero. The kids didn't share my trepidation. They were fascinated.

When it was time to go, Marino told us there was one last thing he wanted to show us before we called it a day. It was dusk and we still had an hour-long boat ride home in the dark. But Marino insisted. We pulled alongside a mangrove island, turned off the motor, and waited, cans of Bintang beer in our hands, not sure what to expect.

A few moments later, Marino jabbed his finger at the treetops.

"There!"

We looked up and spotted a trickle of flying creatures rising out of the trees and passing us overhead. From directly beneath, we could see their perfect Batman-symbol silhouettes against the sky: They were huge fruit bats. Soon a deluge of them poured out, like smoke from a fire. Tens of thousands made their way together over our boat, soaring off in the same direction in search of dinner, a course they followed every single night, according to Marino. It went on for five minutes, then ten, then fifteen. Twenty minutes later and they were *still* emerging by the thousands, filling the orange sky.

The astonishing precision of their routine against the beauty of that sunset, was, to quote my grandmother, one of the damnedest things I'd ever seen. Surreal, magic, humbling. By the expressions on their faces, Willa and James felt the same. The memory of our kids—barefoot, wind-blown, smiling pink cheeks turned upward at the spectacle—is as indelible as the bats.

Later, we buzzed back across the water toward Labuan Bajo in the pitch black, both kids asleep with their heads in our laps, tired and fulfilled. Getting off that boat was, as I noted in my journal, "maybe not the safest thing we've done all year." Teddy, the crew, and I used cell phone flashlights to pass our sleepy kids across wooden boat bows bobbing in the dark, but still, everything about that day, even James's unexpected swim, had been a kind of perfection.

We reached our final Indonesian destination, Maumere, by flying another budget Indonesian airliner. The waiting area by our "gate" featured a pair of *Golden Girls*-era pleather loveseats in pastel pink that did not inspire the confidence I needed. The sole security officer told us inflatable items were not permitted on board and that James would not be able to take his soccer ball on the plane. It was the ball that had lasted the longest so far. We'd purchased it in Paris after the one before it, from Mozambique, disintegrated in a Spanish pool. We were sad to see it go.

"Can you tell him he can keep it if he has kids?" Teddy asked Marino. The guy gave us a big smile of thanks. As we boarded the plane, I could feel that same surge of anxiety. Deep breaths. Keep focused. *It will be fine.* And it was. When we landed, Marino received a text from the security officer, who sent a photo of his toddler daughter clutching her new ball and grinning for the camera.

We checked into Sea World, a beachside set of cinderblock bungalows that hadn't been updated since the 1970s. It couldn't have been farther from the Orlando marine life extravaganza. Our cottage had electricity and running water, but that was the extent of the luxury. It was perfect.

In the mornings, James and Island Ted did their homeschooling shirtless by the water (when they did put on shirts that week, there was usually just one button fastened between the two of them). Teddy hadn't shaved since Singapore, and James's hair was long enough now to be tucked behind his ears. Willa's freckles sprayed over her cheeks, and I was as brown as I had ever been in my life, the skin under my wristwatch bright white. ("It's time to get out of the sun," my dermatologist chided via Instagram.)

Some days we hung out alone as a family, and on others Marino took us out for snorkeling or swimming. He took us to his favorite roadside restaurants and beaches, places where chickens ran around at our feet as we sat on plastic lawn furniture and ate fresh octopus and fish. Willa had recently begun reading aloud to James, and the two of them would sit and read chapter after chapter on the sand or on the bow of a boat, the only other sounds lapping water and the boat crew shooting the breeze in Indonesian. We'd eat mangoes or have a picnic of rice and grilled fish on white sand beaches with no one around, not even a shack selling coconut water.

At dusk, our porch teemed with geckos, which Marino told us were called "chi chas" in Indonesian. We dubbed it Chi Cha Lounge after a bar in DC with the same name, and spent the pre-dinner hours there playing rounds of Yahtzee, which had replaced Rat-a-Tat-Cat, and offering play-by-play commentary of chi chas as they stalked—and nabbed—bugs. When it was time to eat, we could have a full dinner for all of us, including Marino, for $11.

"Where is everyone?" I asked Marino on one of our outings. He'd taken us to a beach that was more of a postcard paradise than anyplace we'd seen in Indonesia yet, but it was empty. He explained that the few tourists who got as far as Flores went to see Komodo Island and left, unaware that farther east there was all this.

"Where's all the trash?" I asked another day. We sat on yet another undeveloped white sand beach that seemed strangely clean, its blue water devoid of litter. Seeing one so pristine was jarring after all we had witnessed. Then I peered just fifty feet around a bend and spotted the standard tangle of bottles and bags. The current had just swirled it out of eyesight.

Before we started our travels we assumed we knew how polluted the world was. We didn't. It was far worse than anything I could have imagined. Forests and deserts were littered with plastic; we'd wade into remote turquoise waters—from Brazil to Mozambique to Vietnam—only to be joined by shopping bag "jellyfish" and other human detritus. Our hotel in Durban, South Africa, offered free milkshakes for every bucketful of beach trash collected.

Even so, we were taken aback by what we saw in Asia. Solid walls of uninterrupted plastic garbage lined miles of roads and coastline, ensnared in seaweed and coating forest and jungle floors. Our laundry would often come back from the wash 'n' fold individually wrapped in cellophane, each pair of socks and underpants in its own package.

One of the hardest parts about seeing all this pollution, right up there with trying to imagine the world in which Willa and James would live as adults, was knowing how our travels contributed. Flying footprint aside, a trip like ours meant consuming countless single-use plastic water bottles. We spent 80 percent of the year in countries where we couldn't drink the tap and unfortunately didn't have a choice. Thirsty? Crack a bottle. Need to brush our teeth? Crack a bottle. All four of us, several times a day, all year.

Indonesia had the worst plastic pollution we saw on our travels. Bali's crushing tourist load overwhelmed systems, but so did everyday life. Markets sold everything from shampoo to cooking oil in single-use sizes because customers often could only afford provisions one day at a time. A fishing village in Flores resembled a landfill more than a town, with rats and goats munching their way across thick layers of plastic bottles and boxes and other trash piled beneath each stilted building. I recalled the carving we were gifted in Mongolia, the one depicting goats grazing on a mountain.

With all the incremental ways in which plastic was so much a part of life, it became impossible to imagine where any of it could go.

Marino understood our desire to interlope. He'd pull over into neighborhoods and towns just to walk around. In one, we stopped to watch a group of kids playing barefoot soccer on a gravel parking lot that overlooked the ocean. Spectators were girls Willa's age with popsicles in one hand and babies on hips in the other, presumably younger siblings. A few toddlers wearing diapers sat on a ledge high above the rocky waters. There wasn't a grownup in sight. Willa and James looked on with envy, not for the first time that year, at the sight of such freedom to play without hovering minders.

A few of the boys playing soccer noticed us and walked over for a closer look. There was some whispered deliberation and shoving among the group until one boy about eight years old, with a streak of dyed blue hair falling over one eye, stepped forward to Willa, put his chin up, stretched out his hand, and offered a loud and clear "Hello!" When she shook it, his buddies erupted in proud cheers, clapping him on the back and laughing.

"It was a dare," Marino explained. "The bravest boy accepted the challenge."

We attracted another group as we continued our stroll, this time a group of about seven middle school girls who giggled as they trailed us. "They've never seen hair this color," Marino told us, pointing to the strawberry-blond ponytail poking out from under Willa's baseball hat.

We wandered to the village's fish market, passing stall after stall selling red snapper, tuna, and squid that had been hauled out of the water just hours before. Locals came by to pick up their dinner, and we joined them, buying a small tuna to take back to Sea World for ours. We also stopped at a stall to buy two soccer balls—one for us and one for a new friend.

"There!" James yelled, pointing out the backseat window of our car as we edged out of town in Marino's car. We turned to see the brave boy with the blue streak in his hair walking along the side of the road with his pals. When Marino slowed our car to a stop, Willa hopped out and ran over to hand him the ball before sprinting back to us, giggling. We watched as the boy looked down at the ball in his hands, then back at Willa, trying to process this sudden windfall, while his buddies again erupted in cheers around him, jumping up and down in excitement.

On our last morning in Indonesia, Teddy went to mass. The owner of our lodge was an eighty-six-year-old Dutch priest who invited him to attend services at the property's cinderblock chapel, and, as our foursome's sole Catholic, Teddy obliged. The service was held in Indonesian and featured lovely hymns sung by a blind parishioner. While Teddy prayed, I packed. It was now mid-October, and after thirty-six days in Indonesia, and three months total in Asia, we were moving on once again, this time on a twenty-five-hour journey to Australia.

The exercise of packing had become a soothing moment at the end of every stay. I used it to process leaving one place and anticipating another. The mood that day was bittersweet in a way that was familiar by now: We were excited to move on to Australia but depressed about saying goodbye to Marino, who had shown us his part of the world with such love and care and so many Bintangs. Our family had once again grown attached to a guide we would miss dearly. The kids cried when they hugged him goodbye at the Maumere Airport and we promised to stay in touch.

AUSTRALIA + NEW ZEALAND

Two months: Australia (Sydney, Far North Queensland, Tasmania) → New Zealand (Bay of Islands, Auckland, Wellington, Kaikoura, Queenstown, Nelson)

Australia

Far North Queensland

It was mid-October and we were stepping off the jetway into the medium-sized Cairns, Australia airport, a building so familiar in its comforts (AC! Bathrooms with industrial-strength flushes! Abundant toilet paper!) that it seemed we could have been in Tampa or Albuquerque. After so long in parts of the world that didn't have these conveniences, and even longer in places where people didn't speak English, it felt surreal.

When we pointed our rental car north and began driving into tropical Far North Queensland, we saw wide, newly paved highways with lanes freshly painted in bright yellow. There was no litter, no smell of burning garbage. We could read and understand the billboards; our car had airbags and seatbelts; the radio played Top 40 songs we knew.

And the grocery store in suburban Cairns! When that automatic door slid open with a whoosh of AC, it was like stepping through a portal back to our old life. Wide aisles stocked with gluten-free crackers … dry shampoo … oat milk. Teddy couldn't stop staring at the dairy section. "They have ten different kinds of cheddar cheese," he said to no one in particular.

We drove in silence up the highway with our bags of groceries. If we hadn't still been wearing the clothes we'd put on in Flores, I might have thought our whole trip up to then had been a dream. "I don't know why I feel so emotional right now," I said to Teddy, who was back to driving us around on the left side of the road. I found myself on the verge of tears for reasons I struggled to explain. "I think I'm … *relieved?*"

It's not as though we had just survived something dangerous. We'd hardly roughed it in Asia. We were just a family who'd stayed in a bunch of hotels for a few months! Yet there it was, a giant exhale I hadn't realized I'd been holding. Teddy said he felt it too. And with it, a little thrill of accomplishment. *We did it. The hard part was over.*

But then there was something else mixed in. A kind of grief. If these Australian seatbelts and aisles of oat milk were any indication, things would be easy from here out. *The hard part was over.*

When we checked into our house, a host named Suzi gave us a tour and told us to keep our pantry locked so bandicoots wouldn't get in. We nodded like we knew what she was talking about, then googled "bandicoots" as soon as she left. There they were: pointy-nosed marsupials the size of cats who liked to rummage for food at night. The hard part may have been over, but surprises still lurked in a part of the world we knew almost nothing about.

Our house was an open-air wooden bungalow in the jungle with a porch overlooking a backyard pond. Our kitchen had only three walls, creating ideal conditions for late-night bandicoot snacking. We flipped through the welcome binder containing information about the house and read that there was a dog on the property: a yellow lab "of sorts" named Gaia. "She is friendly," it said, "But you must use the password, which is 'stick.'"

The next morning, a yellow dog stood outside barking at our porch. "Stick?" I called out to her. She scurried off into the brush, returning a few moments later wagging her tail, a branch in her mouth. Willa and James had finally met a creature whose obsession with sticks matched their own. They spent the next hour playing fetch.

Owners Alan and Suzi came by to give us a full tour of their property. They arrived holding a cardboard box. "This came for you," they said, handing it to James. It seemed improbable, but if anyone were to receive packages out here in the jungle, it was Famous James. He opened the box and peered inside, a wide grin taking over his face. He reached in and pulled out a stiff new Orioles hat. Our friend Phil in Boston had made good on his promise. As James adjusted the hat to fit his head, everything was right in the world again.

Gaia joined us as we set out for a walk together through Alan and Suzi's lush grounds, most of it dense tropical rainforest echoing with bird calls. What had once been a cattle ranch, and before that, a sugarcane farm, was now reminiscent of the Amazon. In a quest to preserve as many of the earth's rainforest flora as possible, particularly plants most useful to humans for food, medicine and more, the couple had spent three decades planting jungles that recreated those found in Asia, Africa, the Americas and, of course, Australia. With the support of the Australian government, they had traveled to more than a hundred countries, collecting seeds for rare flora.

Now the name of their property, the "Botanical Ark," made sense. It was a bank, of sorts, for so many of the rainforest plants now endangered or even extinct around the world. More fascinating was Alan and Suzi's personal history. When they thought about where they wanted to raise their family, many decades before, they made a list of criteria that were most important to them: "Clean air, pure fresh water to drink, suitable land to grow crops free from harmful poisons, and an environment free from crime." They knew they wanted to be somewhere tropical and eventually bought the land on which we now stood.

It was all so specific, yet so open-ended. The rest had unfolded organically, much as it had with Penny, the chef in Bali who had created her dream restaurant and cooking school.

After more than eight months, weren't we tired of all the traveling? People asked us this question all the time. Amazingly, the answer continued to be no, for all the same reasons that had sustained us so far: We weren't working; we went to bed early every night; we moved constantly, which had the counterintuitive effect of keeping our energy up.

Now, though, with so much of the trip under our belts, we could see that two other factors, both accidental, were contributing to our ability to stay invigorated. The first was our itinerary's variety. We caromed among vastly different types of stays: from hostel-ish to five-star; from unplanned days to tightly timed schedules; from modern cities to ancient ones; from apartments to hotels; from city chaos to forest serenity. The constant change kept us on our toes, variety being the spice of life and all that.

The second was especially helpful here in the homestretch: that decision we'd made back in New York to *plan and book most things in advance*. If the calendar were blank, we wouldn't have had enough fuel in the tank to research and book places to go. I suspect that if we'd opted for more of a "winging it"-type trip, we would have gotten to Australia and said, "Let's just find a beach town and chill the rest of the year." Which would have been awesome, I'm sure, but knowing now the experiences that awaited us, I'm so glad we stayed strong until the finish.

The Great Barrier Reef is a perfect example. Under normal circumstances, a day snorkeling on the Great Barrier Reef likely would have ranked as the single most exciting thing we'd do all year. We would have planned and researched and gotten the kids excited and counted down the days. Yet for us, when the day arrived, we kind of wished we could just hang out at our house and throw sticks for Gaia. Travel writer Bill Bryson summed up this conundrum: "Which was worse, to lead a life so boring that you are easily enchanted, or a life so full of stimulus that you are easily bored." Maybe we were a bit spoiled, or desensitized, or weary. Whatever the case, if it hadn't already been booked and on the calendar, I'm not sure we would have put down the sticks and gone.

We drove an hour to Port Douglas, parked and boarded a sparkling white catamaran that comfortably accommodated about three dozen snorkelers. The lead crew member was a muscular Australian named Rick, with white, white teeth and a crew cut, who, as we pulled anchor and set out for the day, flexed his neck and launched into a twenty-minute safety briefing.

I had to laugh. We were on a boat that couldn't have been more than one year old, with a uniformed captain and all the state-of-the-art equipment you would expect on an aircraft carrier. A world-class coast guard no doubt hovered nearby with helicopters and rescue ships at the ready. It felt absurd to get this kind of "SIFE-tee" briefing after all those rickety boats in Indonesia, not to mention the raft in Corsica.

When Rick's talk turned to snorkel protocol, he threw in a few canned "jokes" at the expense of the female crew members. "Don't pee in your wetsuit, folks," he chuckled. "But if you do, be sure you hand it to one of the girls to clean heh heh heh!" We shrugged, now accustomed to this kind of casual chauvinism.

At the beginning of our travels, it had shocked me. "People out here don't even know to *pretend* not to be sexist!" I would tell Teddy. By now, however, I knew how ubiquitous it was around the world and understood how my frame of reference, for better or worse, wasn't the way most people saw things.

Not that it made it any easier to deal with. Sometimes it was outright misogyny, sometimes it was "harmless" teasing, but every day, it seemed, we had to counter messages the world was delivering about a woman's place. I wanted to avoid judging how people elsewhere did things, but I also really didn't want Willa and James to hear this garbage.

After Rick gave it a rest, I assumed Teddy and I would be the only ones to snorkel in that turquoise water. We told ourselves, the kids, and other passengers that Willa and James would not get in the water. "They aren't into snorkeling," we announced. "It isn't their thing." Naturally, James and Willa zipped on a couple of wetsuits, adjusted their snorkels, and dove off the back of the boat into open ocean for long stretches of, yes, snorkeling.

Even for a fish-hater like me, the time in the water was amazing. We went out in pairs, perched on a single noodle float. Our favorites were the starfish and a species of pink parrot fish with a bright blue beak. Our boat made three different stops over five hours, each offering different views of the bright wildlife beneath the surface. We felt excited to see anything, frankly, after a close friend told us he had found the reef "sad" on a recent trip, the warming ocean temperatures killing delicate coral at a devastating rate. When we asked Rick and his crew about the impact of climate change, they looked at us like we were crazy. "The Great Barrier Reef is in *GRITE* health," Rick's colleague said. "It isn't going *ANEEE-WAYAH.*"

This was the exact opposite of everything we had ever read and watched about the Reef in the last thirty years. We asked our conservationist host Alan about it that evening while the kids threw sticks for Gaia. He rolled his eyes. "That's the official line from the tourism industry," he explained. "If they say the reef's dying, tourists won't come."

c—

Australia boasted some of the most extraordinary, and hilarious, animals we saw all year. There were seventy-five bird species living on the Botanical Ark and they all went bonkers when the sun came up, some of their bird calls so foreign they made us laugh, like the one that sounded like a valley girl shouting "Rebecca! Rebecca!" and another that called to mind the *pew pew* of a laser. Birds that look like escaped exotic pets were just Australia's equivalent of pigeons and sparrows.

We needed more of this and headed to an animal sanctuary near the Botanical Ark, where we booked a guide to take us around. As we waited in the cafe at our appointed time, I described to Willa and James how the continents had once been connected and their subsequent split explained the different evolutions of species from place to place. "It must have been so fun to ride," James remarked. I realized he meant the continents. He pictured them cleaving like an ice shelf, and animals surfing giant waves as they gushed in different directions across the planet.

"Sullivan family?" a bright voice asked. We turned around to find ourselves face to face with some kind of angel. Flawless skin, dimples, twinkly blue eyes. Wavy brown hair under a ranger's hat, and tan, fit legs stretching out from khaki shorts. "I'm Shannon!"

"Hi!" I said after doing a double take. I recovered and began to introduce myself and my family. "I'm Margaret, this is my husband, Teddy, and Willa and —" I stopped because James wasn't in his seat anymore. He had scurried behind it and sat on the floor hugging his knees to his chest. It was a five-year-old's physical manifestation of what the rest of us, especially my husband, were feeling inside. Shannon was so beautiful it was startling.

When we finally coaxed James out and walked to a kangaroo enclosure, Teddy and I followed along, chuckling at Famous James's sudden transformation into an awkward middle school boy with a crush, unable to respond coherently when asked simple questions, like, "What's your favorite animal?" We thought we heard him mumble something about hamsters. Teddy looked a little dazed himself. I elbowed him. "What?" he said, laughing. "I was expecting Mick Dundee, not … *Shannon*!"

Shannon was deeply knowledgeable about Australian fauna and spent the afternoon introducing us to the species on site. Willa and James clung to her every word as we met a wombat named Andrew who loved carrots and a kangaroo named Pat. We fed a crocodile named Gregory, and gushed over a koala named Kelly. We laid eyes on our first, but not our last, Tasmanian devil, one of the strangest creatures we would meet all year with their fangs and Quasimodo lumbering. There were other animals I couldn't pretend to name or place. To quote a 1700s English botanist upon arriving in Australia: "One can scarcely meet with any fixed point whence to draw analogies."

These encounters, fascinating as they might have been, were still only secondary to the most dazzling being in our midst that day: Shannon. We weren't alone. When I posted photos and videos of the afternoon on Instagram, many of our followers, men and women, young and old alike, had the same question: "So what's up with Shannon?"

A friend in New York texted, asking where in our travels we'd noticed the most "present" people. A thoughtful question for which we did not have a good answer. That's because by now we'd become pretty convinced that every single one of the world's 8.5 billion people was staring at a screen all day.

Sometimes parents like us romanticize the idea that in far-off lands, kids are somehow healthier and better adjusted because they're allowed to roam free outside, exploring their worlds and discovering themselves in the process. There's been some of that in these very pages. But the truth is, most of the kids we'd seen, from the privileged Sao Paulo kids at the resort in Bahia to the nomadic ones in a yurt in the Gobi, had screentime in common. Everywhere we went, kids got plopped in front of satellite TVs, handed a phone playing YouTube videos, or tranquilized by loud iPads bound in colorful rubber cases.

Not that their parents were any better. The pings of mobile games and talk show audience laughter from other people's phones were the soundtrack to our trip. In most places, we saw necks bent and eyes glassy. People on the bus, behind the counter, on bikes, walking down streets, sitting in idling trucks—all of them glued. "We've seen our planet's zombie future," I wrote in my journal somewhere in Asia, probably using my "Plastic Metal Thing" to do so. For a long time, we weren't really sure we had, or *would* have, a good answer for our friend. How could we tell her that everyone out here was staring at their screens?

But when we drove deeper into Far North Queensland (FNQ), home of denser rainforests and not much else, we thought we might have found an answer. Australia is roughly the size of the mainland U.S., with less than a tenth of its population, and we passed only a handful of cars during the entire four-hour drive to our lodge, a family-owned place converted from a nineteenth century tin miners' barracks. Our cabin had bunk beds, screen windows, and a fan, but no Wi-Fi or a cell signal—by this point a welcome feature, not cause for alarm.

We never would have found this lodge on our own, proof once again that travel agents could be invaluable partners when it came to discovering corners of the world. The only other guest at the lodge was a Melbourne-based travel agent, who was stunned to learn we were Americans. "How on *earth* did you find this place?" she asked.

On our first night there, we drove fifteen minutes down the road to the Lion's Den Pub, the only other establishment for miles. Located on a remote stretch of the kind of highway one might find in rural Florida, the pub was a ramshackle bar with dirty jokes scrawled on the walls and trucker hats dangling from the ceiling—"mementos from about 140-plus years of hard drinking" as one faded article tacked to the wall put it. Like our lodge, it didn't have a cell signal or Wi-Fi.

A Ferdinand-like bull who had escaped his paddock nearby was eating fallen mangoes from a tree out front. "He's here every night," the bartender told us as Teddy and I ordered a couple of pints. We took a seat outside on the deck. It was warm and pleasant and we made ourselves at home.

But then someone shuffled up behind us and leaned close. After a beat, a slow and gravelly Aussie voice asked, "You aren't from around here, are you?" We turned to face a leathery man in a sleeveless tee. He had a gray handlebar mustache and several tattoos.

"How can you tell?" I tried to joke, clutching my fanny pack.

He broke into a wide grin and patted us both on the back.

"Well, in that case," he said, "You prolly never woulda seen one of *these* before!" He reached over the railing and plucked an oversized pink flower out of a tree. As he launched into an explanation, telling us it came from such-and-such tree genus and doesn't it smell wonderful? I cracked up inside and made eye contact with Teddy, who was clearly doing the same.

This was the way things were done at the Lion's Den Pub. Every night, groups of tattooed locals in tank tops and mustaches would wave over new patrons—folks just passin' through—and invite them for rounds of pints and raucous laughter. They introduced themselves and shared what they knew about the area. No one stared at their phones because there wasn't a signal for miles. Lo and behold, people were making real, live human connections and having actual conversations.

We relished being part of a crowd that appreciated the here and now and returned several nights in a row to eat dinner and let the kids play on an old playground outside. We'd listen for the sound of our bull friend trotting down the road and laugh when we spotted the ropes of drool dangling from his jowls in anticipation of mango. We toasted him along with everyone else. *These* people were present.

On our last night in Far North Queensland, we ate a dinner served by lodge owner Hamish. While we waited, he brought out a little box of old books and toys to amuse the kids, assuming we needed something to bridge the gap between sitting down and getting our food. We would have appreciated Hamish's toys earlier in the year, back in the Restaurant Face days when we struggled with always-on parenting.

But things were different now. We had inside jokes to crack, "top three" rankings to update—top three tropical fruits, top three beaches, top three guides—and plenty more about our days to share. We ribbed Island Ted about his unbuttoned shirt and James about his crush on Shannon. Willa admonished Teddy for saying "you know" too much, and James described "facts" about his mother, like, "Mama takes toilet paper from the roll *before* she goes pee pee," the observation of a child who'd stood in countless bathroom stalls with me.

Sometimes we'd update our running "by the numbers" lists like "modes of transportation taken" and "bodies of water swum in." In Far North Queensland, our calculations revealed the number of bodies of water we had swum in that year now totaled 101, with the Great Barrier Reef taking the one hundredth spot, which seemed appropriate. We discussed how such a high figure probably explained why the kids had become excellent swimmers (and gone through so many bathing suits).

Still, when Hamish placed the box on our table, we poked around inside just for fun. I pulled out a plastic toddler cell phone and pretended to hear it ring. I flipped it open. "Hello?" I paused as if listening, then broke into a big smile. "Oh my gosh, *hiiiiiiiiiiiiiiii!*" I covered the mouthpiece and whispered to the kids: "It's Gaia." I pretended the yellow lab "of sorts" from last week was calling to ask about the sticks at our new lodge. Willa and James hung on my every word, half giggling, half secretly wondering if maybe Gaia was on the line. For the next hour, we laughed and took turns accepting pretend calls from other animals we'd met that year, like Cracklin the potbelly pig in South Africa and the spider monkeys who threw branches at us in the Amazon.

Tasmania

As if we needed further proof that Australia was massive, our journey from Far North Queensland in the country's northwest down to Tasmania, an island off its southern coast, took fifteen hours of driving and two different airplanes. Somewhere in there was a three-hour layover in Melbourne, a city I regret not visiting. "If Sydney is the hot guy who doesn't have to try hard," a local told us, "Melbourne is the less handsome but more charming one who'll write you a sonnet, strum you a song, and cook you a delicious meal."

What little we did see of Melbourne gave us a shiver of PTSD: At 4 p.m. on a Thursday, its airport was a hive of business travelers in work clothes walking with purpose, brows furrowed over phones in their palms, efficient little suitcases wheeled behind them. We hadn't seen much of that this year, and Teddy and I had almost the same immediate gut reaction when faced with corporate Australia: *no thank you*. We weren't far from the end of the year, but we were so relieved *not* to be en route to some presentation somewhere, but with our kids instead, all of us looking a little disheveled, about to begin a two-week road trip in Tasmania.

Whenever we tell Australians that we had a two-week Tasmanian road trip on our itinerary, most are surprised. *Tasmania?* It would be like a foreigner coming to the U.S. and devoting two weeks to a beautiful but super-specific state like Oregon or Vermont. It was not on the standard tourist path in Australia at the time, and most of the Australians we met had never been.

A heart-shaped island the size of West Virginia located just south of Australia's east coast, "Tassie" had invested heavily in tourism marketing recently, the same way Mongolia had, ratcheting up efforts to lure foreign travelers to its untouched wilderness and rich historical sites preserved from Australia's convict past. It was one of those places we'd heard of but knew little about. Our travel agent encouraged us to add it and created a plan for us to drive clockwise around the island over the span of two weeks, averaging about two nights in each stop.

"Can we drink the water in the sinks here?" Willa asked at one of our first stops, a working sheep farm in the south. She and James had asked that same question at all of our stops in Australia so far, still adjusting back to the concept of clean tap water. We told her that it was.

Teddy had a question, too. "Should we be worried about the crocodiles?" he asked the farm's owner, pointing to a creek near our cabin.

"Yeah, right!" she chortled, as if in on the joke. Only Teddy wasn't kidding. He was dead serious. We had just flown in from a part of Australia where crocodiles were commonplace, and we all genuinely wondered if we should be careful here as well. As soon as she saw the earnest looks on our faces, she stopped smiling and replied, "No. No, we don't have any crocodiles in Tasmania." We realized later that it would be like arriving in Maine after a trip to the Everglades and inquiring about alligator safety.

Before arriving at the sheep farm, we had made a few other stops, including at a memorable sanctuary outside the town of Hobart, where we met an orphaned baby wombat named Ronda—Australia has an astonishing road-kill problem—a three-legged echidna named Russell, and a Tasmanian devil named Luke. Seeing an actual Tasmanian devil in Tasmania was like seeing an actual komodo dragon on *Komodo Island*—not something we ever imagined doing.

We awoke in the mornings to sheep calling Teddy's name the same way they had in the Gobi Desert: "T-e-e-e-e-e-d." Our hosts gave us a sheep-herding demonstration led by an exceedingly competent dog named Billy, who went by "Bill" in his professional environment. "Ride on up there, Bill, riiiiiii-ide on up!" his handler would command. Later that day we were invited to watch Logan, a tattooed sheep-shearer, at work. I'm not sure what I thought a sheep-shearing would look like. Maybe that the sheep just stood there the way our dog Molly did when she got a bath? Allowing the groomer to scrub and clip without fuss? When Logan disappeared into a corral and came barreling back out through swinging doors dragging a giant ewe by her two front legs, all four of us gasped.

Logan wrestled the sheep down and pinned her under his stocky legs like a gator, running an industrial razor over her body in rough scrubbing motions until nothing was left but, well, a shorn ewe. While he worked, he explained there were eighty-five million sheep in Australia but only 4,000 professional shearers. "The good ones do up to 250 sheep in a day," he said, "And we can name our price." We piled in for an awkward group photo, the ewe splayed at our feet.

The farther west we drove, the better we understood a popular saying about Tasmania: "If you don't like the weather, just wait five minutes." It rained off and on, the ocean either shimmering with sunlight or moody and rough under dark clouds. The air was especially crisp for the same reason the waves off its coast were especially massive: Both had traveled all the way from Argentina, uninterrupted. Around us towered pine forests with floors carpeted not in trash but in moss and ferns. It reminded us of Norway, South Africa, and Peru.

In a town called Strahan we rode a sightseeing boat down the Gordon River to learn more about Tasmania's two biggest claims to fame: the Tarkine temperate rainforest, which boasted thousand-year-old Huon pines, and a brutal convict history defined by terror and heartbreak.

"Hi there, miss!" said the captain as he welcomed James on board. He was the second person that day to mistake James for a girl. Earlier, an elderly woman had smiled at our kids and said, "Such darling girls." Famous James's hair was now almost shoulder-length. With his floral shirts, pink knee socks, and long eyelashes, he looked like the second daughter we never had. Not that he noticed or cared.

This part of Tasmania was beautiful in an eerie way, haunted by ghosts of nineteenth century murderers and shipwrecks. We stopped for a tour of Sarah Island, a defunct version of Alcatraz where they once sent the worst of the worst: English and Irish convicts, already exiled from their homelands to faraway Australia, were sent here if they continued to break laws (or merely offend the powers that be, it turned out). Sarah Island was the end of the earth, and for most, a miserable death sentence. We were surprised to note it marked our second island prison tour of the year after Robben Island in Cape Town.

One stop in the Tarkine rainforest would be the most remote of our stays all year: Corinna, a "town" unchanged from the 1890s, when a gold prospector described it as, "The very roughest place it has been my experience to strike." Our cabin was a former pub belonging to the original Corinna Hotel, opened in 1895, and hadn't changed much since, more of a diorama from some pioneer museum than a lodge. It had tiny doors and low ceilings and an outhouse, but no heat or Wi-Fi. I kept a little fire going in our cast iron fireplace, adding "Fire Tender" to my list of jobs.

The enchanted Tarkine outside our cabin beckoned us. We hiked through its moss-covered fallen branches and ghostly pines, sometimes enveloped in mist and stepping along thick ferns bordering frigid brooks. Creatures called pademelons, which we learned were miniature fuzzy kangaroo cousins, nibbled grass and hopped away when we got too close. It was so cold we wore gloves while we homeschooled and slept in our jackets and hats, humbled and cozy.

I have a fun-loving aunt and uncle who always warn: "Don't invite us anywhere unless you mean it because we *will* show up." We had adopted that sentiment and expanded it to include, "And don't recommend anything to us unless you mean it because we *will* go." When a laundromat owner back in Stockholm said to try her favorite neighborhood restaurant, we went. When a gas station attendant in Tasmania insisted we see this one waterfall, or when someone in Bali suggested a surf film festival in town, we went. The many strangers who made these recommendations were our best shot at getting off the beaten path to interlope. We only had to be open to saying yes.

About halfway through our Tassie road trip, we were staying in a town called Launceston (lawn-SESS-tin). Ten thousand miles away in the U.S., the Washington Nationals were playing the Houston Astros in Game Seven of the World Series. This was exciting for Teddy, who missed sports. Sure, we'd seen that Cape Town Stormers rugby game, and we'd gone to a Real Madrid match in Spain. We'd streamed the Super Bowl on an iPad in Santiago, Chile, and Teddy had even set alarms in the middle of the night to listen to audio of March Madness while in South Africa. He called around to a couple of Launceston's sports bars and found one who agreed to put it on. No one else was there on a weekday morning to protest.

Meanwhile, the kids and I went to a playground, where we befriended a local family. It was Halloween, Day 299 of our trip. We'd barely chatted with these nice people for ten minutes before they invited us to trick or treat with them that night. "Halloween's not really a thing in Australia," Renee, the mom, explained. "But our neighborhood celebrates every year." We were supposed to be driving out of town that afternoon, headed to our next destination a few hours east. The old Margaret would have found relief in that fact. *An easy out.* But the new Margaret texted Teddy and told him to get a costume ready.

Teddy texted back a thumbs up, and let me know that, against all odds, the Nationals had just pulled out a 6–2 win against the Astros. "The crowd in this bar is going absolutely bonkers," he wrote, attaching a video panning an empty tavern.

We cobbled together *Harry Potter* costumes for the kids from the aisles of a KMart—Hermione for Willa and Dumbledore for James—and spent the evening strolling the streets of suburban Launceston, a place I'd never heard of until the week before, Teddy, Renee, and I with glasses of prosecco in our hands, chatting with neighbors about life, weather, and school. Willa and James dashed door to door with a pack of witches and superheroes and Transformers collecting candy.

Everything about that day had a dream-like quality to it: Teddy drank alone in a Tasmanian bar on a weekday morning; the underdog Nationals won the World Series yet nobody cheered; it was Halloween—in spring; we went to KMart; the kids trick-or-treated for candy with names like "Freddo Frogs;" the sun didn't set until after eight.

There were several more stops and still more end-of-the-earth dramatic scenes, both natural and historic: natural arches and wild, angry Southern Ocean waves slamming into cliffs. "I've never hiked so much in my life," I wrote in our blog, appreciating how far we city slickers had come. The kids were growing physically stronger and seemed far more at ease going two hours on a trail. Occasionally we came across some of the animals we had learned about, like echidnas, those porcupine-looking characters with anteater noses, or our favorite, the fuzzy pademelons.

Two weeks of driving long, quiet roads through Tasmania offered us the chance to see a part of this world on our own time, making stops recommended by locals and discovering things we couldn't always explain, like a hand-painted sign on the side of the road advertising, "Horse poo: $400." ("$400 seems like a lot," Willa said. "Yeah, why would horse poo be so famous?" James replied.) We slowed through pioneer towns that could have been mistaken for old Western movie sets, with their theater marquees and general stores.

All that driving did more than show us Tasmania. Teddy and I were able to do something we hadn't done all year: talk seriously about Life After the Trip. Until that point, we were so locked in the present that we could scarcely focus on what we were doing the next *day*, to say nothing of when we returned to New York. But now we felt ready to start having the conversation, and, lucky for us, long car rides were perfect for such meandering "life chats." While the kids listened to audiobooks on headsets in the backseat, we filled hours crossing forests and farmland, bandying about every "what if we…" and "here's a crazy thought" that came to mind, no idea off limits.

Our plan had been to move back to New York. But now we weren't so sure. Did we want to go back to the grind? Or should we start a more manageable (and affordable) life somewhere else? Somewhere we wouldn't have to compete quite so much—or at all? Somewhere slower? Then again, did we *want* slower? We seemed to *like* doing a lot. Plus, we adored New York! That's where most of our friends lived! Where the kids' school, which we loved so much, awaited their return.

We needed a sign of some kind, but none came.

The fact was, it was impossible to answer any of this without first solving some bigger, existential questions. Namely, what did we want? What mattered most to our family? Teddy and I talked about people we'd met that year like Penny in Bali and Alan and Suzi here in Australia—people who had laid out their lives in intentional ways, literally writing a list of what was most important to them and working backwards from there to design lives that fulfilled them in ways only they dictated. We admired their focus and envied their results.

Driving through Tasmania, we abandoned the idea of devising a plan and started brainstorming a bulleted list of priorities we could refer back to when making decisions about our future—more guidepost, less blueprint. The more we drove, the more we imagined what those might be. What had this trip revealed about us? What could we now see mattered? What had we once considered important and now viewed as irrelevant? What could we discard? What did we need to fight for? We started to put pen to paper.

Sydney

We flew to Sydney on a Monday, the Opera House clearly visible from our seats as we descended. "We have eight Monday mornings left," Teddy noted that morning before our flight. Monday mornings had never gotten old. Each time, we would look up from whatever warm weather perch we happened to be enjoying—that day, Hobart, Tasmania—and say out loud, "Monday morning." It was a weekly reminder to appreciate our break from the intensity of work and school.

On the drive in from the airport, Ariana Grande's song "God is a Woman," came on the taxi radio. Willa listened to the lyrics while watching Sydney go by out her window, all water views and lush greenery. She was pensive, and I wondered what was going through her mind.

"Mama?" she asked at last. "Is she saying … 'God is a *wombat?*'" Later, Daft Punk's "Around the World" came on. Famous James had recently discovered the nineties dance hit and adopted it as his personal theme song. He asked the taxi driver to please turn it up.

Sydney struck us as San Francisco meets Cape Town, a breezy beach vibe on a large urban scale, with cliffs and crashing turquoise waves, but also skyscrapers and international crowds. The best of all worlds, as far as we were concerned. Everywhere we looked, there was sky and water. The apartment our travel agent found was tucked up the side of a hill in Rose Bay, one of the city's "eastern suburbs." When I unpacked and went down the street for groceries—where I proceeded to spend what felt like our life savings on three days' worth of food—the place was abuzz with neighbors greeting one another with questions, like, "Ready for summah?" It was early November, and the Sydney summer was just a few weeks away.

Soon Lobsy landed, ready to complete her sixth and final installment of visits. "Are you sure you want me to come again?" she asked for the tenth time before flying back to this side of the planet. The answer was a firm yes. She was by now an established member of our group, in on the jokes, along for so many of our memories and mishaps. She *got* it. In Sydney, she also fit right in—everyone in town was somehow tall, fit, and blonde. And none of them seemed to be working! (That's how we fit in.) Cafes and restaurants brimmed with beautiful goodtimers wearing "sunnies," eating "avo toast" and drinking green juice. They wore trendy straw hats and cute tops. The scene reminded me of LA or Williamsburg, Brooklyn, where I'd always been tempted to ask someone sitting at a cafe on a workday afternoon, "Who are you and why aren't you in a cubicle right now?"

James and Willa were thrilled at Lobsy's return, naturally, and got right down to business teaching her to speak with an Australian accent. "If you say, 'rise up lights' like an American," James instructed, "It sounds like you're saying 'razor blades' in Australian." It was a party trick an American expat friend of mine had taught him.

"Also," Willa added, "if you want to say 'amazing,' you have to say 'uh-MIZE-ing.'"

We took our time exploring Sydney's neighborhoods, often by ferry, the preferred way to get around for commuters and tourists alike because of its stunning panoramas and efficient straight-shot routes. Lobsy was intrigued by signs on the ferries threatening "on-the-spot fines of up to $400 if you do the wrong thing." Australia had *a lot* of rules. It was a safety-conscious place that seemed even more preoccupied with not getting sued than our own litigious country. When I posted the scoldy signage to Instagram, an Australian friend back in New York replied, "Welcome to the nanny state!" (Better than the American friend living in Dubai who'd welcomed our arrival there with, "Welcome to the police state!").

Laws and safety ruled here, which might be one reason Lobsy loved it so much. There had been the long safety talk on the Great Barrier Reef, the bartenders who measured regulation thimbles of spirits into cocktail orders, and the childrens' surf school on Manly Beach where policy required instructors to grip the back of learners' boards at all times. Watching this inflatable-underpants-level display made us appreciate Brazil and South Africa, where instructors had sent Willa and James rocketing across waves alone to fend for themselves. God forbid our kids wipe out and actually learn something!

And then there were the foam-padded playgrounds. As Willa and James ran around them with "interchangeable blonde kids in school uniforms," as Lobsy put it, we recalled the playgrounds in Europe, which were just as new but at the opposite end of the safety spectrum. They boasted high towers and precarious ledges without railings, nothing far below but mulch. The Germans and Dutch had seemed to enjoy a borderline-sadistic "pro-risk" view of play, embracing the notion that kids could learn a lot by experimenting with danger. What would those Dutch parents—the ones socializing over beers as their kids played and got hurt—make of all this rubber padding? What would the Indonesian kids playing barefoot on gravel in that fishing village think?

By this point, our kids were regularly wandering up to anyone who looked interesting, usually a grownup, and striking up a chat. At a park in Sydney, they befriended an adult woman and her border collie. For nearly half an hour, the three of them chatted and took turns throwing a stick. "To be a fly on the wall over there," Lobsy said quietly from the bench. She was appreciating all the changes in her grandchildren. They were good travel companions. They tried so many foods. She noticed how peaceful our morning homeschool sessions had become. Not only did Willa and James do their school work without a fight, they took out their books and worksheets and journals on their own and just got down to business.

She was also amused at their language, which, after countless exchanges with foreigners, included quirks. Willa complained that James was "driving her mad!" and everything was "a bit" this and "quite" that. It was more pronounced in James, for whom everything was "about three meters tall" or "ten kilometers away." He casually called our flashlight a "torch," the trash "rubbish," and his bathing suit a "swimming costume." The bathroom was "the toilet." I always looked for signs that he was joking, but this was no act. One evening at dinner, when a server said the day's special was "Toe-MAW-toe soup," James, who'd seen his parents befuddled many times that year, leaned in to offer some help. He met Teddy's eye and whispered, "toe-MAY-toe."

"What is your clearest memory from this trip?" asked our friend Greg, who happened to be in town for work from California. The kids didn't hesitate. Willa described celebrating her birthday in Madrid with Lobsy, and James offered a play-by-play of The Piranha Story. As they talked, I was grateful to Greg for asking a refreshing version of that same question we got all the time: "What's been your favorite stop?" We were asked it so frequently that it had become an almost nightly dinnertime debate. *Did* we have a favorite place? Well, it depended. What were the criteria? Best place for kids? Best weather? Best food? Best hotel? Best hike? Best view? It was an impossibly broad question for the scope of our trip. We had been traveling now for more than 300 days.

Instead, we tried to find answers to questions like, which stops will the future-you picture when you close your eyes at night? Where did you feel emotional highs? Where will you return because you loved it so much? Where could you see yourself living for six months? Where could you see yourself living for two years?

Where were you happiest?

New Zealand

Bay of Islands

We landed on the North Island of New Zealand in mid-November, where the weather was cool and crisp. Lobsy would be with us for another week before returning home, after which we would stay there for another three weeks. Our route, plotted by travel agents, started far in the north, in the Bay of Islands, then headed south with stops in Auckland, Taupo, and the country's capital, Wellington. After that, we would fly to the South Island for Kaikoura, Queenstown, and Nelson.

Like everything we'd seen in Australia, these New Zealand forests and coastal enclaves were trash-free, a state we would never take for granted again. Though the Bay of Islands' turquoise beaches looked like a tropical paradise, the weather was closer to a brisk Colorado fall. We wore windbreakers and scarves, high socks, and wool hats.

One day we sailed among the islands with an easygoing skipper named Dave, who we found online. Our agent had proposed a private cruise, but we preferred to join a small group on a more affordable, laid-back visit around the area's many uninhabited islands. Rather than baby us, Dave told us that if we felt like we might fall off the boat, we should "just grab onto something!"

Whenever we'd anchor to explore, Willa and James searched for sticks on beaches with Lobsy, while Teddy and I hiked up tall, grass-covered hills to see the view from above. Dave encouraged us to try these hikes barefoot, saying the grass was soft ("and we don't have snakes!"). Indeed, the ground beneath our toes squished like the padding on a Sydney playground.

An Australian couple on our boat asked where Lobsy was from and were surprised to discover that Washington state and Washington, DC, were two different places. This prompted a great debate later that night at dinner: Should people from Australia know America's geography? Lobsy thought definitely yes, while Teddy and I were not so sure anymore. We'd seen how most people out in the world didn't know, or frankly, care about, other countries' history or geography. Yes, even ours! They had their own lives and worlds.

On our way to the Waitangi Treaty Grounds, widely considered New Zealand's most important historical site, I noticed James staring at my legs with a funny look. "Did you just get those pants?" he asked. Yes, I said, I had picked them up in Sydney for the cooler New Zealand weather. We wore the same clothes every single day, and when one of us put on anything different, it was more discombobulating than ever. About thirty minutes later, I caught him staring again. "You look like a new person," he said. I looked at his long hair and floral Balinese shirt and bit my tongue.

The Treaty Grounds tour was a revelation. It was there, we learned, that in 1840, British settlers and chiefs from the Indigenous Māori people reached an agreement on moving forward peacefully as a single country, "not a single shot fired." Where we came from, what few Native American tribes had survived the arrival of colonists represented only 2 percent of today's U.S. population—and rarely crossed our radar unless it was to debate sports team names or the merits of Columbus Day. Life for New Zealand's Indigenous people today looked different than in the U.S. The Māori made up nearly 20 percent of the population and had representatives in parliament. Their language was one of the official languages of the country, taught in schools and featured on highway signage. They had National Māori Day.

Willa and James may have dug in the dirt with sticks on that part of the tour, but they snapped to attention when dancers started performing the Haka, the ceremonial Māori dance of rhythmic stomping and chanting. They sat agog at the dancers' bulging eyeballs, flexed pectorals, and bared tongues. This was no side show for tourists. The dance, just like the Māori culture in full, was revered by all. It was even performed by sports teams from rugby to basketball, including by white athletes, with no one crying cultural appropriation because it was so deeply integrated into all Kiwi culture and performed with pride and respect.

Auckland

As we made our way to Auckland from the Bay of Islands, we stopped at Sheepworld, a suggestion by our New Zealand travel agent. Sheepworld was a farm (or "station" as they're known in New Zealand) where tourists like us could visit and learn first-hand about wool, the country's most important export. Lobsy was skeptical. "*Sheep*world?" she asked from the backseat, where she rode in her usual spot wedged between Willa and James.

We took seats in a small barn-like amphitheater among a smattering of other families and tourists. A twinkly-eyed sheepherder in his sixties came out and welcomed everyone, introducing himself as John through a TED Talk microphone, then pointing to his dogs, also onstage: Border collies named Boy and Mac and a large brown goofball named Grizz. "Boy and Mac here are my Ferraris," John said. "They're elegant, smooth; they're smart and they're fast." Then he turned to Grizz and smiled. "Grizz, well, he's more like a bulldozer driven by a drunken Irishman—strong and loud, but not particularly sharp or coordinated."

John enlightened us about New Zealand, about the biology of sheep, about the history and tradition and business of sheepherding. He punctuated his delivery with jokes the kids could understand and rounded it out with details, like how sheep needed to be sheared to avoid overheating and to prevent infection; how thousands of years of human intervention made the species reliant on us.

I wondered if this, like the Great Barrier Reef crew's insistence that the ocean was perfectly healthy, was a tourism board party line, but then I was distracted. Grizz the dog walked over to a sheep John was now shearing—his technique gentler than what we'd seen in Tasmania—took its hoof in his two front paws, and sat down as if to comfort the animal. When the shearing was done, we watched as the dog appeared to munch happily on bits of shorn wool scattered around the stage. "He likes the protein," John joked. We capped the tour with a walk out to his pasture to witness John and his dogs at work rounding stray sheep into a paddock.

When a small child in our group asked, "Which of the dogs is your favorite?" John paused and said, "No one has ever asked me that before." He seemed to think for a moment and then said, "I've never told this story." He described the day he picked up his border collie Boy as a puppy. It was the one-year anniversary of a close friend's death, he said, and he drove with his new dog to pay his respects at a cemetery. Farmer John appeared to be baring his soul, and we all leaned forward.

"I couldn't find the gravestone anywhere," he said. "I looked all over, walking from headstone to headstone—and finally, well, I gave up." Another long pause. "I yelled up at the sky, 'I miss you, mate, wherever you are!'" Right then his new puppy started barking. Boy was sitting and wagging his tail on a gravestone. His friend's gravestone, it would turn out. John stared at the ground for a moment and wiped his eyes. "So, yeah, I guess you could say Boy and I have a special bond." Boy wagged his tail as John patted his head.

Sheepworld was our family's best tour of the year. It was a new gold standard—a holy grail of tours. "Why?" Lobsy asked. She'd liked it too, but … *best tour of the year?* No question. Sheepworld had nailed all four of the key elements we knew by now actually made a tour kid-friendly.

The first was brevity. A small child's birthday party when booked at a playspace or gym is one hour long. For the happiest moment of their year! No one, therefore, should rationally expect two kids Willa and James's ages to be engaged in a 106-degree walking lecture about ancient Egyptian pharaohs for *three-plus hours*. Sheepworld's tour was forty-five minutes.

Next, it had incorporated one of the following: nature, food, animals and/ or music. When we were in Peru at Lake Titicaca and did a five-hour tour of a floating island village built and inhabited by the Indigenous Uros tribe, there was a lot of whining. The next day, when guide Alberth rowed the kids around in an aluminum boat looking for bird nests in the reeds, Willa and James were filled with wonder. Sheepworld had sheep *and* dogs.

The third was that Sheepworld was a simple place. Ask anyone who's watched a toddler spend Christmas morning playing with cardboard boxes from the trash pile: It doesn't take much to impress small kids. We went to the chocolate-making lesson in Cartagena and all James wanted to do was kickbox the plastic AC door flaps. We went to Machu Picchu and the kids only cared about the centipedes. We spent a small fortune on safaris, but Willa and James had been just as astonished by that dreary Durban petting zoo. At Disneyland, one of their biggest thrills was a duck pecking at grass.

Finally, Sheepworld nailed the final, and most important, element: It had delivered a charismatic guide. John's talk fascinated us. He spoke plainly, clearly and told vivid stories that helped us understand the subject matter. He made us laugh. He made us cry! We "'standed" everything he said. Not only had our kids *not* dug in the dirt with a stick during this tour, but they also wanted to *watch it all over again*. When we signed the guestbook before leaving, Willa wrote, "I can't wait to come b-a-a-a-ck."

Finding a tour that met all four of these criteria had eluded us for almost eleven months and six continents. But at last, we had found it. And now we knew what to look for.

⌒⟋

We were told that Auckland would be "an ugly Sydney," but after a few days in the city, I didn't agree. It was clean and surrounded by blue waters, but on a miniature, manageable scale. With just one million residents, it was about the size of Charlotte, North Carolina. When the former prime minister ate lunch a few tables down from ours at a restaurant, there was no security detail and no fanfare, as if he were the mayor of Mayberry.

We spent several days there, staying in an apartment hotel downtown and exploring the city by foot, Uber, and even one Hop On Hop Off bus. We took the ferry one afternoon to Waiheke, a small island known for beautiful vineyards and stunning natural scenery. We attended a rose festival, had a blind-friend-date for brunch, and found still more, equally padded, playgrounds, confirming earlier observations that New Zealand had just as many, if not more, rules than Australia.

And then, it was time for Lobsy to leave.

It was always sad when Lobsy left us, but this time felt even more so. With just six weeks left of our trip to go, the next time we would see her would be back in the U.S. On her last night we ordered Peking duck from a local Chinese restaurant and ate it at a table in our apartment. We reminisced about Lobsy's "Year of Living Dangerously." She had joined us six different times across eight different countries, flying on thirty-one flights, and staying in seventeen different places in the process. She completed twelve long-haul flights, which were twice as many as we would. And throughout it all she had been a willing tourist and babysitter, a walker and an adventurer, always ready to add a touch of glam to our rumpled foursome. As we cleared our plates from dinner, Lobsy spotted a rainbow out the window. We ran to the balcony and took pictures, amazed at the timing of such a fitting tribute.

Just twenty-four hours after we put Lobsy in a cab to the airport, Teddy's phone rang. Auckland is known as "The City of Sails," and the four of us were wandering a marina filled with handsome sailboats, getting ready to meet up with Pete and Jeff, the Kiwis we'd befriended on our Hong Kong food tour.

"It's yesterday here!" Lobsy said from her kitchen in DC when he answered. It was a video call and we all piled into the frame to see her. To us, home felt so far away at that point—more of an idea, or some vague memory—yet Lobsy, with us just yesterday, was there. It was like she had appeared and disappeared via some magic portal, reminding us that while the world was huge, tens of thousands of international flights took off every day, and seeing faraway places was often just a matter of boarding one.

We came across the most Americans all year in New Zealand, especially once we hit Auckland. Many had rented camper vans for roadtrips. This seemed to be the "thing" for American tourists to do when in New Zealand, just as we had by now learned that the "thing" for foreigners to do in our own country was to drive Route 66 in a rented Mustang.

Most tourists appeared to be looking for adventure. There was hiking and biking and zip-lining and bungee jumping and more, all designed to provide adrenaline rushes for fit, helmeted types.

For all the thrills, one was unlikely to get hurt in New Zealand, thanks to its many rules and regulations. The gentle slope at a neighborhood park we visited had a marker stuck in the grass warning people of the danger of tumbling.

We opted for the occasional toned-down thrill—like white water rafting with a company that offered a "family float" ("If zero is a bathtub and six is Niagara Falls," our guide said, "then we're a two!")—but mostly found different kinds of excitement, like the "Craters of the Moon" geothermal fields in the center of New Zealand's North Island, where we could actually hear the ground water boiling and bubbling like a cauldron. "It smells like the time you dried our gloves on the stove," Willa whispered to me, referring to an incident when I almost burned down our Tarkine pioneer cabin.

Taupo

Like Australia, New Zealand had a different feel from so much of our year. No lingering smell of burning trash and never any chickens running in the road. No mystery meat or kids riding on motorcycles. We had seatbelts, air-conditioning, and English. This part of the year continued to be just, well, easy.

We'd not only pared touring way back, but also found that the parts of our days that once sucked up a lot of energy, we now completed in efficient little bursts. Like homeschooling and writing the blog. Even just a few months before, writing the nightly Wordpress entry had still felt like a lot. *Is this really how we want to spend our precious kid-free time at night?* But then an old friend wrote us this note:

Keeping up every day is the only way. I know from long trips that if you miss more than a day or two you will regret it years later. Keep putting details in. I have a journal of a trip across the country in 1982 and in one place it says that [my daughter] got in trouble for "being bad." She was 6 and now I wish I knew what she could have done that was that bad."

Her words motivated us, and now the upkeep was just a habit. Good thing, too. Looking back, the single best decision we made, besides actually taking this trip, was to remain so disciplined about documenting it.

Best of all, our days hummed because Willa and James could now amuse each other for long stretches on their own, making up games. One day I overheard Willa propose to James a game she called "Boring Grownups." ("Ooh!" he replied. "I'll be … um … 'Steven!'"). We could declare two and a half hours for "quiet time," a concept that might have been hard even a month before, and they could reliably read their books, watercolor, or play with the few games we packed. They might get their swimsuits and go in the pool. We'd be nearby, but no longer required to watch every cannonball.

All of this—the peace of mind, the autonomy, the efficiency—left us with more time for uninterrupted reflection. We used it to discuss that Big List of Sullivan Life Priorities we had started brainstorming back in Tasmania. It had taken weeks to distill, not to mention almost a year of travel to conceive of in the first place, but at last it had come into focus. We had created *our* list of essential criteria; the things we felt we needed to create the life we wanted to live when we got back:

- Time with the people we cared about most
- Good physical and mental health
- Creative pursuits and lifelong learning
- Owning our time
- Giving of our resources to people who could use them

We agreed that any and every decision we made about our future would have to be informed by this list. "If it's not tied to these," Teddy said, "let's not spend time or money on it." The list allowed us to envision our return and decisions began to take shape. We began with the kids: After such a year of constant change and newness, a return to something familiar would be best, so we would put them back in their beloved school in New York.

Besides, weren't most of our friends in New York? Wasn't it nice and close to our families in DC, whom we now vowed to visit more frequently? It was decided: We'd rent a new apartment, not buy, and then think about jobs. It would be a challenge to see if we could maintain our new rules for mental peace and owning our time. If we decided in a year that we didn't like it—or couldn't hack it—we gave ourselves permission to leave and do something else.

Wellington

When I was twenty-three, I ran a marathon. Things were going great until I stopped to use a port-a-john at mile eighteen. In those two short minutes, my leg muscles seized up so completely that I almost couldn't complete the race. I did end up finishing, but it was a good lesson: Don't mess with momentum in the homestretch.

It was now November. We arrived in Wellington on day 325. We'd taken more than sixty-five flights, visited twenty-seven countries, and stayed overnight in more than ninety places by then—and had more than a month left to go. The thrill of constantly arriving in new places still provided a shot in the arm, but we'd reached a point where we knew that if we settled down at all, we'd risk stalling. That's how I recall our relatively lackluster week in Wellington, New Zealand's capital city at the southern tip of the North Island with a population equivalent to Des Moines or Spokane.

Our travel agent most likely put us up here for five nights as a budget breather to stretch our dollar in this pricey country. We celebrated Thanksgiving at a restaurant surrounded by the Thursday lunchtime work crowd, took the kids to the national museum, and saw *Frozen II* in a movie theater. Though there was good interloping to be had, five days felt long. We felt the urge to press on.

Attempting to keep the energy up, I booked a "seal safari" we found online, where we met Rachel and Jo, two women from DC on their honeymoon. They loved to travel, they said as we jounced around in the back of a four-by-four. We compared notes and talked about places we had both been. When I shared our itinerary, they listened with longing. "Wow, we'd *love* to go to some of those places," Rachel told us. "But so many of them just aren't safe for us." When we got back to the hotel I looked it up: Seven of the twenty-nine countries we went to criminalized LGBTQ "behavior" at the time, and at least one punished it with death.

I thought of the discrimination we had seen already that year. The widespread disdain for Chinese tourists; the driver in Bali who'd sniffed at our "lady boy" hotel manager; the Beijing tour guide who thought traveling to Africa would get you murdered. I thought of the Random Traveling Black Guy and the message of his t-shirt. I was embarrassed to admit how long into our trip it took us to appreciate that we could just bop along carefree—doors opening and people welcoming—all because we fit some non-threatening stereotype: White American mom and dad with daughter and son, blue eyes, able-bodied, dollars to spend. Not everyone could do what we were doing, but not only for the obvious reasons.

Queenstown

When we arrived in Queenstown, a city in New Zealand's South Island, we spotted a familiar figure in the airport—6'5" with gray hair and a blue Patagonia puffer coat. "Beepaw Jim!" Willa and James yelled as they ran up to him. This was no mirage: My dad had made good on his promise to fulfill a lifelong dream of fly-fishing New Zealand's rivers. (Grammie stayed behind in Washington. "Why would I fly halfway around the *world* to see people who look just like *me*?") Beeps would be with us for our last two weeks in New Zealand, and we were thrilled.

Everyone told us Queenstown was gorgeous, yet still it managed to surpass our expectations, more a village than a city, plunked down among dramatic skies, snow-capped peaks, and soaring evergreens. We could see the sapphire blue lake from a balcony in our apartment rental. The afternoon we arrived, Mother Nature flexed her muscles and delivered a rainbow. We thought of "Lobsy's Rainbow" in Auckland, and the others we had seen and noted on a list, including one over a vineyard near Bordeaux and another that arched over our *ger* in the Gobi after a thunderstorm. I looked at the spray of color and cursed my mom for being so stubborn and missing out.

The friends who'd invited us trick-or-treating in Launceston, Tasmania, told us that when we visited Queenstown we had to see Milford Sound, located within the vast Fiordland National Park. *Don't tell us to go somewhere unless it's good, because we* will *go.* Even if the outing required a thirty-five-minute Cessna flight, as this one would. I had not flown on anything that small since South Africa, and I dreaded it, but got the tickets anyway.

When we showed up, Captain Hank was waiting for us, a Kiwi Sully Sullenberger-type who assured us that we were on "the fleet's newest plane, flown by its oldest pilot," words I needed to hear. As we flew, Hank stayed low to show off the park's full glory, our plane seeming to skim the tops of pointed green hills, then, later, snow-capped mountains. I tried not to think about how tiny and meaningless our tin-can plane was out there in the big, windy sky. I tried not to think of *Alive*.

But when we landed and our waiting catamaran began crawling between fjords so tall they reduced seagulls to white pinpricks high above our heads, I knew it was worth it. The waterfalls! The albatross! The crisp air! This was postcard New Zealand. Cover of the guidebook. And that was before the dolphins showed up. Hundreds of them swarmed our boat, leaping and surfing in our wake. They raced along, and looked up at us with one playful eye as they skimmed the surface of the water. Willa and James leaned over the front of the bow to watch the show, perhaps one of the most extraordinary any of us would see in our lives, right up there with the flying fruit bat migration in Flores. I fought to hang on to the moment when Hank informed us the wind had picked up and we'd be "rockin' and rollin'" the whole flight home.

My dad hadn't seen Willa and James since the Middle East and was amused by the changes in them. Every time Willa used the words "quite" and "a bit," or whenever James emerged dressed in his favorite outfit—knee socks decorated with Tasmanian devils pulled up high over leggings he inherited from Willa, one of his floral shirts from Asia, and shoulder-length hair under his O's hat—my dad would look at me with a smile as if to say, "Seriously?"

He sketched with them and applauded their jump-roping skills; he showed them how to cast a fly-fishing line and watched their silly dance routines at bedtime. When we set out for our afternoon exploring, he tagged along when he felt like it and peeled off to do his own thing when he didn't.

Our outings were usually outside, not surprisingly. We rented bikes—electric ones with "half bikes" for the kids hitched to the back—and pedaled through the countryside, which bloomed with wildflowers, and across suspension bridges straddling deep ravines. We rode a gondola up to the peak for a view of Queenstown one day and drove out to the sleepy, picturesque town of Wanaka another. My dad and Teddy went fly-fishing with an American expat guide named Declan, who was also, it turned out, a professional magician who hosted us at his place one night for a vegan dinner and some card tricks.

Many of the Americans we encountered in Queenstown were dressed as Mr. Travel Guy, a costume we had read about earlier in the year in a hilarious book called *Turn Right at Machu Picchu*. Mr. Travel Guy was, according to author Mark Adam, "the fellow who strides through international airports dressed like he's flying off to hunt wildebeests—shirt with dozens of pockets, drip-dry pants that zip off into shorts, floppy hat with a cord pulled tight under the chin in case a twister blows through the baggage claim area." We had seen Mr. Travel Guy wherever American retirees ventured—Machu Picchu, yes, but also airports in Norway, Chile, South Africa and now, New Zealand.

The consistency of Mr. Travel Guy in Queenstown amused us, but none of us begrudged him his sun hat. The hole in the ozone over New Zealand combined with the lack of any air pollution meant exposure to direct UV rays was especially dangerous. Free sunscreen dispensers hung on every wall, as ubiquitous as hand sanitizer. I bought a new straw hat for the occasion. Assigning each of us a letter one day at lunch, James told us he was "F," for funny; Willa was "H" for Harry Potter, a series that had consumed her since Indonesia; Teddy was "E" because, in the absence of hotels, he had been making a lot of scrambled eggs lately; and I was "S," for "scarecrow"—a reference to my new sun hat.

There was one excursion that brought us in from the sun to total darkness: We wanted to see a kiwi bird. I had thought kiwis were common in the country, the same as echidnas and wombats in Australia. They're the national bird, after all! But, I soon learned, they're also nocturnal, skittish, and very endangered. We were never going to see one in the wild. We booked tickets to a bird sanctuary in Queenstown instead, one that featured a "nocturnal house" where visitors could observe kiwis in captivity.

The nocturnal house was a small single-story space in total darkness. When we stepped inside from the blinding light of a Queenstown afternoon, I couldn't see my hand in front of my face. "Please take a seat on one of the benches," a guide said, pronouncing it "beenches." We felt our way alongside other blinded tourists shuffling in, shoulder to shoulder, tripping over one another and bumping heads. I managed to get Willa and James seated but when I went to take a spot next to them, I backed down into the lap of a woman who squealed.

"Oh my gosh I'm so sorry," I whispered. I scooted over and managed to squeeze in.

The guides switched on red infrared lights inside the enclosure, and we feasted our eyes at last on two real, live kiwi birds. The room oohed and aahed. And tittered. The birds were funny—about the size of large hens, with shaggy brown feathers that looked like fur and long, arched beaks. I could have watched them go about their purposeful kiwi business all day: digging up grubs, sniffing the ground, rustling in the leaves, their mole-like eyes and loping gaits so goofy and endearing. About halfway through all this, I wondered where my dad was. My eyes had adjusted to the dark, and I scanned the room. There he was, all the way on another side. He was sitting next to a young woman about my age. Sitting way too close, in fact. I watched as he occasionally leaned over to talk in her ear, despite the fact that she seemed to shrivel smaller every time he did.

He thinks that's me, I thought.

When it was over, he exited alongside this woman who was not me. "I'm going to tell mom you were picking up ladies at a bird sanctuary," I said from behind him. He jumped at the sound of my voice, then did a goofy, kiwi-like double-take at the stranger next to him.

Kaikoura

We flew north to Christchurch and rented a car at the airport for the drive to Kaikoura, a one-stoplight town put on the map by whale-watching. Our car was a cacophony of sneezes and sniffles. In fact, the sound of people blowing their noses will probably always make me think of New Zealand: Teddy and James were still fighting their year-long battle with seasonal allergies, and my dad, whose symptoms were worse than both of theirs combined (or so he proclaimed), brought his particular brand of fog horn nose-blowing to the chorus. The abundance of sheep everywhere we went in New Zealand convinced James he was allergic to the animal. When restaurant servers asked, "Any allergies we should know about?" he would reply, "Sheep."

In Kaikoura, the kids taught Beeps petanque, a game they had first picked up in South Africa and had honed over their months in Australia and New Zealand. Famous James showed off his ability to drop bombs, or as he said, "bop droms," on his opponents. We played cards. We skipped stones. The kids showed off their Yahtzee skills. When it came time to go whale-watching, we rode out into the South Pacific where the shelf drops several miles into the depths and saw a sperm whale and a humpback, not to mention another pod of hundreds of rollicking dolphins having the time of their lives showing off their twists and leaps.

The winding route to our last stop, a countryside inn outside Nelson, took us deep into farmland with few houses and even fewer cars. We wondered where the heck we were going and how travel agents even found places like this. When we pulled up, we stopped questioning anything. This was the "vacation" to end our time in Australia and New Zealand, an English-style home, perfectly appointed on the interior, with rolling gardens of roses and mazes of wildflowers outside. Our hosts were Bobbie and Peter and their black lab, Chili. Cocktails were served at 6:30, and dinner followed on the porch.

Teddy and my dad went fly fishing that week, once again relishing the experience despite not catching anything. "I'm not even experienced enough to explain why it's difficult," Teddy told me that night. But he appreciated the similarities to baseball and other sports where timing and relaxation were more important than "muscling" your way through the technique. "I could hear my high school coach as I was casting," he said. "'Teddy! You're playing baseball like a linebacker! Relax!'"

The inn was the kind of place that even a few months ago might have been a recipe for restless kids and whining—no pool, a tad stuffy, lots of downtime. But the afternoon my dad and Teddy fished, Willa and James spent five hours amusing themselves by painting and making "perfume" out of lavender, all without mom steering any of it. Was there anything better than doors open, birds tweeting, kids quietly engrossed in their own projects? This was no manufactured image from a mom blogger's perfect Instagram feed. This was actually happening! Was this the result of our travels? Or were they just naturally maturing and getting older? We'll never know.

Of course, that night James was ready as always to show me how, for all his quiet afternoons painting, his table manners, his good posture and eye contact—for all the "library voices" and pleases and thank yous!—he actually knew exactly how to be a five-year-old boy. When Peter walked around our dinner table wearing a crisp Oxford shirt and serving oysters, he expressed surprise that Willa and James were eating them. Naturally, I beamed.

"What other adventurous foods have you tried this year?" he asked. Willa told him in her now very grownup way about the silkworms and the crickets, the snakefish and the pig ovaries—"and butt poop!" James interjected with an impish grin. Everyone froze, oyster shells midway to our mouths. Peter recovered quickly and pretended not to hear, which just made it worse.

New Zealand felt a bit like a last hurrah. With my dad flying home, it seemed we should be too. But no. Ahead of us was a flight to Auckland followed by an eleven-hour daytime flight to *Japan*. Somehow this trip was still going.

We had a favor to ask Beepaw Jim before we parted ways: Would he interview Willa and James about their year? We wanted a record of their stories and their memories, in their own voices, and knew they would only oblige if a non-parent did the asking. So, my dad, a career litigator with thousands of depositions under his belt, pulled out a legal pad one day and hit "record" on my phone's dictaphone app while Teddy and I disappeared out of earshot. He wound up collecting nearly two hours of material.

He asked about their favorite animals ("Let the record show that Willa is demonstrating a dung beetle's poop-rolling technique"), places where they wished they could have stayed longer ("Casa Teatro," James deadpanned, referring to the shag-carpeted Amazon hostel we'd hated) and things they did to be punished with Minutes ("accidentally biting James"). When asked if they could impersonate their parents, both kids hammed it up: "Put on your socks! *PUT. ON. YOUR. SOCKS!*"

"You learned how to do one important thing this year…" my dad said, turning to James.

"Ride a bike?" James replied.

"No…"

"Surf?"

"All those things are probably true, but I'm thinking of something else you couldn't do before the trip, and now you *can* do…"

"Blow bubbles with bubble gum?"

"No…"

"Jump rope?"

"I learned how to do my own ponytail?" Willa offered.

"Something to do with books!" my dad clarified, growing impatient.

"Read!" James shouted with pride.

My dad asked if they liked temple tours. An emphatic no.

"When we go to temples, [Mommy and Daddy] try to make us believe it's going to be really good," Willa said.

"—Even though it's going to be sixteen hours long and sixteen temples a day," James added.

"They say [high, squealing voice]: 'Can you *believe it?* We're going to a temple! *C'mon*, it's going to be *really good*!'" Willa performed.

"But then it's just some big rock thing," said James.

"Why don't you like temples?" my dad asked.

"Long and boring," Willa replied.

"—and it takes like millions of ages until it finishes," James added.

"—and it's like they're speaking another language we don't understand—"

"—and temples are just rocks but carved to look like a *building*—"

"—and it's always at least 106 degrees every day. I basically go mad!"

"Can you do an impersonation of a tour guide?" asked my dad.

"I don't hear anything, so it's mostly, like 'blah blah blah blah blah blah blah,'" said James. Then, adopting the lofty air of a professor, "'This is the house of the brother's king we talked about yesterday!'" Then, back in his normal voice, "But I don't even *remember* yesterday!"

"Every thirty seconds you have to say 'As you can see...' Like, "'As you can see, this is a sculpture of Egyptian history!'" Willa said.

Then a pause and some reflection from James: "But a 'pro' is—"

"—James! There is no 'pro' of a temple tour!—"

"—a 'pro' is the *reward*."

"Oh, yeah," Willa conceded. "Sometimes if we're good we get a Coca-Cola or a piece of candy."

"Were there *any* temples you liked?" my dad asked.

"We went to this old castle in Cartagena," Willa replied after a pause. "[The guide] had hidden plastic toys all over for us in little holes in the wall and we had to get them, and we learned about tunnels. At the end we had a huge pile of toys!"

"If you could live in any of the places you visited, which would you choose?" my dad asked, changing the subject.

"I would say Australia," Willa replied. "So I could work with animals with Shannon."

"I want to work with Shannon, too," Beepaw replied, laughing.

"My daddy thought she was pretty," James said, his voice suddenly soft.

"Um, so did *you*!" Willa replied.

"NO, I DIDN'T!" he bellowed back too quickly.

When asked about their favorite part of traveling around the world for a year, Willa thought for a long time before replying, "We get to be together."

"And the only work Mommy and Daddy have to do is write the blog," James added.

ASIA (AGAIN)

Japan

Kyoto, Hakone, Tokyo

The Sullivans who landed in wintry Kyoto after a twenty-hour journey from New Zealand are my favorite version of our family: relaxed, present, and inseparable. James called Kyoto "kia ora," which is the Māori-language greeting New Zealanders use, and to his credit, did sound similar (he also got "Pinocchio" and "Tokyo" mixed up). The jolt of arriving somewhere so different reminded us that this trip was still very much in progress. Just because we were close to the end did not mean it was the end. We developed a new mantra: *We're not back until we're back.*

This was the first real cold we had experienced all year, but we had shopped for a few extra layers in Tasmania and New Zealand, none of it particularly flattering or matching. Teddy and I proceeded to wear the exact same outfit every single day for our two weeks in Japan—from Kyoto to Hakone to Tokyo. We simply woke up and put it all back on. The kids, meanwhile, wore a hodgepodge of whatever layers kept them warmest, resulting in some truly interesting sartorial choices, even by their standards. We had simply stopped caring.

We scheduled no tours in Japan. Our travel agents selected hotels and suggested an itinerary, but we figured out the rest. "Are you sure?" they asked. "Japan can be really tough to navigate." We'd never been more certain of anything in our lives.

We wandered around, stumbling into places, taking the occasional wrong train. We drank heated cans of coffee from subway vending machines and spent more time than I ever would have imagined inside 7-11s and video game arcades. Sometimes, we'd detour towards a temple, not to go inside, but simply to add what I started to think of as "texture" to our walks. You could stroll past the Brooklyn Bridge for a New York experience without having to take a two-hour historical tour of the thing.

"Everyone is staring at me," Willa whispered to me one morning. "It's making me kind of uncomfortable." It's true, there weren't many non-Japanese people wherever we went, though I was surprised Willa cared. By now they knew what it felt like to be outsiders. How often had we been the ones who did not speak the language, could not understand what was happening, and generally did not fit in?

I, for one, had shed my self-consciousness. At a Kyoto arcade one day I noticed racks of colorful mini dresses lined up next to photo booths decorated with glamour shots of smiling, posing Japanese teenage girls. This, Google told me, was *purikura*, a phenomenon popular with Japanese teenagers. Girls rented dresses from the rack, styled their hair and makeup at one of the vanity stations lining the wall, hairdryers and mirrors at the ready, then used the booths to pose for portraits that they could then airbrush and decorate with hearts and other emojis. They printed their favorite images on stickers and trading cards.

The old Margaret would have noted all this with an amused shrug and moved on. The new and improved one wanted to try *purikura* for herself. While Teddy and the kids played air hockey and worked a claw machine filled with Harry Potter toys, I made my way over to a bored attendant looking at his phone behind the counter. He didn't speak any English, but I pointed and gestured enough to rent a "sexy" Santa outfit—a red velvet mini skirt and matching jacket lined with faux white fur—and get him to explain how the photo booth worked. Willa, James, and Teddy drifted over to see what Mommy was up to.

I used a changing room to put on the velvet outfit, then flung the curtains open to reveal my look. "Oh my god," Teddy said. The skirt was two sizes too big and sagged to my knees. The shapeless top smelled like Febreze. It was decidedly *unsexy*. Undeterred, I strode into the booth, and hammed it up, serving my best peace signs and kissy lips. I airbrushed them and added some pink lollipops to my background. Then I hit "print." What came out of that machine were the most hideous wallet-sized photos of me ever taken. I treasure them and everything they represent.

A satisfied feeling of joy permeated our days in Japan; we did only what we wanted, keenly aware our time was winding down. Japan had nailed "cozy," and our winter weeks there were filled with steaming *shabu-shabu* bowls, warm and inviting restaurants lit with the glow of paper lanterns, quiet streets, and Suntory highballs.

We took a train to Nara outside Kyoto to feed the famous sacred deer that roamed its streets and went vintage clothes shopping with Japanese Gen Z'ers. We watched schoolboys play baseball, the first of the sport we'd seen all year. We rode a municipal bus to a geothermal field in Hakone and later that day took a family dip in our inn's hot springs. We discovered the depths of James's allergies at a cat cafe in Kyoto (sheep no, but felines definitely yes). We sang our hearts out in a private karaoke room in Tokyo, booked by a travel agent at our request. If we ticked any tourist boxes, we ticked them on our own damn time.

Willa and James rolled with the unfamiliar traditions, happy to wear Japanese robes and sip tea at a traditional inn, or *ryokan*, where, mercifully, they were by then just self-aware enough to behave in a country where decorum reigned.

There was very little English spoken in Japan, yet people still bent over backward to help us. In Tokyo, we spent an afternoon wandering around a fancy department store where I made one of my few but favorite purchases of the entire trip, a Christmas present to myself: a set of pastel pink "marshmallow gauze" pajamas made of the softest fabric I'd ever touched. When I realized with horror an hour later that I had misplaced my shopping bag, I used the Google Translate app to ask a shop lady for help. She instantly took pity on me, trotting around making urgent phone calls and gathering other colleagues to discuss the matter in Japanese. Ten minutes later, she had located the bag, so giddy I'm not sure which one of us was more excited.

On Christmas morning, we woke up late, the kids on their futons, just the four of us in our Tokyo hotel room on a Wednesday, a YouTube "fireplace" video playing on our TV. All of the kids' Christmas gifts fit inside a small tote, which I'd been filling since Auckland. It'd felt weird to set out such a measly pile the night before as they slept—a sparkly headband, a remote-controlled fart sound machine, some fluorescent gel pens, an action figure, and a few erasers—but of course, it was a treasure heap to Willa and James, who'd kind of forgotten about toys. We sat around in our robes and counted our blessings. We were heading back to the U.S. in a matter of days, and we felt ready.

NORTH AMERICA

One week: United States (Kauai, Hawaii)

Hawaii

Still groggy from our overnight journey from Japan, we boarded a domestic plane in Honolulu bound for Kauai. "Go O's!" a man bellowed from a first-class seat. He and his extended family were all wearing matching Orioles-themed Hawaiian shirts and gave Famous James fist-bumps from both sides of the aisle as he walked to the back of the plane. It felt like a sign: *Welcome home, buddy!*

Settled into our cottage near Hanalei Bay, Teddy and I would turn to each other every morning and say, "Can you believe we were supposed to be skiing in Japan right now?" A quiet stretch of reflection should be a requirement for the last week of a trip like ours. We had few plans and used the time to think back on the year and mentally prepare for reentry. At night, we'd cook at home, sitting around the table, just the four of us, talking about our favorite memories and stories from the year. We'd had these conversations all the time, but now they felt more poignant and more complete. We pulled out our lists and shook our heads at all we had seen and accomplished.

We also spent our week discussing the many things we were most excited about returning home to. Family and friends, of course, including many who'd had babies while we were away. Teddy told the kids they'd be able to have a whole bookshelf of their very own books. Willa stared in disbelief, then turned to me for confirmation.

"Wait," she said. "Can we really have our *own* bookshelf of our *own* books?"

When I dropped the concept of a library card on her, it was almost too exciting to bear.

Also, food! Like bagels and breakfast sandwiches and tacos. And ESPN! And safe tap water! We couldn't wait to *not* have to write the blog every night. To walk into a room, turn on the lights, and *not* see half a dozen lizards scatter. We couldn't wait to enjoy everyday situations where we knew *exactly what to do and say.*

Friends back home wondered if we were sad to come home; I, too, had worried that our final weeks could get weepy. But our trip had wound down gradually, without the heartbreaking abruptness I'd been dreading. We carefully, gratefully counted down our "lasts." Last country. Last big hotel. Last small hotel. Last breakfast buffet. Last immigration line. Last rental car. Last rental house. Last laundry. Last suitcase packup. Last Monday morning. We'd savored them all. There were twinges of apprehension, of course, but mostly we felt fulfilled, at peace. On our last day, while floating in a flamingo innertube in our pool, James looked up at me and said, "Mama, this is a good life." We were ready to go home.

We beamed as we descended into DC (not least of all because I knew it would be my last flight for a while). Willa pointed to the Washington Monument out her window. When we bounced onto the runway, I leaned back against the headrest, closed my eyes, and smiled. When I opened them, Teddy and I looked at each other from across the aisle and exhaled. There's a video he took of me as I rolled my suitcase off the plane and through the yellow-beamed corridors of Washington's Reagan National Airport, pumping my fist in the air, my skin a deep brown, my stride confident.

At baggage claim, I walked up to a stranger.

"Excuse me," I said. "Would you mind taking our picture? We're just back from a big trip."

Part Three

New York

We delayed the start of school, and our New York lives, by five days so we could spend time with family in DC and beat the jetlag. I monitored our emotions carefully for any signs of sadness or letdown but didn't feel or see either in the kids or Teddy. We were feeling good—giddy, even. Everything in DC was reassuringly just as we'd left it one year before: Christmas decorations still up, our parents' houses cozy and quiet, cousins and siblings reuniting, childhood homes the way they always were. It was as if time had stopped while we were away.

When it was time to head to New York, our car buzzed with nervous excitement. The four of us drove up the New Jersey Turnpike on a Friday, Teddy and I fielding questions from the backseat like, "Where are we gonna live?" and "Can we go to Imagination playground?" Willa and James played their new favorite song, an Idina Menzel number from *Frozen II* titled "Into the Unknown," over and over again. We'd seen the movie in New Zealand a few weeks before, and its refrain offered an apt, if unsubtle, reminder of what awaited: "Into the unknooooooooooooooown! Into the unKNOWWWWW-WWN!"

After a year of pre-booked itineraries, we now faced the blankest of slates. We had an Airbnb for ten nights in our old Lower Manhattan neighborhood, and Willa would start second grade and James kindergarten on Monday. But after that, what lay ahead, including basics like where we would live and what we would do for work, was indeed unknown.

The car got quieter as we emerged from the Brooklyn-Battery Tunnel into Lower Manhattan. I turned Idina down. We inched into the neighborhood, a place where I knew every tree and ATM and bench, and scanned for signs that we'd made the right decision to return. People talked on cell phones and bike delivery guys buzzed by. A beeping MTA bus hissed as it lowered to pick up commuters in puffy coats. A guy in khakis and a vest carried a to-go salad.

I'm not sure what I expected. Fireworks? A ticker-tape parade? A banner draped on the Brooklyn Bridge saying, "Welcome Home, Sullivans?" None of these people had any idea—nor, frankly, gave a damn—that we had just experienced a life-changing year away together. Whatever longing I may have had for a friendly welcome or acknowledgment of our trip was irrational, I knew, but somehow the indifference still unsettled me.

We circled for parking, then walked to lunch at a neighborhood spot with a wood-burning oven cranking out pizzas for the lunchtime crowd. The host squeezed us into a table against a back wall between groups of boisterous co-workers catching up after the holidays. I looked around at my family.

In just forty-five minutes we had a meeting at school to meet the kids' new teachers, and after that, an appointment with a real estate broker to look at apartments. I didn't want to do either of those things. I wanted to stay suspended exactly where we were, the four of us, huddled over lunch in our travel clothes, interloping in a crowd, forever.

When we leave the restaurant, I thought, *it will all be over.*

I tried not to look at my watch as we ate and talked about what school would be like, how soon we'd see our friends, what kind of apartment we might find. I joined the conversation with a smile. When everyone finished, Teddy took the kids to the bathroom, leaving me alone at the table to sign the check. I stared at it, knowing this was it.

I started to cry.

Teddy bought a book about how to manage major life transitions, in which the author described "suffering through a confusing nowhere of in-betweenness." That perfectly described those first few days. We seemed to be floating through a haze, unsettled and disoriented. The trip was over, but "home" did not feel like home at all. Our Airbnb was gloomy. Our car door got dented in the garage. We thought we'd found a great apartment, only to see it fall through. Reuniting with friends lifted us, but their "I-can't-believe-you're-back-already" responses just reinforced the feeling that life in New York had rocketed onward in our absence. Did we fit into this place anymore? How?

On our travels, James had asked every night, "What are we doing tomorrow?" Now he didn't need to ask. He knew that school was his new tomorrow, and he, like his sister, did not take to this sudden return to routine. Not only were they being pulled apart from their parents, they were being separated from each other. They both cried every day at dropoff that first week. We navigated all this the only way we could think to: Put one foot in front of the other. Take the kids to school, look at apartments, eat, sleep, do it again. Maybe if we kept it up, something would click?

Fortunately, rays of sunshine began to poke through. One afternoon Willa bounded out of school hugging a little girl with bangs, shrieking, "Mommy! I made a new friend!" On another, Famous James's teacher played "Around the World" by Daft Punk so that he and his classmates could dance together. And while there would be no ticker tape parade, there would eventually be more meaningful interactions with people who'd not only been "with" us on the trip—following our social media and blog—but who'd also been personally touched by it.

Like the Colombian barista in our neighborhood who cheered when we walked in one morning. He'd followed our trip on Instagram and wanted to reminisce together about Bogota. A mom from school who'd known Willa since she was three told me how moved she'd been to follow Willa's growth on our blog. "I'm just so proud of how brave she was," she said. Another friend, a hard-charging executive with two small children, cried during a ramen lunch when I described the peace we'd found. "Sorry to get crazy on you," she said, wiping her eyes. She explained that she'd been questioning her path lately, and longed for something more fulfilling. Not one but two different people we didn't know at all stopped us after recognizing Willa and James—or, rather, Famous James in his signature Orioles hat. Both were distant acquaintances who had followed our trip on Instagram. They wanted to talk about where we'd been and what it had been like, right there on the sidewalk.

Our loneliness disappeared even more when friends we met overseas continued to check in, sometimes in ways we never expected. Like the Moroccan Uber driver we met in Amsterdam who shared our love of travel. We'd swapped stories as we sat in traffic, and he went on to become a regular cheerleader on Instagram. One day when we were back, he messaged us:

> *Thank you for sharing your fantastic journey. Sometimes you meet people who make you realize life is more than chasing financial goals but enjoying it and taking time to value and appreciate the little things. Thank you so much! You've been/are an inspiration! Thank you, I can't say enough!*

After a few weeks we found an apartment and moved in. In the midst of all this getting settled, we heard reports of a deadly virus in Wuhan that was spreading rapidly. "Is being a grownup scary?" James asked me around this time, seemingly out of nowhere.

Having shed my Invincible Mom facade somewhere on our trip, I met him where he was. "It does feel scary sometimes," I said. "Definitely."

Not long after, COVID engulfed our city. James's question replayed in my mind as the screaming ambulances out our window began and didn't let up for weeks and the refrigerated morgue truck parked up the street in front of NY Presbyterian Downtown Hospital seemed like it would hum there forever. Before we'd been back for two months, before we had any real sense of what returning from our travel life to the intensity of a full-throttle Manhattan existence would be, before we really knew if we could have hacked it, we found ourselves locked down and facing the same unknowns as everyone else: About school, about work—about life and death.

It was not the return home we imagined. Yet, for all the fear, the pandemic gave us an unexpected gift: a pause. Here was a chance to be still and to reflect. As we did, we hung onto the togetherness: We ate three meals a day together, played board games and cards, wrote letters and chatted with friends on video calls. We were conditioned to spend hours outside every day getting fresh air, rain or shine, and the habit remained, just when we probably needed it most.

Someone commented we were lucky we'd stored up a year's worth of beautiful memories to sustain us through those challenging days. She was right. We told stories about our trip every night at dinner—about Famous James's funny encounters and Willa's courageous episodes; we pulled up photo slideshows on our TV screen, going through batches of snapshots I'd categorized by topic, like "Signs," "Food," "Animals" or, my favorite, "Bloopers"; we read aloud from our many lists, rehashing inside jokes and funny quotes; we played "WhatsApp Roulette," scrolling hard and fast through our endless 2019 threads and stopping abruptly on, say, Ari and Camila from Bogota or Bongani from Johannesburg, just to pick up the conversation and say hi.

And every day, dressed in my sweats and sitting just outside the frame during Willa's and James's remote-learning Zooms, I'd put my headphones on and peck away at my book, returning to a boat on Lake Titicaca, a playground in Amsterdam, a wall in China.

Before we committed to taking our trip, one of the negatives on our endlessly debated pro-con list was the fact that our young kids, especially James, probably wouldn't remember most of it. What would be the point of taking them all the way around the world for a year when their memories would be fuzzy and disconnected at best?

A wise friend swatted that logic down. "They might not remember it," she said. "But it will shape them."

She was right.

Sure, they were exposed to a lot—as little kids, both could tell you a lot about Genghis Khan and the Amazon rainforest, about Nelson Mandela and koalas—but saying that is how the year shaped them would almost demand a comeback like Matt Damon's in *Good Will Hunting*: "You wasted $150,000 on an education you coulda got for $1.50 in late fees at the public library."

The transformative effects I'm talking about are more nebulous than that, harder to pinpoint. Maybe not even the result of our trip. But here's what comes to mind.

I think a year of carrying their own stuff created a lasting habit of personal responsibility. *Your stuff, your problem.* Nevermind that wearing backpacks all the time these days makes them look like tourists. "Where are you visiting from?" a pizza guy in Chelsea asked Willa when we stopped for a slice. When she replied, "Lower Manhattan!" he said, "Oh wow, I thought you were from, like, Ohio." If they can carry it themselves—or, for that matter, say it, do it, or ask it—they generally do.

All those Tough Questions asked and answered, the ones about war and disease and terrorism, about orphans and about the United States not always being the hero, set a precedent for frank-talk in our house. Willa and James expect the unvarnished truth, even when it's ugly, and can usually be trusted to grapple with it. They understand that humans, for whatever reason, can be violent toward one another. They take the concept of their own immortality in stride. "I didn't exist eight years ago," Willa said one night as COVID raged. "I didn't really *mind* not existing, so if I died, I probably wouldn't care."

For a while it seemed their reflexes had been honed to view any outing smacking of culture with suspicion and a reflex of opposition. Had we ruined touring forever? Willa and James are indeed astute about excursions. When faced with a steep downhill at the beginning of a hike, their first question is always: "Is this one-way ... or round-trip?" But mostly those "reps" from 2019 have translated into a kind of muscle memory for touring. At museums and landmarks from the Museum of the City of New York to Ellis Island, they linger and ask questions. As a fourth grader studying the Silk Road, Willa pulled me along to inspect obscure rooms at the Met featuring fourteenth century Iranian artifacts, seeming to forget that she was supposed to "hate" museums.

There's an ease there with grownups. They love to shoot the breeze with anyone who'll listen. Willa will compliment a stranger's dog, kicking off a back-and-forth I have to interrupt. In a typical conversation, seven-year-old James asked an antique shop owner polishing silver behind the counter if he found the task "satisfying." When the guy laughed and said, "As a matter of fact I do," James lingered for another thirty minutes to discuss this or that rare baseball card.

They don't usually need to be coaxed to ask strangers for help or directions the way I always had to ("Now, Margaret," my mom would say, nudging me toward the library's checkout desk while I stared at my feet. "Tell Mr. So-and-So you'd like to apply for a library card.") Not only had they seen their mom and dad ask for help everyday for a year, to them a Mr. So-and-So behind a desk was the best kind of grownup: a captive audience.

I can also see the ways in which they stayed exactly the same. Despite my pride at their capacity to behave in places, like restaurants and museums, our trip did not transform our children into perfect angels. They still have a genius for knowing how to frustrate us in a million ways. The simple act of getting *dressed in the morning* remains challenging. No amount of Woody Woodpecker motivation can spare us the dallying, the complaining, the wasting time, the avoidance of Just. Putting. On. Your. Socks.

I have to assume at some level the trip impacted Willa's and James's perspective and worldview. But then again, who knows. Maybe the more recent, disruptive experience of COVID overrode all that. Or maybe Willa and James just are who they are. But if nothing else, the goal of spending more time together as a family—*what could be more valuable?*—worked. The fierceness of our bond today means that, for now at least, we're a package deal. What's more, it's given rise to a strong family narrative: *We did this. This is who we are.* Our adventure is the story Willa and James tell about themselves and about us. The details may fade from memory, but the significance will only intensify.

As for me and Teddy, the changes between "before" and "after" are easier to identify. Some are small—where I used to whine about the cold, I now quote the Danish: "There's no such thing as bad weather, only bad clothing." And where we were once too scared to ride bikes in New York, we now own an electric cargo bike to shuttle both kids in and out of traffic around town. But beyond these minor adjustments lies a deeper rewiring of our worldview.

A year spent mostly far from cities, including in primordial places like the Tarkine Rainforest in Tasmania and Robberg Nature Reserve in South Africa that had been there for millenia and would, hopefully, be there long after we were gone, allowed us to discover our planet's natural beauty and appreciate its enduring strength in a way we simply had not before.

The creatures we met had the same effect, down to the last dung beetle. After so many sanctuaries, reserves, and rescue operations—not to mention farms, butcher shops, and wet markets—I not only lost my appetite for seeing animals in cages, I lost my appetite for them period. After a year of eating everything put in front of me, from those cold pig ovaries in Hong Kong to raw horse in Japan, I gave up meat for good. It just seemed a form of cannibalism somehow, not to mention unsustainable for our planet.

While we'd been aware of Earth's deterioration before, it was mostly in a superficial, sloganeering kind of way ("Save Earth!" "Go Green!"). Now, the plastic-clogged oceans and jungles we saw haunt me. We still buy things, but

I can't help but view every purchase the way Jerry Seinfeld put it: as "future trash." Useful for a heartbeat of time before being shipped to a landfill or joining the rest of the garbage we saw swirling around in the surf.

We discovered how befriending strangers could be one of the most surprising joys in life. We made dozens of new friends and learned that speaking up or introducing ourselves could lead to, well, you never knew what it could lead to, which was the point. We are less cynical and make fewer assumptions, firm in the belief that, for the most part, most folks are just trying to do right by their families and, if needed, strangers, too.

Countless people who came to our aid that year shaped this view, beginning with the lifeguard in Kingston who cracked open the almond pod to show Willa and James what grew inside, and the Jamaican business travelers who made James feel better after he spilled cherry juice at breakfast. I think with soul-deep gratitude of the tourist who handed a weepy Willa candy at Machu Picchu; the grocery store cashier in Cape Town who ran off to find me that bag of charcoal; not one but two leather-clad bikers who surprised us with gentle displays of kindness—the one in Amsterdam who fixed Willa's bike and the other at Australia's Lion's Den Pub who wanted to tell us about that indigenous flower. There was the shop lady in Tokyo who found my missing bag; the bus riders in Saigon who offered wipes after James threw up; the parents of all those children who played with ours; and so many others.

When we started traveling, I'd left with a dim view of the direction the U.S. was taking and felt outraged at the many injustices and silly politicians. But one of the trip's unexpected outcomes was a new appreciation for our homeland, especially New York City. Our country is not perfect, not by a long shot—but it turns out nowhere is. No, not even Denmark with all its happy citizens. At least, not by my new criteria for what made a place great, which includes diversity. I hadn't realized how homogenous the world could be until our final flight from Los Angeles to DC, which had a greater mix of humans in one place than we'd seen all year.

New York's diversity in particular is more striking than ever and not just because it is a microcosm of the planet, offering a way for anyone to travel the world just by taking the subway, but because of its diversity in every regard—interests, styles, walks of life. "I forgot how people are just so unapologetically themselves here," a visiting friend remarked on a walk through downtown.

As for us and the way we move through the world, that's changed, too. Before our trip, I recorded Willa and James answering a few questions about their parents. What were we like? "Daddy's always working on his computer and doing phone calls," four-year-old James said at the time, adding, "He always goes to exercise, he always brushes his teeth, and he always eats chips at night." Of her mother, Willa described a woman who was, "Busy, funny, and cold," as in needing a jacket or a heated blanket. James added, "And always looking for her phone and wallet."

Disciplined, distracted, and "busy?" Sounds about right. We'd been on a particular treadmill, the kind where certain trappings felt important and any misstep seemed to have serious implications. We're not immune to getting caught up in that old script, but the trip forced a radical assessment: we are small, probably inconsequential in the grand scheme of things, and life is short. I got Teddy a coin to carry in his pocket inscribed *memento mori*, Latin for "Remember that you will die." Is there a better way to get clarity? What greater incentive to *carpe diem?*

The list of priorities we developed helps, too. It informs the decisions we make, providing a framework so obvious I have to remind myself it took us nearly a year to distill. Letting go of concerns and "goals" that once consumed us, like owning one or multiple homes or distinguishing ourselves as "asskickers" at work, has not only been a relief, but it has also been profoundly gratifying, the emotional equivalent of laying your arm on a cluttered table and pushing everything off in one large sweep. Nothing broken, nothing to clean up, just a way to proceed undistracted by mess.

When we unpacked on moving-in day and saw with fresh eyes all of the stuff we had paid to put in storage for a year—the books, the toys, the furniture, the clothes for every imaginable occasion—we decided to give most of it away, keeping only what we used and genuinely liked. "I never want to do another purge like that again," Teddy said when the last box was gone, happy to be back to our fighting weight.

These days my work is of the solo creative variety—writing a book, freelance illustration, photography, and photo organizing. Teddy avoided the temptation to take a job he felt he was "supposed" to, instead holding out for a business role that allowed him the chance to be creative, learn something new, and be flexible with his schedule.

And then there is our outlook on parenting. What I hadn't realized before our trip was that Willa and James have just as much to teach us as we have to teach them. Today our foursome operates with that understanding. And while there's so much pressure to raise kids in a particular way—and only getting more intense as ours get older—we're generally able to catch ourselves whenever we start to sweat things like carving "paths" for Willa and James to attend "good" schools and colleges. We remind ourselves of the countless people we met while traveling who were leading remarkable lives, none of whom fit such a narrow vision. If we give Willa and James a safe and loving home, teach them right from wrong, and arm them with skills like coping with disappointment and doing laundry, the rest can be up to them; if our kids can fend for themselves in life, and do so with integrity, we will have done our job.

A close friend joked that we've "turned into hippies." There is indeed less makeup in my life and more used furniture, not to mention a freezer full of plant-based "meat." But we aren't willing to give up this new way of moving through the world for anything. The challenge today is whether we can hold firmly to it, or, as one fellow family traveler put it, "keep fighting for our new normal."

Not everyone will have the chance to travel the world with their family for a long period of time, but there is something everyone can do to make the most of the time they are allotted. They can slow it down. We're all familiar with how whole periods of our lives can go by in the blink of an eye. How many times have people posted photos from a child's birthday or graduation to social media with captions like, "And just like that, so-and-so is ten?"

Our year away did not fly by. It plodded along at a satisfying pace. Even in hindsight, years later, it seems epic, not fleeting. And I think there's a lesson there. Every day that we traveled required navigating new streets, figuring out new protocols, calculating unfamiliar currencies, seeing, smelling, tasting, and processing things we'd never encountered before. All that newness forced us to be acutely aware of every passing minute in a way we hadn't been back when every day held the same conveyor belt of commute, work, bed. How many Mondays through Fridays had I sleepwalked to my office and been unable to recall the subway ride?

According to the scientists and philosophers who study this kind of thing, an auto-pilot routine can make life seem short, whereas memories, when accumulated, stack up to make life feel fuller. Because we usually only remember the things that stand out from the ordinary—a vacation, a celebration, even a funeral or illness—the more of these there are (ideally not the funerals and illness), the richer and longer one's life seems in retrospect.

French philosopher Jean-Marie Guyau said that the best way to lengthen time was to "fill it, if you have the chance, with a thousand new things." And well before him, the ancient Greek philosopher Seneca offered another way to think about it: "It's not that life is short, it's that we waste a lot of it." The fact that our trip did not "fly by" demonstrates that not only had we *not* wasted our time, we had discovered the secret to slowing it down: Turn off the auto-pilot switch and make memories instead. An act as small as taking a different route to school, strolling a new neighborhood, saying yes to an invitation (even when the couch seems more enticing) can do the trick. Newness might seem like more of an effort, but it has a way of jolting us back to the present and creating memories for the future.

I'm reminded of this every time I think back to a dinner we ate on a warm February evening in Valparaiso, Chile, seated on a patio overlooking the Pacific. Midway through our meal, we began chatting with a retired couple from Boston at the table next to us. They asked all about our trip and we answered as many questions as we could. It was early days and we still had plenty to figure out.

After a pleasant exchange, we bid our farewells and the couple headed out for the night. But just as we were turning back to our food, the man stopped and took one last look at Willa. His blue eyes crinkled into a smile.

"I have a daughter your age," he said, pausing. "Problem is, she's thirty-seven."

Then he turned and walked away.

I pulled Willa in for a hug, grateful that she was still six and not thirty-seven. Grateful that we'd decided to take this leap—that we were making the most of this very brief window when she and James were still kids, and we were all alive and healthy. Grateful that we were slowing time while we had the chance.

These days, when I close my eyes at night, I feel that same gratitude. I can still summon the memories that bring me peace, like watching the kids swim on a late Rio afternoon, or laughing as they skipped rope in Bali, big goofy smiles on their faces backlit by a setting sun. And, of course, my cherished memories of cooking dinner in our Cape Town kitchen.

There was an evening in Amed, Indonesia, when James sat wrapped in a towel, his hair wet from swimming and his cheeks sun-kissed. He was sleepy at the end of a long day and stared out at the ocean with his chin in his hands, head tilted like a puppy. I was cooking dinner, and the Beatles song "I'll Follow the Sun," played quietly on our speakers. I probably wouldn't have noticed it, but James was listening carefully to its mournful lyrics.

"*We're* following the sun," I heard him murmur to himself.

He was merely repeating a line he'd heard us use to describe our warm weather itinerary. But in that sliver of time, during a mundane evening as I watched the water boil and stirred some sauce for our pasta, his observation felt more poignant, all hopeful and childlike and optimistic and radical in its simplicity. He understood not only how our great adventure was organized, but was it possible he had also intuited something more meaningful? That all of this beauty was ephemeral and would not last? Probably not. But hearing him make this quiet statement to himself made my eyes well with tears of love and pain. Our tomorrows would most certainly have rain. For now, though, we were following the sun.

Appendix

PACKING

"How do you pack for a year away?" Our approach was to bring as little as possible. A trip around the world seemed hard enough. Why add the burden of huge suitcases? We went light. Very, very light. One carry-on suitcase and one backpack per person.

Teddy and I purchased one international carry-on-sized roller each. We settled on black Briggs & Riley roller bags with four wheels, which are soft-sided instead of hard and designed to open like a chest with a well and lid. We avoided hard-cased clamshell styles, which I find unwieldy. The kids each got roller carry-ons with two-wheels, which we regretted. Two-wheelers were harder for them to pull on their own.

Each of us got a backpack. Importantly, these backpacks *fit under an airplane seat*. Teddy and I each used a 35-liter model with compartments for laptops and other items. We opted for a dark gray style that gave more "work trip" than "Appalachian trail." The kids' backpacks were very small, a deliberate move to keep us from over-packing. If they were too heavy, the kids wouldn't carry them.

Packing cubes were new to us but turned out to be the key to our success. Organizing our belongings into these individual zip-up containers meant everything fit in its proper place, just as it would in drawers at home. Underwear in a small bag, t-shirts in another, all things swim in a third. We could pack and unpack in minutes; we never had to rummage through an explosion of clothes to find, say, a deck of cards. There was a cube for those, and we knew exactly where to find it.

We grownups also each had a smaller daypack that could be unfolded once we arrived somewhere new and used for stuff like snacks and sunscreen during walks and tours. This way we wouldn't have to lug our larger backpacks around with us. I picked up a medium canvas tote for this same purpose that I could use as a slightly more elevated alternative when in cities.

Each person had a medium-sized drawstring laundry bag.

Finally, I bought a fanny pack. For someone prone to misplacing stuff, that fanny pack proved the single most important item I brought. In it, I fit my phone, a small card carrier with just a credit card, debit card and driver's license and few extras like hand sanitizer, a hair elastic, a tampon, a few bandaids, a small pack of wipes and an extra contact lens. On travel days, my passport fit perfectly.

PACKING APPROACH

When it came to clothing, here was our approach (and some of what we learned along the way):

- We packed about one week's worth of clothing each.

- With an itinerary that followed the sun, we mostly prepared for warm weather with a few layers for chills here and there. We ended the year in Japan where it was winter and bought coats in New Zealand just before flying to Kyoto.

- Surf shops, rather than outdoor or athletic clothing retailers, turned out to have the right mix of comfortable, relatively inexpensive traveling clothes.

- We tried to keep our clothes to solid colors. Mostly for simplicity's sake and easy mixing and matching, but also because logos, patterns and slogans don't always age well in photos.

- While our clothing didn't vary much for weather, it did for our surroundings. I had white leather sneakers and lightweight slacks for cosmopolitan cities like Madrid, Paris and Singapore, and surf-y joggers and flip flops for more casual beach locales. Teddy had lightweight trousers and a few casual button downs for cities; shorts and tees for more laidback, rural environments.

- One was enough: One sweater. One scarf. One bathing suit. One hat. I started the trip with three sundresses, which seemed logical at the time but turned out to be a major waste of space.

- As a woman, I decided to err on the conservative side when it came to clothes. I didn't bring shorts or tank tops. T-shirts and lightweight ankle-length pants worked just fine.

- As for makeup, I had an eyebrow pencil and mascara that I wore every day, but nothing else.

- A well-traveled friend advised us to overpack underwear. We did and he was right.

- The only jewelry I wore was a gold wedding band. I left my diamond engagement ring at my in-laws' back in the US. While I did buy some cool earrings and jewelry on the road, I shipped it all home to wear when we got back.

- We didn't need to start the year with a complete wardrobe and kit. We underestimated how much we could, and would, buy as we went.

PACKING LIST

Here is the complete list of what we had in our suitcases at all times:

Margaret's suitcase

- 6 tees (2x white, 2x black and 2x gray)
- 5 lightweight solid-color/neutral pants (breezy, lightweight, loose ankle-length)
- 1 thin sweater
- 1 sundress
- 10 pairs neutral/tan undies
- 8 pairs white ankle socks
- 1 nude everyday bra
- 1 sports bra
- 1 pair workout leggings
- 1 short nightie
- 1 bikini
- 1 beach coverup
- 1 lightweight windbreaker/rain jacket
- 1 lightweight pullover puffer
- 1 thin scarf
- 1 wool beanie
- 1 foldable straw fedora
- 1 pair sneakers for walking/working out
- 1 pair white leather fashion sneakers
- 1 pair flip flops
- Bathroom kit (three-compartments; unfolded to hang from a hook)
- Tweezers
- Cuticle cutters
- Nail clippers
- Hair elastics (10x)
- Toothbrush/toothpaste
- Floss
- Face wash
- Face moisturizer
- Zit cream
- Deodorant
- Vaseline/lip balm
- Eyebrow pencil
- Travel-size mascara
- Small concealer
- Flat hairbrush
- Travel dry shampoo (when I could find it)
- Disposable razor
- Contact lenses*

Teddy's suitcase

- 6 solid color cotton tees
- 4 casual button-downs (used as a layer, often over t-shirt; a linen option was his MVP)
- 3 lightweight casual slacks with some stretch
- 1 pair lightweight joggers
- 2 casual shorts
- 1 belt
- 1 lightweight puffer
- 1 raincoat shell
- 1 shirt-like fleece jacket
- 1 light beanie hat
- 1 baseball cap
- 2 workout t-shirts
- 1 workout short
- 1 bathing suit
- 1 shorts/swimsuit combo
- 1 long sleeve UV-protection rash guard
- 1 long sleeve workout pullover
- 1 pair goggles
- 7 pairs ankle socks (with some polyester which help them dry faster/not smell)
- 3 pairs calf-length socks
- 10 pairs underwear
- 2 cotton handkerchiefs (seasonal allergies)
- 1 pair casual/lightweight cloth slip-on shoe/loafer

- 1 pair sneakers
- 1 pair flip-flops
- Bathroom kit
- Toothbrush/toothpaste
- Deodorant
- Face wash
- Face lotion
- Hair gel
- Shaving cream
- Several razor blades
- Small electric trimmer
- Nail clipper
- Contact lenses*

*We both wear daily contact lenses. That's a lot of contact lenses when you're talking about a whole year. We ended up bringing a six-month supply each, layered at the bottom of our suitcases, then had another six months' worth shipped to a friend's place in Singapore, where we picked them up halfway through the year.

Willa's suitcase (7 years old)

- 2 tees
- 4 pairs shorts (to also wear under dresses)
- 2 pairs long leggings
- 4 dresses
- 1 cardigan
- 10 pairs undies
- 6 pairs socks
- 1 pair PJs
- 1 raincoat
- 1 pair sneakers
- 1 pair waterproof hiking-type sandals
- 1 pair aquasox
- 1 sunhat
- 1 wool beanie
- 2 bathing suits with UV rash guards
- 1 pair goggles

James's suitcase (5 years old)

- 5 tees
- 4 pairs shorts
- 2 pairs long pants
- 1 sweater
- 1 raincoat
- 10 pairs undies
- 6 pairs socks
- 1 pair PJs
- 1 baseball hat
- 1 wool beanie
- 1 swim shirt
- 2 swim trunks
- 1 pair goggles
- 1 pair aquasox
- 1 pair sneakers
- 1 pair rubber waterproof slip-on shoes
- The kids shared a bathroom kit (also a three-compartment hanger):
- Toothbrushes/Toothpaste
- Hair elastics (10x)
- 2 small hairbrushes
- Tea tree essential oil for hairline to ward off lice

"Kit" Items

We traveled with a number of items that were not clothes. We bundled this additional stuff—which we came to refer to as "kit"—into packing cubes by category and distributed them among our four suitcases. They included:

Tech

- Multi-outlet power cube
- Universal converters
- All relevant chargers
- Extra portable battery pack
- A small flat zippered case for cords .
- A small portable Bluetooth speaker

Games

- Constantly revolving:
- Deck of cards
- Plus Plus blocks
- Travel-sized games like Otrio, Rat-a-Tat-Cat, Spot It, Tiny Dot, a few logic puzzles
- A soccer ball

When we got to a place where we'd be staying for a while or knew we'd be road-tripping instead of flying, we'd buy a ream of printer paper and let the kids draw and paint as much as they wanted. But we didn't fly with blank paper.

School (one packing cube for each per kid)

- Workbooks
- Journals

Skin

- Sunscreen
- Bug spray
- Neosporin
- Bandaids
- Cortizone
- Iodine disinfectant cream
- Gauze + tape

Medical

Crossed-out = items we packed but never used

*Most-replaced items

- Advil*
- ~~Alka Seltzer~~
- ~~Aquatabs~~
- ~~Benadryl~~
- Dayquil
- Cough medicine (for kids too)
- ~~Dramamine~~
- Excedrin
- Cough drops
- Imodium
- ~~Pedialyte~~
- Pepto Bismol tablets
- Tylenol for kids
- ~~Thermometer~~
- Visine
- All of our prescription Malaria pills, antibiotics and altitude sickness meds

Should've packed: Prescription for UTIs, drops for swimmers' ear and extra Claritin.

Housekeeping

- A clothesline
- A headlamp and flashlight
- An extra packable market bag (for grocery shopping and other random needs)
- About 5 packets of detergent
- Sewing kit (used once I think)
- Two inflatable booster seats for the kids

Here's something we bought on the road and used religiously, but wouldn't have thought to pack before we left: One of those magnetic phone holders for the dashboard of a rental car. So handy for GPS on a road trip.

Also, if you have room for a small set of binoculars, add them. Only too late did we realize how awesome these would have been to have.

Documents

In Teddy's backpack, we carried a sealed plastic file envelope with important documents and cash:

- Passports
- Photocopies of passports
- Photocopies of driver's licenses, back and front
- Original birth certificates (this would be easy to overlook, but many countries require you to carry them when traveling with children as an extra precaution against trafficking)
- Photocopies of birth certificates
- About $2,000 in USD at all times—hundreds, twenties and some ones, fives, and tens for tipping. American cash got us out of a few jams when credit cards weren't accepted and we didn't have anything local, including for visa fees at borders.
- Vaccination papers proving we were up to date on all required shots, required for entry in many countries.
- International drivers licenses from AAA

Kids' backpacks

- Tablets for movies and games
- Headphones
- Kindles
- Pencil cases (set of colored pencils, one pencil sharpener, 4x mechanical pencils and 4x black felt pens)

Grownup backpacks

- Tablet with portable keyboard (Teddy)
- Laptop (Margaret)
- Kindles
- Headphones

Photos

I love this shot, taken at a stop on our road trip through South Africa's Western Cape, because it captures a feeling: the joy of sitting around long after a meal has finished, cracking up with one another over some inside joke, the grownups present, the kids equal members of the conversation.

Back when we were debating whether or not to take this trip, a friend of Teddy's cut through our paralysis by asking a simple question: "What could possibly be more valuable than spending a year away with your family?"

His question, and more so, the fact that we hadn't thought to ask it ourselves, forced us to acknowledge that maybe our New York days and weeks had become a bit too transactional: commute, work, bedtime, playground, socializing, rinse, repeat.

This new clarity helped us understand how a year-long adventure would mean we'd all get to know each other, not just better but more deeply. More than anything, it would allow us to make the most of this fleeting chapter of our young family's story. To future-proof against regret.

We assumed that a year of travel without jobs would translate to lots of free time for grown-up pursuits like watercoloring. We were wrong. There was no free time.

At least in the beginning.

With our children around all day and night, requiring meals, schooling, and support in unfamiliar environments, it seemed as if we couldn't write or read one sentence without one of them hollering at us from the pool or the couch to show us a trick, tattle on the other, or ask when we were going to join their game. We wondered: How was it impossible for them to just play on their own for thirty freaking minutes?

But by the end of the year, things had changed. We could declare two and a half hours for "quiet time," and they could reliably read their books, draw, or play with the few games we packed. They weren't needy for our attention anymore, plus their tolerance for long boring stretches had increased after so much experience. Here they are in New Zealand on a boat enjoying a post-lunch reading session that would have been unheard of at the beginning of our year. I think Teddy and I even took a nap while this was happening.

This is Restaurant Face, which appeared whenever our hungry little boy's meal took too long to arrive. Lunch and dinner were almost always in a restaurant because we were living in hotels or, if we had a kitchen of our own, weren't in town long enough to stock much beyond cereal and milk. Not only were restaurants convenient, they allowed us to eat local food.

But they weren't always easy, especially early on. Teddy and I would either overeat or order too much food—or both. We wasted a lot of time scanning menus for dishes that the kids, especially picky James, would eat. And we probably made things harder on ourselves by having a low tolerance for loud and disruptive behavior. We were on them constantly: Don't play with that, sit down, lower your voice, say please, say thank you, shhh!

Eventually their endurance—and their table manners—caught up. We stopped catering to pickiness and, lo and behold, they stopped being picky. They started ordering for themselves, cutting their own food and got really good at using chopsticks. Teddy and I improved too, always ready with a plan for our next meal before someone uttered the dreaded words, "I'm hungry."

The kind of safety precautions that earnest, fretful American parents demand for their kids don't exist in most of the places we visited. We started the year with good intentions, bringing along things like inflatable booster seats, but they ruptured in the high Peruvian altitude just a few weeks in, and we tossed them. There were limited functioning seatbelts at best and few, if any, booster seats the rest of the year. We had to adjust our expectations. Early in our trip I openly worried about the kids playing on a seesaw in Chile (*top*), but not long after that they were swimming in the Amazon River and riding on the back of motorbikes like this one in Vietnam. They managed to survive—and their parents lightened up in the process.

Here are a very excited Willa and James posing with two threadbare, second-hand stuffed animals they won at a festival in Mongolia. They were dazzled by these matted friends, proof that their relationship with toys had been completely recalibrated by this point in our year. Six months earlier, when they had a New York City toy closet brimming with plastic toys, such tattered stuffies probably wouldn't have gotten a second look. But after living with little more than a soccer ball and a deck of cards for so long, they couldn't believe this windfall. They spent the next two weeks in Mongolia doting on these creatures, tucking them into bed at night, carrying them all over.

Here's Willa doing some math on a boat in the Amazon. If you'd asked us six months into the year how homeschooling, or "roadschooling," was going, we'd have replied: "Awful." It turns out kids don't want to learn from their parents. We eventually got better at it over time, thanks in part to rewards. For example, for every six great school days without attitude or tears, Willa earned a new iPad game. We hated this at first because it felt like bribing (*they shouldn't get kickbacks for work they're supposed to be doing!*), but it worked. Soon enough the improved behavior stuck. Or maybe it was that our kids simply surrendered. They'd fought valiantly, but we broke them in the end. Our unwavering consistency—ninety minutes of schooling each morning on non-travel days—showed them school would happen, whether they threw a tantrum or not.

By the end we had to admit that homeschooling was one of the most rewarding parts of the year. Teddy taught James to read! The kids got customized instruction that suited their learning style and pace of understanding. Not surprisingly, with that level of individual attention, both surpassed their grade level in a matter of months. Plus, we parents gained a better sense of how our kids learned and what their areas of strength and weakness were.

This is Willa examining Nelson Mandela's solitary cell in South Africa. We quickly saw how the world doesn't come with trigger warnings, and that difficult topics could arise at any moment, often when we least expected them to. On day two of the trip we toured Bob Marley's house in Jamaica, which had seemed innocent enough—we sang "One Love" and got to see his recording studio!—but ended with us fumbling to explain the words "assassination attempt."

We decided after that to lean into their Tough Questions by offering honest, blunt answers. Willa and James could be trusted to grapple with facts about murder, war and disease and terrorism, about orphans and about the United States not always being the hero. No sugarcoating, no beating around the bush. As one friend put it, "You can't kid-proof the world, so you may as well world-proof your kids." It's an approach that set a precedent for frank-talk in our family.

Our favorite kind of travel was when we could just be anonymous wanderers in far-away lands, observing the goings-on of everyday people. We loved seeing what was what. A shopping mall! Dog parks! The unvarnished, unsexy, real-life gas stations, public pools, fitness classes, convenience stores, and city buses that made up people's real lives. The equivalent of going to a little league game in Memphis instead of the Statue of Liberty.

We started calling this style of travel "interloping." It wasn't quite the right word, but it stuck. Not glamorous or sexy or Instagrammable, interloping was the art of para-chuting, Zelig-like, into someone else's quotidian existence, where no one was putting on a show for tourists, but rather living their lives that day in their corner of the world. We got to feel their rhythms, what mattered, and experienced a taste of what it would be like to be from there.

Grocery stores and markets were the best for interloping. Here's James stocking up somewhere in southern Spain.

We fully embraced the help of not one but many, many travel agents over the course of the year. We don't regret doing so—their help with ideas and logistics was essential with so many stops—but some agents overscheduled us with tours and "experiences" like calligraphy demonstrations and basket weaving, which felt more like tourist filler than anything authentic.

Here we are in Hue, Vietnam, at a master kite-maker's home for what felt like the four billionth such "experience" that week. We faced a heap of Vietnamese kite parts and spent more than two hours "making" four of them, aka, assembling pre-made pieces with rubber cement. It was past lunch and we were miserable.

People talk a lot about the difference between "tourists" and "travelers," the former being those who sightsee along a comfortable circuit, the latter more likely to wander off the beaten path, making friends and eating local food. We wanted to be, and would eventually become, proficient at both. But finding the right balance between the two styles wasn't easy.

Traveling with little kids meant spending a lot of time at parks. After a morning spent homeschooling, we'd often anchor our afternoons with an outing in search of a cool playground or two. Most of the time they would make friends. Here they are living it up at a Launceston, Tasmania, playground they ranked in their global top three.

Here are Willa and James playing a game of pickup soccer with some local kids in rural Yunnan Province, China. James's preschool teachers emphasized that academics weren't a concern at his age ("Just keep reading to him"), but that peer socialization was vital: "Make sure you create as many opportunities for him to play with other kids as you can," they told us. "We can't stress this enough."

We quickly learned the value of carrying around a soccer ball—if you were a kid and you had a ball, you could make friends—and packed one with us all year despite our small bags.

Some days we'd wander a city with a ball, eventually enticing new friends to play pickup. Other times we asked service folks—a groundskeeper in Indonesia and a housekeeper in Vietnam come to mind—if their kids wanted to come over to play. In almost none of these situations was there shared language between the kids, but it didn't matter.

Clockwise from left: Grandma Lobsy and Teddy atop Machu Picchu in Peru; Willa and Grammie after emerging from the Great Pyramids in Egypt; James and Willa with Lobsy and Beepaw Brendan in Copenhagen, Denmark; and Beepaw Jim with both kids in Queenstown, New Zealand.

Having visitors on our trip wasn't always easy—hosting had a way of altering the rhythm of our days and the feel of our adventure—but grandparents were always welcome. Not only did the time together allow us to create memories, but it also provided grandparents a way to parachute into bucket list destinations hassle-free. Teddy's mother in particular relished the opportunity, joining us six different times across eight countries on five continents.

A trip like this isn't for couples who have a tough time getting along. Anyone considering doing what we did should first take a hard look at their marriage and ask, "Are we good?" If we hadn't seen eye-to-eye on everything from spending to disciplining our kids to schedules, we would have spent the year at each other's throats.

To help keep the marital peace, we created a "jobs" system where we each held distinct roles and had specific responsibilities. Teddy was in charge of "finance" (eg, withdrawing and carrying local currency, tipping, etc.) and "logistics and ops" (eg, devices, IT, navigation). I was responsible for "content," (eg, photos, photo organization, Instagram). He packed James's bag, I packed Willa's.

Roles prevented things from falling through the cracks. Not to mention seething resentment. There was no "I thought you were handling that" or "How come I end up doing all the work?"-type bickering. Because we both had our fair share of unglamorous assignments, we were always grateful to the other for dealing with this or that task.

And, no, the lack of childcare did not prevent us from spending quality time together just the two of us. We actually wound up alone together more than we ever had in our relationship, chit chatting every day on playground benches, shooting the breeze while the kids played. It's how I imagine retired couples might be, just enjoying each other's company in an unhurried fashion.

Top: Petra, Jordan (taken by my dad, Jim Bensfield); Bottom: Flores, Indonesia

Acknowledgements

I genuinely believed I could bang this book out in thirty days. Just crib from my blog posts, bullet out some tips, mash it all together, and voila! How hard could it be?

When reality set in, I was lucky to be surrounded by so many cheerleaders and willing readers. To Joanna, Julia, Jessica, Camille, Amanda, Robin, my mother Llewellyn, father Jim, and Teddy's parents, Lila and Brendan: I am eternally grateful that you read this thing, some of you more than once. I also want to thank my proofreader Katrina, my book designer Joia and my talented friend Liam.

I am especially indebted to my editor and friend, Marianne, who forced me to write a real book, not just a memo about packing tips. It's hard to imagine this book existing without her wit and relentless encouragement.

And to Teddy, my biggest fan and most ardent supporter: I love you.

Made in the USA
Middletown, DE
05 June 2024

55324661R00150